BEHIND A GI

THE ANATOMY OF A SUICIDE

By Dorothy Schwarz

All rights reserved, no part of this publication may be reproduced by any means, electronic, mechanical, or photocopying, documentary, film, or otherwise without prior permission of the publisher.

Published by:

Chipmukapublishing

PO Box 6872

Brentwood

Essex

CM13 1ZT

United Kingdom

www.chipmunkapublishing.com

Copyright © 2005 Dorothy Schwarz

ISBN 1-904697-20-8

CONTENTS

Zoë's family, friends, lovers, colleagues and doctors.

Zoë's family

Nana - grandmother

Walter - father

Dorothy - mother

Habie - eldest sister (partner Simon Hamilton)

Benjamin – elder brother (partner Fredy)

Tanya - middle daughter (partner Niall Murphy)

Zachary - younger brother (partner Maria Eldred)

Mickey and Jan - uncle and aunt

Simon, Penny, Julia - cousins

Zoë's closest friends

Mylène - French

Sarah -English

Kelly - English

Florence - French

Corinna - German

Eleni - Greek

Zoë's boyfriends

Matthew - English

Sam – Anglo-French

Kingsley - Nigerian

Simon - Welsh

Francis Winston - Jamaican

Francis- Anglo-Nigerian

Tolis - Greek

Henrik – Japanese/Dutch

Jamie - English

Hicham – Moroccan

Zoë's animals

Daisy, Tigger – the cats

Napoleon - the goat

Minny, Zugi, Kismet, Amigo, Shah Jehan - the horses

Leah and Dac – the German shepherd dogs

Zoë's colleagues and bosses

Helen Seaford – Runnymede Trust

Liz Hosken, Ed Posey – Gaia Foundation

Su Sayer and Tania Mitchell, Bob Tindall – United Response

Zoë's doctors

Paul Rasor in Colchester

Felix Ghazouan in Marrakech

Cahn Vasudevan in Colchester

Sally Mathieson in Colchester

Cover photograph by Habie Schwarz

This book is dedicated to Zoe's father Walter, without whose love, support and help it could not have been written.

FOREWORD

Most of us don't discover what helplessness really means until we become a parent. We think we know how to solve problems, how to get things done and be in control. Then we become responsible for a small scrap of humanity and we discover that there are problems we don't know how to solve, things we don't know how to do, and events for which we are responsible but over which we have no control. As the small scrap of humanity becomes a child, a teenager, a young adult, our sense of responsibility becomes greater as our ability to solve problems and be in control of events becomes less. Even if our child is strong and healthy and deals with education, work and relationships competently and happily we have some inkling that all of this could fall apart and we wouldn't know how to put it right. Being a parent is an impossibly difficult task because what determines a child's behaviour isn't what parents do but how the child interprets what parents do. This is something over which parents have no control whatsoever. Nevertheless, as the years go by, we feel the helplessness that accompanies the thoughts of 'If only' and 'I should have'. When things do go wrong we vacillate between the guilt of 'It was my fault' and the helplessness of 'There was nothing I could do.' In guilt we feel the archetypal terror of punishment that we deserve, while our helplessness awakens the ancestral terror of being prey to an unknown but an immense, ravening beast. And then there is sorrow, the sorrow of a loss for which there can be no recompense or reward, and the sorrow of no forgetting. This is the experience of loving parents whose child has lost his grip on his life. It falls apart, and the child, despairing, kills himself.

Many parents who experience this keep their suffering private, and in so doing can feel that there is something peculiar about them because they suffer so. They don't want to risk being condemned by others or leave themselves open to the thoughtlessness of others, and so they don't discover how universal their suffering is. Dorothy Schwarz experienced all this when her beloved daughter Zoë killed herself, but celebrating Zoë's life, showing how little the extremes of mental distress are understood, and how badly such sufferers are cared for by those who say they are experts in the field were far more important to her. All this she has achieved in this courageous and vastly important book.

These experts, the psychiatrists, say that there are mental illnesses, or, as they are now called, mental disorders, which are the equivalent of physical illnesses. When parents are told that their child has a mental disorder they may assume that this means that their child is suffering from an illness for which there is effective treatment. However, they soon discover that, though the psychiatric language used may be that of physical illness, what actually happens is not like a physical illness at all. When we are physically ill most of us do whatever we can to get better. Most of us see our doctor, follow his instructions, ask family and friends for advice, and we rest and take care of ourselves, but those who are said to have a mental illness resist all help. They refuse to see a doctor and, if forced to do so, they neglect to follow his advice. They reject psychotherapy, or else see a therapist but resist the wisdom and understanding of that therapist. They may go into a psychiatric hospital, but then the parents discover that little happens there and that patients may be abandoned at the moment they need help the most. Physical illnesses have a natural progression which a doctor can describe but with mental illness none of the professionals can give any kind of prognosis. Psychiatrists may talk to chemical imbalances and manic-depression genes, despite the complete lack of scientific evidence for any of this, but then they urge the patient to try harder, even though no amount of trying ever cured cancer or even the common cold. Watching all this, the parents oscillate between hope and despair, and always with a sense of utter helplessness.

The cure for helplessness is to take control, if not the situation itself but of something relevant to the situation. In the last fifty years the greatest improvements in the care of those in extreme mental distress have come, not from the professionals, but from the sufferers themselves and from their family and friends. These people have seen that their greatest asset is their experience, and that what they need to do is to work collectively and change not just the psychiatric system but society itself. Extreme mental distress is not an illness but part of what it is to be a human being who lives in an uncertain and dangerous world, as we all do. *The Glass Wall* is not merely an account of the tragedy of a young life cut short but a challenge to us all to understand ourselves and thus learn how best to care for one another.

Dorothy Rowe

October 3, 2005.

PROLOGUE

After you died, we found on the top shelf in your bedroom six cardboard boxes crammed with papers in no particular order or dates, diaries in hard and soft covers, notes on loose sheets of paper, dated and undated, birthday cards and postcards, souvenirs. Business letters, bank statements, certificates won at school, medical records, letters received and letters you'd written. Maybe sent, maybe not. A box of several hundred photographs, mostly of people and animals, a few places, some of which I recognised; many I didn't. I had no idea that you'd kept this stuff; you were such a private person. Your elder sister Habie knew. So did your friend, Kelly; I didn't. Reading those papers brings you alive again.

You wrote two months before your sixteenth birthday:

Sunday 18th October [1987]

Woke up at 8.30. Read Lawrence's criticism in the morning. It was a lovely day. Had lunch. .... The family was all together. The lunch was delicious. Mum & Freddie chatted in the greenhouse. Dad, Bups and me had coffee and some of my cake. We went for a walk around the reservoir. It was stunning. Two swans crossed the sunray upon the water.

I brought the horses in. Diana came. We had more of my cake and some of Dad's bread. We talked, had tea and went to bed. It was a lovely, magical family weekend.

One month after your birthday, you wrote about your school friends:

12

Friday 6th January [1988]

Saw everyone again and we talked a lot. We had a really funny conversation at lunch about who was going to lose her virginity first. Everyone is either in love or going out with someone so we can talk about it a lot which is really nice and fun.

A few years later, recovered from your first breakdown and back at university, the diary entries are matter-of-fact, whom you met, what you ate, what pleased you, proud to win games of pool, happy with your friends.

At twenty-two, you wrote about them and us:

Saturday 4th May [1994]

Mylène [oldest friend] *and I had a chat in the end sitting room. Zac* [brother] *came home. We went to Vagabonds and I asked to work there. Mylène and I had dinner at Monty's.... We came home and watched the end of 'Revenge', which is unbelievably sexist. Completely happy to find Tigger purring on my bed.*

Nothing melodramatic – just content with your life and loving the people around you.

Sunday 5th of May

Mylène and I woke up late. We spent the afternoon chatting in the Peldon Rose. After dropping her at the station did some typing.

... Tigger sleeping in my bed.

Being close to Mum and Dad.

Mylène being happy. Adnan kissing me on the cheek. Zac showing me his design projects.

Out of many entries that read, *'chatted with Mum,'* I can't recall whether the chats were fruitful and loving or whether we argued. And during your last illness, when we brought you back to Greenacres in the spring and you died in the summer, the first summer of the new century, during those five months you spoke little and wrote almost nothing.

You left those boxes on the top shelf in your bedroom where you knew they would be found. Your Dad believes you were too modest to think anyone would bother to examine them and we'd just throw them away. None of us would have done that. One of my oldest friends, Heather, and one of your closest friends, Kelly, came to help me. We sorted the papers into foolscap folders – in rough categories - letters, love letters, diaries, notebooks, mementos. We didn't keep every single birthday card and postcard (there were hundreds). Although it hurts to see your handwriting, I have no qualms about reading your diaries and letters or even publishing parts of them. You did not die in a fit of florid madness or rage; you planned your suicide with care and left a hand-written list of forty friends whom we were to contact.

Perhaps those papers represent an unconscious sort of last present to us as well as a rebuke; we did not understand you well enough and not everything you wrote was complimentary. From a young age, you had a wickedly sharp way of slicing through pretension. A least one person, amongst those few to whom I've shown some of your writing, has said, "don't print what she wrote, it's too hurtful." And in so much of what you wrote in your twenties, when outwardly you seemed happy and successful, inwardly you were grappling with demons. You gave them human faces; they resemble people you knew including your parents.

Two days after your death, we found an Internet site that claimed that one in five manic depressives eventually kill themselves. That statistic isn't a classified secret, although we never discovered it during your lifetime. Were we, as well as you, afraid? You wanted to believe that your illness at eighteen was 'cured'. You didn't want the label of 'someone suffering from mental problems'. We accepted

14

that and went along with the idea; easier to refer to Zoë's breakdown NOT Zoë's first episode. Easier to let our pleasant life slide on.

I've rearranged the contents of those cardboard boxes many times, sorted out letters, cards and photos and mementos and made up four scrapbooks from different stages of your life. Did you imagine when you left those papers, unsorted, untitled, we wouldn't read every single sheet? Use a magnifying glass on the indecipherable bits, trying to find answers to the unanswerable *why* which haunts every case of suicide? I scrabble amongst your papers looking for answers to questions that only you can give. Sometimes I'm angry; other times I cry.

After your death, well-meaning people trotted out clichés: that we had given you a happy childhood; that we had done the best we could; that you knew we loved you and so on. And the one that helps the least: time heals. No, it doesn't; it merely habituates. Nothing can cancel the horror of your final act. It is murder and I remain enough of a Jew to remind you of the commandment which says, 'Thou shalt not kill,' even if murderer and victim is the same person. How could that happen? How could you kill *anyone* – even yourself? What stops survivors (anyone of your friends or family) from taking the same decision?

Is there enough evidence in your diaries, in your papers, in the scrawled notes you wrote in the Moroccan hospital, in our memories? Is enough left about your life for anyone to understand why you chose to end it? I doubt it. Examining the facts might yield enough clues to find an answer. I doubt that it will. But I am forced to try. In the boxes, amongst the photographs are several pictures of horses and ponies. The top half of the rider has been cut out; you were the rider. It looks odd and nasty - the silhouette of a horse with only your lower leg. Why did you do that? The photos frightened me; I tore them up. And another oddity – in the diaries you rarely mention birthdays - neither yours nor anyone else's, although you've kept hundreds of birthday cards, as if you did not want to mark time passing.

15

But this book isn't meant to be a complaint against someone who can't answer back. The anger that you must have felt against yourself, us, the world, is mirrored in the anger we feel against you, ourselves, the world. *Someone should have been able to save you.* Your parents, your doctors, yourself! And anger is only a subterfuge - so much less important than grief. We allow ourselves anger because we can't bear grief.

Grief is the most boring of emotions; it simply hurts and rarely leads to any positive outcome. Before grief can heal there must be acceptance. Having read and reread your papers, I have learned aspects of your nature that I never guessed when you were alive. And a fear that you hid from all of us including yourself. Amongst your papers, I found your enormous anger masked a grief that you never fully acknowledged or worked through. What caused such grief? Brain malfunction, hereditary weakness, bad childhood experiences, inadequate parenting - all of these or simply none – bad luck alone, a star-crossed fate? My anger with myself, the family, the medical profession remains because *you have killed yourself.* I am angry with you, too. Underneath the boiling anger are granite blocks of grief which are far harder to deal with.

My way of acceptance has been to search amongst the papers and photos, the diaries and letters. I want to recreate the child you were, to retrace your steps in the weak hope that a pattern emerges from that light-hearted dance that started so brightly. As a little girl you were often dancing. You had a way of holding out your skirt in each hand and putting your head on one side. So many photos show you in that pose.

When I write about you - just your name – Zoë - you come alive; when other people read about you, you are alive. Your name is the Greek word for life, which suited you so well. You were such a loving and loved child and many people loved you when you became a woman. Love shouldn't get lost.

16

Can reading about your suffering help anyone else endure the same illness? Could our efforts to explain to you (wherever you may be) or to ourselves, help other carers (especially parents) who feel the same draining inadequacy that your dad and I suffer because of how you ended your life? If your story (and ours) helps readers the telling is worthwhile. One of your most endearing characteristics was pleasure in helping people so skilfully that they never resented your help. But something happened over time that cut you off from the rest of us and robbed you of hope. You stopped believing that you had a future. And you never made us understand. During your final summer, you tried but we missed the signs. After your death, when Dr Vasudevan admitted to us you'd spoken of suicide to him, he believed he had 'negotiated' you out of it. Not parents, not siblings, not friends, not doctors, could give you the reassurance that you craved and so you severed the link between us.

Writing down blunders and mistakes or efforts doesn't erase them. But I want and need to tell this story – for you, for me and for the others.

CHAPTER ONE

"…this golden dust called love…"

In the final weeks of Zoë's life, during the summer of 2000, neither in writing nor speaking could she communicate. She became almost mute. I tried to persuade her to write down anything. She wrote almost nothing. We found a few post-it notes in her bedside drawer and a brown notebook that I'd given her with only a few pages filled; a couple of stylized pen drawings of a woman's head, a page describing her depression and a page of jobs to do and two pages giving a retrospective of her life, as if she were weighing up the pros and cons. The letters are so cramped that the words are almost undecipherable. The retrospective reads:

Born   5/12/72 India

1972-74 India – happy baby

1974-84 France - happy, well-adjusted child

1984   Move to UK difficult 3 months then very happy at school

GCSEs 6As 3Bs

1988   Summer: mild depression

1988-89 excellent year academically, socially, sports, etc.

1989-90 happy but stopped studying hard. Put on a lot of weight. Lots of friends

1990-01 Year out. Very happy holiday interacting with Kelly but promiscuous and binge eating

Glandular fever – depression - hospitalised – recovered

1991-92 Bristol depression, dropped out, suicide attempt, hospitalised, recovered

Summer in the States - happy but very promiscuous

92-93 Bristol 'manic' delusional – prostitution. Fetched by Dad. Insurance job. Met Kingsley, moved in with him

1993-96 Essex 2:1 Happy years Lots of friends. Sociable

1996-97 LSE MSc Distinction. Happy year. Lots of friends v. Sociable

1998   Worked for four months at the Gaia Foundation good job sacked -

   Dope with Jamie. Busy, social, quite happy.

 Briefly back with Francis

1999   SSE - United Response - Very good job - became dope-head -

   Promiscuous busy social life - a bit happy

2000   Morocco beautiful time with Hicham. Became disillusioned - manic

   - Hospitalised

      Back in UK. Clinically depressed. Diagnosed as manic bi-polar depressive

   July: slowly resurfacing. Afraid that I've missed the boat career- wise and that I'm not up to my friends. Where do I go from here? I have enormous potential and I am in an enormously fucked-up situation.

   Plus points: interpersonal skills/intelligence/looks/wonderful friends/health/supportive family/ good degrees /some relevant work experience. Points to consider: no job, no money, no vocational training. Longest job at age 27 only one year.

That entry isn't dated but she must have written it sometime in July in the middle of a depression that had began on the tenth of May. We were expecting a mood change; the doctors had explained that depression generally follows a manic episode. What none of us, and especially Zoë, were expecting, was the length of that depression and the pain it caused her.

When she was a child and young woman, you could not imagine that she would suffer a severe mental illness and breakdown in her late teens.

72-74 – India – a happy baby

There were three children, a boy and two girls when Zoë arrived. She was unexpected and unplanned for. My husband Wal had been correspondent in Jerusalem for *The Observer* and *The Guardian* and Habie, Ben and Bups (Tanya) went to Hebrew school, Bups, my youngest was five and although we didn't use any sort of birth control, I hadn't got pregnant again. Wal had had enough kids. I was keener on riding my two Arab ponies than I was on childcare so I started taking a contraceptive pill and wasn't bothered when my next period didn't arrive. Six weeks later, I felt a hard swelling just above my pubic bone. I was too scared to mention it. Cancer terrifies me. That spring on a visit to my parents in London, I made an appointment with Tony Woolf, family friend and a gynaecologist. I told him, trying not to cry, about the lump. He examined me:

"You're sixteen weeks pregnant."

"I can't be. I started the pill the first week of March."

"Dorothy, my dear, I've been a gynaecologist for thirty years and I should know the difference between a tumour and a foetus."

What a relief! I must have conceived three days after I started the pill. The pregnancy continued normally.

Wal accepted a new posting that was to cover the Indian subcontinent, so we moved with three children and bump to New Delhi.

Zoë had an uneventful birth at the cottage hospital in the grounds of the British High Commission.

"Stop pushing," cried the nurse. "Doctor isn't here yet."

"I can't."

Doctor arrived putting on his mask just in time to catch Zoë's head.

Photographs of her first birthday party show a fat regal baby wearing a Rajasthani mirror-work dress of embroidered red cotton. Her nickname was Baby-ji - the Indian honorific as in Ghandi-ji. Like her elder brother Ben, her hair was daffodil yellow, though like Ben's, it ended up mid-brown.

Habie, the oldest child, went to the British School, her younger brother Ben to the American school. We thought that the more relaxed atmosphere would suit his naughtiness better. He and his friends thought it funny to scatter nails in front of visitors' cars and pee into my riding boots. Tanya, who was still called Bups, went to a posh kindergarten where well-to-do Indians sent their kids in cars with drivers and white-sari-ed ayahs. Zoë had an ayah called Parvati. I didn't want to employ two ayahs, so Bups had to manage nursery school without a personal attendant.

Habie has sent me an extract from her diary. At eleven years old she wrote:

Oct 16 1973

Dear diary,

...Today I feel like telling you all about my two younger sisters. First there's Babyjee (Zoé), who's absolutely adorable! She's now ten months and a bit. She learnt to crawl ages ago. Now she spends most of her spare time (that is, when she's not eating, sleeping or howling) climbing up the stairs or crawling around the house making mischief. In looks, she's also lovely. When she laughs properly, it's a truly enjoyable sound to hear. She also has an extraordinarily strong personality, you know. For

example Bups tried to take something out of Babyjee's hands, but the little creature is unbeatable! And then there's Bups. Oh Bups, she's... she's, she is the one person I love most of all. She's just so kind and obliging. Sometimes she just fills my heart with tear-bringing love. Once, for instance, it was early in the morning and the baby woke us up. It was dark, and I was awfully tired and I just began to cry. Bups then said: "Don't cry Habie, If you want to go to sleep I'll look after Babyjee for you" (she was just as tired as me).

Yours ever, Habie

New Delhi in the seventies provided an agreeable, slow-paced life for expatriates, if you could pretend not to notice that you were incomparably richer than most of the population. Our money stretched; we had plenty of domestic help to take care out of 'childcare'. Zoë, an easy baby, seldom cried and was never ill. I breastfed her for eleven months, so that whenever Wal suggested I go with him on a trip, she had to come, too. We took her tiger watching in Corbett Park. The tiger sauntered into the clearing at midnight, posing like a film star before it killed the tethered goat. But two-month old Zoë never opened her eyes.

Zoë aged eleven in Wales

She slept in a Moses basket next to my bed for a few months and then shared a room with her elder sisters. She must have started sleeping through the night quite early because I don't recall having to get up to feed her.

Parvati, the ayah, treated Zoë as if she were her own child. I was too occupied with parties, horse riding and buying silks to wonder whether Zoë believed that Parvati was her *real* mother. Years later we read about that experiment in which baby chimps were given milk from wire-framed models of mothers but cuddled by soft cloth imitation mothers. The baby chimps grew to prefer the cuddling mothers to the milk-giving ones. I never related any of that to how Zoë was treated. I fed her but Parvati cuddled her.

The Ayah rarely saw her own nine-year-old son, who was cared for by relatives while his mother worked. The same situation applied to Anthony, our cook, a South Indian Christian, whose wife and children lived in Kerala and whom he visited for one month of the year when he went on leave. We accepted such unfairness casually because it was 'the custom.' Working for foreigners was considered a plumb job. Someone working for an expatriate could expect a present of money or in kind if he recommended a relative or fellow caste member to a vacant post. Everyone who worked in our house had come via Anthony. We paid higher wages than the local going rate and gave the servants a day off a week. Walter didn't like our children being waited on but I said that it would make them self-confident like Edwardian aristocrats. Certainly as a baby Zoë had every whim catered for and was never left to cry. Our experience was not unusual. Most memoirs of a European childhood in India refer to that glowing, jewel-like quality of life. Habie, the eldest child, certainly remembers India like that. Zoë only repeated memories second-hand from family stories and photographs.

Parvati the ayah would say how much she longed for a daughter and fair-haired Baby-ji seemed a harmless fantasy substitute. I would breastfeed the baby with Parvati hovering at my side ready to whisk her away for changing nappies, love and cuddles. Baby-ji adored her and would stretch out her arms to be carried off.

24

We moved to France when Zoë was almost two. For the first few months she cried a great deal, unlike the smiley baby photos taken on the pile of red cushions on the veranda in New Delhi. It never occurred to us to wonder whether separating from the ayah had traumatised her. We had substituted a grey toddlerdom in the place of a golden babyhood. It always seemed to be raining in northern France - me busy breeding horses, Wal chasing political stories and the kids learning to speak French.

Our first home in France was the chateau of Blincourt. We joined a group of eight Parisians who wanted to set up a sort of artistic commune. It suited us at the start. I had the horses and Walter kept a tiny flat in Paris and came home at weekends. Venu, who'd worked for us in Delhi, came too. He was twenty-three and wanted to better himself in Europe. We had a flat over the stables. While he was stretching across the narrow kitchen table, Venu knocked off a pot of boiling coffee. It spilt on Zoë's tummy, first degree burns. For three weeks she and I had to stay indoors. The gauze stuck to the burned flesh had to be pulled off every twenty-four hours. Whether you eased it off or ripped in one yank - the result was the same: Zoë yelled. She'd never had cause to cry in the arms of her Indian ayah, Parvati. Now, this cold grey rainy place and this 'Mum' who hurt - not like her other mum. She had no words; she could only scream. The bubbled skin covered half her stomach. By her twenties it had faded into a small patch of dry scar tissue high under her ribs. Venu, when we left Blincourt for Normandy and then Vaugenlieu, stayed with us for a couple of years, learnt to speak French and got a job as an embassy driver in Paris. Zoë became a quiet and good child, tagging along behind her siblings.

74-84 France - happy, well-adjusted child.

That's what she remembers and we, too. The nine years we spent in France seemed happy and busy. Walter had a job he adored as foreign correspondent for *The Guardian*. I was a housewife with writing ambitions and horsey inclinations with four, then five kids. My first baby,

25

Nicola, had died in 1961 of complications arising from
Spina Bifida. Zoë's baby brother was born in 1980. She was
eight, too old to be jealous. She adored her little brother.
The whole family did. A late baby (I was forty-three)
Zachary Asher Tobias weighed in at over four kilos and was
cherished from the moment of birth. He still is. I tried to
count how many kisses different family members gave
eleven month old Zaco in the course of a single day and
gave up at 152.

We had a passion for large, old houses surrounded
by their own land. In France they are often cheaper to buy
than modern, smaller houses. When the scheme of renting
Blincourt collapsed, communes not being the easiest form
of social living, we moved to a semi-detached, manor house
in Normandy and when that failed (we were too isolated
from Paris and useless as small farmers) we moved to
another mansion outside Compiègne – only eighty
kilometres from Paris. This was called the *Chateau de
Vaugenlieu*. It wasn't really a castle, it was what would be
considered a manor house in England. Big it certainly was.
Our friends teased us for having delusions of grandeur,
moving from one large house to another three times but
everyone enjoyed visiting and staying in these isolated
mansions and writing the address on their postcards home.
Our overlarge houses seemed strange to outsiders, I
suppose, we were tremulously trying to escape our inner
bourgeois selves. We were a bit late for the sixties but I
scrambled to keep up and Wal, although he was never
trendy, found it amusing to live a rackety lifestyle, earn a
good salary and have several pretty kids running around the
place.

The Chateau de Vaugenlieu where we lived for the
last five years of our stay in France had two wings with
shutters at the high windows. Some of the catches were
missing and the shutters would bang in the wind. There
were two hectares of paddocks and gardens. Habie was a
teenager and finishing her baccalaureate. Ben went to the
Lycée where he soon met Frederique, the prettiest and

cleverest girl of her year, whom he married five years later. Tanya, still called Bups, was busy, happy and clever. Zoë came at the end of the line. (Zachary would arrive two years later.) Once we had moved to Vaugenlieu, she had grown out of the difficulties she'd had when she was two. She had learnt the lesson that no one was exclusively available for her.

I took a holiday to Australia and she dictated a note to Wal to send me: *me and Daddy having a beautiful walk to a lake. It was all covered in ice and in the middle there was a little bit of snow fallen down on top. We went afterwards to the river. After we came home I gave the birds some crumbs because it is so freezing that the birds cannot find any food so that is why I myself give them their food. Lots of love to my dear Mother and thank you Zoë.* She was seven.

It was also at Vaugenlieu a couple of years later that she wrote five pages in her diary. Until I found it eighteen years later, I'd never known of its existence - a small pink diary with a padlock and key. Seven envelopes containing letters are neatly stuck on pages decorated with crayoned flowers and hearts. Before the letters were pasted in, Zoë wrote some short pieces in the copperplate writing French schoolchildren are taught. Habie has translated the text; her French is perfectly idiomatic – mine isn't.

My love affaires from the age of 6-9

The first boy that I loved was Romeo. He was very handsome and it was for that I think I loved him. In growing up, I loved him less and less; also I loved another who was called Olivier and so I realised that it was looks that I loved not him. At first Olivier didn't love me. We were mates afterwards friends and we loved one another.

The Belgian Frontier

One day the school organised a trip to an amusement park near the Belgian border. In the bus, I sat next to Eric not

because we wanted to but because a teacher had told us to.
In the bus he asked me whether I preferred him or Olivier.
At the amusement park I was with both of them all day.
Coming back I was with them in the bus and he told me that
he loved me and did I ? Yes.

Zoë kept seven of Eric's letters in their original envelopes, neatly stuck into the pink notebook. I remember Eric as a good-looking, fairhaired, polite boy. They had met at the village primary school.

The first letter reads :

Zoë,

I love you madly. I hope forever. Squeeze my hand and tell me out loud if you love me. Yes or no.
I want my noodles.
Age 11 years. Date of birth 2 December 1970.

On the facing page, two tiny photos of Eric and Zoë are decorated with a crayoned red heart. I don't know what were the noodles that Eric wanted.

His last letter reads:

Zoë, Did you find the letter I wrote you interesting?
In my bed I am alone, it's better when there's two of us. I wish I could see you every evening. I'm going to tell you one of my dreams, just between us. I dreamed we were on a faraway island and there were black and white horses and we slept in a tree in a tree house we had made.
I love you
I hope you and me is forever. Eric

One of her nicknames was 'Sugar-Plum Fairy.' She had a physical grace about her that stayed throughout her life. Although she had kept Eric's letters for eighteen years, she never mentioned him again.

After she died, several people remarked how they've never forgotten the first moment that they saw Zoë. Mathieu, an Argentinean musician, said, "I was eight; she must have been six. She ran down the stairs wearing a long dress and a necklace and I thought she was a princess." Judy, one of my Colchester friends, first met her at thirteen. "She walked into our sitting room and I thought she was the most beautiful young woman I had ever seen."

Along with beauty grew Zoë's love of animals, cats and horses in particular. In France I had five horses. We managed the expenses of oats, hay and farriers by breeding a couple of mares and selling young stock. Ben at the age of thirteen broke in Shah Jehan bareback because he couldn't be bothered to clean the saddle. Habie, Ben and Tanya shared my enthusiasm to begin with but gradually gave up one by one. Zoë started riding at seven. She was the only child who didn't outgrow a passionate love of horses. Why do horses inspire such terrible devotion in some and not others?

Zoë wrote at nine:

Madame Minny

My pony, my pony of Wales who is white as snow. Good as gold. As speedy as the wind. As pretty and as dainty and as fine as a fairy. That's Minny.

Unfortunately, it wasn't true. I'd bought the pony from Madame Boucqillon an Englishwoman married to a French landowner, who bred Welsh ponies on her huge estate. Her grand manners intimidated me: the pony was a bargain... the high price 3000 francs justified ... splendid first pony, etc. etc. I was rooked. The pony was unridable most of the time because of chronic laminitis. We had bought it in one of its rare periods of soundness. Zoë spent

29

hours grooming the lame animal; maybe she blamed herself. We had to get rid of it. Could Zoë have guessed its destination was probably the abattoir? In France they eat horses as well as ride them!

Zoë's privileged childhood suffered similar losses and mishaps. After Minny was sold, I bought her a pygmy goat that she adored and carried everywhere. Napoleon would jump on the dinner table, upset the dishes and have to be chased off.

At Vaugenlieu, we hired Maria, a Portuguese cleaner, who crammed herself and several family members into the gardener's cottage besides the gates. Zoë was fond of her. We came back from shopping one day to find that Maria's husband and brothers had shot every songbird on the property; a triangular pile of tiny corpses was stacked in front of the door. We sacked her. Neither she nor her men folk could understand our distress and anger. When she finally left in a fury, having hit me over the head with an aluminium pipe (luckily too light to do any damage) she stole as much from the cottage as she could carry in their van and Zoë's goat was included. We learned later that she and her family had eaten it. Again Zoë never spoke of her lost pet.

And then - the catastrophe of the cats. We'd moved to Vaugenlieu from Normandy with a nice tabby. Within weeks he disappeared so we got another. That one went missing, too. Zoë was the greatest cat lover amongst our children. I wanted to breed pedigree cats so I imported a pair of Abyssinians kittens from UK. Stately creamy brown kittens with unfriendly natures, we called them Ra and Sheba. They, too, vanished within a year. I replaced them with a pair of local moggies, brother and sister. Zoë named them Snowflake and Bluebell and they used to perch in the apple tree outside the front door, playing with each other's tails. When they were half-grown, they vanished. All in all, we lost nine cats at Vaugenlieu over three years. When Bluebell and Cornflake disappeared, Zoë refused to go to school for a week. Her face was white with shock. We

30

found out what had happened. Our neighbour from Hell, a rich and nasty farmer, had shot every single cat. No legal recourse because, as he boasted, cats are considered vermin.

In spite of what seemed to us then, these minor tragedies of childhood, Zoë was always amongst the top students at school, had many friends, a sunny disposition and a sense of humour.

When *The Guardian* sent Wal back to London after nine years in France, she never complained at losing her friends and leaving her dog behind. We only learnt years later that Zoë felt let down because we had sold her childhood home.

We bought Greenacres in rural Essex in 1984. Zac was four. Zoë was eleven. The previous owners had built the house for their young family and added a granny flat for his old parents; they were astonished when Ben, aged eighteen, and Tanya, aged fifteen, arrived a couple of weeks before the rest of us and cleaned the grubby house and fenced the fields. If Zoë kept a diary of her early months in England, it hasn't survived.

Our first years at Greenacres started out well. At first it seemed odd to be living in a bungalow, even a large one, after Vaugenlieu. There were no corridors for Zac to ride his tricycle down. We soon grew used to low ceilings and Zoë began to love Greenacres. She was growing up surrounded by space and she loved that. The previous owners had planted many trees on the seven acres and we built a stables and an outdoor manège. There was even a plastic-lined, 20 metre long swimming pool that required as much care as an ailing pet. Walter was working on *The Guardian* and I registered to do an MA at Essex University. Ben started a Music degree at Colchester Institute and spent every available free moment rushing back to France to see Fredy, who had begun her medical studies. Habie was finishing off a BA Hons at the London School of Economics and living in London with Nana, her maternal grandmother.

Colchester still had (and at the time of writing still has) selective grammar schools. We assumed Tanya and Zoë would be accepted. Tanya at fifteen with superb grades in Physics, Maths and Chemistry from her French school was given a place in the Lower Sixth of the Girl's High School but Zoë had to take the eleven plus. Wal drove her to Chelmsford, where she sat by herself in a large room with an invigilator, puzzling out questions in English, many of which made no sense to a French speaking schoolchild. She couldn't supply the ending to: 'a rolling stone gathers no …?' or 'a bird in hand is worth…?' She failed.

We believed as good *Guardian* readers should in state education but the local Comprehensive sounded dire with pupil violence reported in the local newspaper and high teacher turnover. Eventually we solved the problem with the sort of manipulation that middle class *mores* allow. The headmistress of the Girls High agreed to interview Zoë. She was accepted. Her French was immaculate, in spite of its Picardy accent, her maths excellent, her spoken English fluent as a second language and her charm irresistible.

With bureaucratic illogicality, the school took her into Year Two, although she was only eleven and had failed entry into the first year. So she went through her secondary schooling as the youngest in the class. We were confident that Zoë would be able to keep up.

We learned many years later that her first months in England were miserable with homesickness for France; she never told us.   Amongst the letters she kept were those from her old French schoolmates. Her closest friend, Mylène wrote in big, round schoolgirl writing.

I miss you so much. You absolutely must come and stay with me this summer.

Their friendship continued while they grew up on opposite sides of the channel. At Zoë's funeral, Mylène, who has the grace of a gazelle, spoke in her French-accented English:

"Zoë my wild Zoë,

"Zoë l'indomptable.

"How are we going to live without your smile, your warmth, your great ideas, sometimes crazy ideas?

"You were looking for perfection and for a world which does not exist. Of course, this impossible quest made you angry and rebellious…But you made this world better for all the people who came across you. I know you realised.

You were too aware of the absurdity of life but lived it to the full anyway.

"What a life, Zoë! Full of laughter, full of doubts sometimes, full of excess up to the end…

"Quelle vie! ma cherie, ma belle.

"Thanks for your energy, your unconditional support, your precious love, and your freedom.

"Merci d'avoir eté tout çela.

"A beautiful part of me has now gone, but I will fill the big hole you left with all our memories together.

"You came on earth like a shooting star and you covered your dear family and friends with this golden dust called love, so that we never forget you…

"Zozo my friend, Zozo the sister I have never had, I shall learn how to live without your light and guidance.

CHAPTER TWO

"... as warm and wholeheartedly generous ..."

Zoë was the opposite of moody; she laughed a lot. Like my Dad and her younger brother and unlike both her parents, she'd remember the punch line of jokes and tell them at the family dinner table. She loved her family, her horses, her friends and she developed a fervent love of God. Her manner of seeing through pretension became and remained one of her most appealing qualities. No one could bullshit Zoë.

Her judgements could be harsh. My mother dominated my father ruthlessly; he was as henpecked as the little guy on a seaside postcard. All my children loved their doting grandparents who spoilt them rotten.

We found a scrap of paper in one of Zoë's boxes, written after a weekend spent with her grandparents. She was fourteen. I don't come out of it too well either.

The Well-Matched Couple

The door opened and my grandmother sighs, "Max, time for your walk, would you like the bike or the chair? Don't forget your hat and scarf. Zoe will go with you."

Funny how when people grow old they return to infancy.

As a young woman she'd always been the dominant one and now for him at eighty-two she was his goddess. I looked at my grandmother. What a silly woman she was! Rather pathetic with all her hopes and aspirations. Her superior airs were ridiculous because she couldn't carry them through. When she spoke she spoke in what she thought was a grand tone and very slowly to give importance to her words. She had gone into a fantasy life because her own world was and had been boring for years.

All her stories were of self-glory, self-love and self-adoration. Never we but I.

My own mother has inherited quite a few of her mother's mannerisms, which always annoys me. And often she bears that same silly expression of self-importance that she can't even look people in the eye.

My lovely grandparents that I had adored as a child. Oh, I love them even now, or at least parts of them. She is warm and Jewish, very loving and Grandpa would never hurt anyone except himself. But at fourteen I could see through them. Like transparent children they sat before me.

Max was in his chair all stooped and like most old men his neck had shrunk into his shoulders. Each time Nana uttered a word, his eyes glazed and a pathetic look of slavish adoration swept over his face. I didn't really feel sorry for him. In fact he irritated me more than she did. Human beings are usually attracted to qualities such as beauty, harmony, style. He had none of these. He had let himself be dominated. You couldn't speak to him without her butting in and answering instead of him. But that was the way he wanted it.

Zoë didn't stand out amongst her siblings. She wasn't the eldest; she wasn't the baby in the family; she was the middle-child. That Zoë was more reserved than the rest of us was accepted, rarely discussed. We were noisy, argumentative and full of ourselves. Tanya, as elder sister, hogged in the limelight and Zoë never fought to get more for herself.

We are not a family who takes lots of home movies but Zoë appears in a couple of videos. Habie, as a young woman, wanted to be a filmmaker. One spring weekend, she came to Greenacres, where she hoped to shoot a short film, which would gain her entry to film school, a simple story about a five-year old boy with Zachary as the star. Habie arrived with two young male film students. But Zac refused to cooperate and the plan seemed set for disaster.

Zoë aged fourteen at Greenacres

He would neither speak to camera nor learn his lines. Habie, with only a couple of days' shooting time, tried to salvage the film by turning it into a documentary about *why* Zachary wouldn't take part. She interviewed me, Tanya and Ben and herself questioning whether Zach had

been spoilt as a child. Wal was away covering a bishops'
conference somewhere. Ben and Tanya thought he was
rather spoilt; Zoë and I said that he wasn't. (Habie was
subsequently offered a place at film school but went to work
at the BBC instead.)

Filming through mirrors and windows is a
trademark of Hab's work. Shot through the glass windows
of the sitting room out into the garden, Zoë aged thirteen
canters bareback on Shah Jehan. She wears long black boots
and a white tee shirt. She sits Shah as if she grew on his
back. The Japanese cherry tree is in full bloom. As her
horse ducks under the tree, Zoë snaps off a spray of
blossom. She threads the blossom through Shah's bridle and
taps on the window to attract her little brother's attention.
Zac, in his grey-striped pullover, is sitting scowling with
crossed arms on the red-striped settee. Aware that someone
is behind him, he won't look up from watching *Little Big
Man* on the TV. Zoë grins and canters off. The thirty-second
scene glows with sunshine, blossom and the subtle
interaction of beloved baby brother and elder sister. The
spring is so lovely you could cry with joy, the garden green
on green in an amazing range of shades.

In a later sequence, Habie interviews a poised Zoë,
on her thought as to why her little would not cooperate?
Didn't she agree with the young filmmakers that he was
spoilt?

Facing the camera, Zoë replies in her husky voice
with all the confidence of thirteen years: "it depends what
you call spoilt. He's not obedient but he's not spoilt in the
way some kids are - they cry all the time.

"The best thing about Zaco is he's open; he's shy
but after a while he's very friendly to people. He opens up
really well; he's fun to play with. He can be bossy with his
friends. He grew up with so many older brothers and sisters
he needs a sense of power. He does have friends in the
village – the point is they always come when he asks them

round but they never ask him back. I don't know if that's because he's not one of them. They all come from completely different backgrounds. ..."

She fidgets a little with her necklace. "Me? I had a nanny in India – I don't remember about that. I came to France when I was about two years old – I had a lot of freedom. I was also the littlest. I was a lot more obedient than Zaco.

"When I was little I always wanted to go with Mum when she went out shopping and so on. Zac wants to stay home.

She tosses her hair and grins, "right now I'm going to bring the horses in, make some phone calls about horse shows, and ring some friends up..."

Habie remarked later that Zoë's polished performance including its few hesitations and giggles was due to the fact that she fancied the cameraman rotten.

As she grew from childhood into adolescence, Zoë and I became as close as we would ever be because of horses. In England, we wondered whether we could still keep them; Wal's salary without the hefty expense account of a Foreign Correspondent was halved now that he worked in the London office. We could probably afford to own a couple of horses if we stabled them at home and did all the work ourselves. A subculture flourishes in British rural life, ranging from pigtailed little girls keeping fat ponies in fields to tweedy ladies and gents riding top quality show jumpers and Three Day Eventers. We slotted uneasily somewhere in the middle. Zoë's love of horses equalled my own and she soon became a bolder rider and enjoyed giving me lessons.

An entry when she was sixteen.

Came home from school and sorted Mum out on Shah.

Zoë grew too tall for her pony and we bought her first horse when she was thirteen. Zoë called the fifteen-hand brown mare Zugi, one of our family's nonsense pet names. Although the mare had a somewhat spiteful nature, a long neck, was hard to catch and tended to kick, she adored her.

That summer, Zoë was registered to attend Pony Club summer camp with Zugi. The week before camp began, she had an accident. The girth wasn't tight enough. Zugi tripped, fell onto her side and trapped Zoë's foot beneath the saddle. The foot was broken.

An enforced bed rest of three weeks compelled her to write a Mills and Boon novel, it would be set in Kenya so she could describe lots of wild animals and tell a love story, none of it from personal experience. She dictated the text to her Dad who typed it onto his computer. Only five exciting chapters were finished and they are lost. I'd love to read them again.

Three years later, I persuaded Zoë we should sell the mare. I had sound reasons. We had brought Nike back from France already in foal. That colt was a splendid well-grown animal and now old enough to be ridden. I never trusted Zugi's stable manners. She once aimed a vicious kick at the blacksmith's head, missed but could easily have killed him. Zoë agreed and Zugi was sold for twice what we had paid for her.

Zoë aged twelve riding Shah Jehan at Greenacres

This is what she wrote shortly afterwards, which she showed no one. She often wrote in French when the subject was something she felt deeply about. I've left the passage in the original because I like Zoë's French.

[1986] '*J'ai monté un peu Shah. J'ai pleuré pour Zugi. Elle me manque. C'était très dure. Je m' était tellement attacheé à ma jument et je repensais à tout nos souvenirs: quand je l'ai monté de bon matin dans la fraicheur, comme je l'aurais dressé, quand elle m'avait gagné le cross, ses deux classes de dressage.*

Je me suis dit qu'il fallait que je fasse un gros effort avec Najem car Zugi était partit et il était un petit (grand) cheval magnifique.'

[I rode Shah for a bit. I cried for Zugi. I miss her. It's so hard. I adored my mare and I keep thinking of our past times: when I rode her in the early morning, how I trained her, how she won the cross country and two Dressage classes. I keep telling myself that I must make a big effort to get on with Najem because Zugi has gone and Najem is a super big young horse.]

Sunday 8th

We took Najem to his first Hunter trials at Krissimmons. He was very good. Did pairs with really nice man Nick Scott. Both horses stopped at the last jump. On his own Najem was unable to jump no 22 because of the angle I took him into it.

Was I insensitive to sell Zugi without understanding the depth of Zoë's attachment? But why didn't she tell me herself? She gave up riding a few years later, after her recovery from her first episode of bi-polar illness. She said that she was sorry to hurt my feelings. "I no longer want to ride." No reason. In the cardboard boxes, we found an undated note, which must have been written after her suicide attempt.

"Six years ago we sold Zugi. That is the greatest regret of my life. Not only did I genuinely care for her; she also symbolises the most productive phase of my life. She was the principle factor that made that positive attitude possible.

Zugi is not a great horse; and I am not a great rider. But together we were great. We won a Cross Country in optimum time 3.56 minutes. The day we sold her we won both our dressage classes. Everyday before school, I woke up at 6am to feed her, brush her and exercise her. We rode in the manège overlooking the lake. And at that time of day everything is crisp and fresh. Those moments are stuck in my memory as some of the most happy of my life.

I have come to the conclusion that Zugi and I formed something of a perfect union. My parents have a

*nice mare Kismet who is similar in many ways to Zugi. But I
cannot bring myself to relate to her. The thought of taking
her into a competition is painful because Zugi's memory
comes to mind wiping out the present.*

*When we sold Zugi, I lost interest in riding and I do
not believe that I could ever regain it. Perhaps this is purity
and fidelity; perhaps it is just insecurity.*

*We tend to be aware of happiness only in
retrospect. I let Zugi go because it was not until she had
gone that I realised that she was the greatest part of my
happiness. "*

At the time, I didn't interpret her giving up horses
as more significant than the commonplace decision pony-
riding girls make when they exchange ponies for
boyfriends. And boyfriends were something Zoë never
seemed short of, starting from primary school.

Her elder sister Tanya's first serious boyfriend was
Tom, a garrulous, lanky chap, who badly needed to grow
into the successful barrister he later became. They had one
of those touching early romances that leave a lavender-
scented memory for the rest of your life. Their birthdays fall
on the same day and two decades later, both happily
married to other people, they remain great friends.

When a group of Grammar School boys - sixth
formers - dashing fancy waistcoats, furtive smoking, full of
energy and promise visited Greenacres, Zoë met Tom's
friend Matthew. Zoë at fourteen, not really in their set, was
allowed to hang on as a sort of pretty mascot. Zoë and
Matthew began a romantic friendship which burgeoned into
a voluminous correspondence; Zoë had kept enough letters
to fill two folders. One of Matthew's letters (he intended to
be a poet at this stage in his life) reads in part:

Dear Zoë,

*Lately there seems to have been a lack of (verbal)
communication between us. This, I realize, is almost*

entirely my fault and I am taking steps to iron out this difficulty in order to understand you a little better.

(Could it be that when you are near I am so overwhelmed by your presence that I cannot manage to produce anything more than muffled banalities?)

This uncomfortable distance between us may be partly caused I think by the coldness and distance that accompany poetic creation. Love that proves itself in rhyme often finds it difficult to express itself to its own object. I have for several weeks now been labouring to produce a set of poems written entirely in your honour. I cannot tell you when they will be finished. I am finding the villanelle difficult and am at present writing an immensely complex 'spiritual' poem.

However I hope that I can give them to you soon in true lover's passion...

Your love- struck suitor, Matthew

Maybe I can bring those poems to you beneath your window by moonlight?

Zoë understood our young poet's self-absorption. Her ironic self only deserted her at the end of her life. There's a letter she wrote in July 1987, which is probably the draft of a reply.

Dearest Matthew,

Although it's Monday and I am at home, Mum said she didn't mind because of the gorgeous weather. Anyway, I'm only telling you this to set the scene. Since I was at home lazing around I reread parts of the letters you sent me.

Although perhaps slightly pretentious in parts (I don't blame you for this since I seem to remember that my letters to you were gruesomely pretentious and I do hope that that has changed.

43

They were really rather charming and lovely. I also liked you humour and your paintings and I don't think that I appreciated them or you at the time or gave you enough credit for what you are, But anyway I think that is enough flattery for you now...

Zoë never talked to us about Matthew, neither then nor later. It was one of the paradoxes of her nature, apparently chatty and always articulate (until depression hit her) she kept her deepest feelings to herself but in that unfurling part of adolescence; Zoë wrote a lot about them. Although Kelly and Habie knew that she wrote diaries and poems, she never showed us and I suppose if she hadn't died, we may never have read any.

She wrote more about Matthew a little later and you can guess she must have been reading Jane Austen. [From a letter dated January 1988]

...It was exquisite indeed to be held in your arms by the light of the fire. So much so, that the alternative family life is not so rewarding. Though no doubt was this house to be graced with your wit and your unfailing charms, the Schwarz family would appear as angels before my eyes. (Do not allow such immodest flattery venture into your head lest it should 'Pop'.

I am listening to Bach's Concerto in C minor for violin and oboe. It is beautiful I would love to listen to it with you.

I could carry on writing for many pages yet but sleep is drawing close.

Goodnight and goodbye. I love you more than ever.

Zoë

How she would have loved to read that again in middle age!

Amongst the cardboard boxes we found an exercise book –
a diary for 1987 with the beguiling subtitle from Oscar
Wilde - *For **one should always have something quite
sensational to read on the train.*** Zoë could be quite an old-
fashioned romantic in her early teens. The first entry is 31st
of December 1986 and the last one five months later. She
puns on Mathew's surname Small.

*Matthew is beautiful he knows many things. His
conceit is not small and his confidence not very big.*

*Self-love he perpetuates through a young girl and
she – well that is her secret.*

*While the wind was blowing and the horses
munching I told him: 'tonight anything is possible. Fortunes
to be made or lost, virtues to be broken but in our case my
pretty jeans boy I think they were lost.'*

*He didn't understand. It was simple though. He was
taking more notice of himself than of Zoë – and that with a
pampered young girl will not do.*

*Through Dylan Thomas he softened me and inflated
himself – keen pride grew as he read his favourite lines.*

*My mother and I said to each other, 'If a man loves
you, you have him right round your little finger but if he
does not, love and kisses won't change him.'*

*Mathew is intelligent, well read and casts a
scornful eye on Macaroni cheese.*

*His lips are not full but none the less exquisite. His
eyes are wide and green and shaded with long lashes. Must
stop - sounding like a practise for Mills and Boon.*

<u>*Sunday 11th January*</u>

I would like to be with you now. But I had an afternoon and evening with you. I can ask for no more.

From this moment onwards I sign my soul to you to do with as you will. If you were to die now I would die too.

Do not kill this love. It is yours. My heart is in your hands,

Mozart Requiem

Zoë has just had her fifteenth birthday. And sadly and inevitably early love didn't last.

<u>*Thursday 4th January 1987*</u>

With Vivaldi Concerto for Flute and mandolin I am transported to the 18th Century court. Reposing in lawns of ivory-fresh scented flowers and sweeping trees. A handsome musician in a flowing white shirt, jodhpur trousers and boots and as fine wig of luxurious black curls plays the mandolin. The courtiers in silk gowns and powdered hair watch entranced.

The Scarlet Pimpernel and Magritte make love by the great oak tree.

I am about to close the Matthew chapter of my love forever. Blow out the flames that kept it burning and leave only ashes to be thrown on the roses.

Today I learnt the lesson that most women are taught I am sure. When young men say they love you they love themselves still more. In Matthew's case a pretty young girl fed his inflated self. Keen pride grew as he read his favourite lines.

To be denied on the verges of love hurts both emotions and confidence.

There is no crueller torture for she who loves than to be parted from her lover and for days I have seen the sun rise, live and die without him.

But such a weak character does not deserve to be mourned; as he used me I can use him. Think of him as an 'experience'. It is sad indeed but I will no longer be so free with my emotions.

To Matthew

You came and sparked creation

But you left only desolation!

But dear, from your dead indifference

You shall rise a hero before mine eyes.

For he that is unknown unseen

With fruitful qualities is blessed.

Tuesday 31ˢᵗ December 1987

The more one learns the less one knows. Such is the fate of most mankind. If all truth were to be a large beautiful cornfield, Man holds one blade of that paradise.

Evident but important observations I have made throughout the last few months:

- *Searching for perfection may be noble but expecting it of anyone may be presumptuous.*

- *Do not be disappointed by family or friends. They rarely behave as you would like them to. Do not be too rash in casting anyone aside. Look for the mistake in yourself first. If you find no fault here (as I rarely do) only then should you seek out the other's inadequacies.*

This afternoon I felt happier than I have for weeks.

I woke up at nine in a warm comforting bed, enveloping down like a mother's womb. In the same way that unborn babies do not want to leave their mother's womb, adults do not want to leave their beds and I read a small book describing painters from the 13th century to Picasso. The book discussed the effects they had on their own period and periods to come. I then proceeded to re-read Matthew's poem. After which I brought breakfast in bed to a luscious young Frenchman. I had an exquisite fruit salad for lunch. I went round Glebe House on Shah. When I came back I revised some French verbs for my O-level then to pamper myself still further I wrote all this down.

With all these privileges who could possibly complain. What is more - Mel Brookes is on the Tele tonight. I cannot comprehend why all this is granted to me whilst other less fortunate souls are dying of hunger and general neglect from our so-called 'caring' western civilisation. I think the greatest self-fulfilment is through helping and working for others. Perhaps like my godmother Sarojini I will work for UNICEF or Amnesty International.

I'll turn in now, more of this later.

Zoë's godmother (one of my closest friends) was one of Zoë's role models. They loved one another dearly. Zoë's second name, of which she was proud, was Sarojini : she who lives in a Lotus flower.

I had first met Sarojini in 1957, a year after Wal and I were married. She was then married to Abu, the cartoonist and living in Bayswater. She was, and still is, one of the most beautiful women I've ever known. She has always kept a grace and warmth about her. When her daughters were ten and twelve, her marriage broke up and she brought them up alone, working and living abroad in foreign postings for UNICEF. Not so unusual in the twenty-first century but rare enough for an Indian woman in the nineteen seventies. She was a brilliant administrator. I used to visit her in various postings and often took Zoë. We went to Ankara when Zoë was thirteen. Sarojini took us to visit projects UNICEF had set up in villages. Zoë wrote in a journal:

April 16ᵗʰ [1986]

During Ataturk's time the women had 'opened' out and were less suppressed but now the population is retreating to religion and strict tradition. Before being allowed into a villager's house, we had to have the consensus of the man as in all things. In contrast to the village, the interior of the house was very clean and cheerful. The women (separate from the men) were joking and laughing and very hospitable. We were offered hot fresh milk with sugar. Visiting the village one really got a feel for life and attitudes in an eastern Turkish village.

For Zoë in her early teens, the world was opening up towards art and friendship as well as love; there were no apparent shadows. And if her grasp of modern history was a bit shaky, her sentiments were not.

January 13ᵗʰ 1987

If the Nazis had read Owens poems, the First World War might never have taken place.

I am discovering poetry, classical music and great literature. I am very fortunate to be able to do this and I am very grateful.

At this stage of her life Zoe reminded me of a rosebud opening out to the sunshine. Although her favourite poems were those of the Great War poets - poems dwelling on death and destruction rather than love, I would never have called her morbid.

It is quite phenomenal how much one changes and matures in adolescent years. Over the last 4 months I feel I have changed a lot. When I look at things I wrote less than one month ago, I can look at them from the viewpoint of a much older person and say, Ah how sweet, at something like the page opposite....

And already at the age of fifteen Zoë knew she was pretty and intended to capitalise on it.

February 25th 1987

Both times I have been recently ill, I have profited by it. Summer '86 when I broke my foot I wrote a book. [The unfinished Mills and Boon mentioned earlier] *And now I have discovered a book, which had I not been ill I would not have read. I think it will help my riding a lot. I really must lose ½ a stone. I am not overweight but normal weight as opposed to very slim. Being figure conscious as much as I am, it is irritating me. To be confident which is an ingredient towards happiness I have to have the total self-assurance that I am beautiful which if I was half a stone less I would have. Vain and teenagerish this may be but I do not blame it on myself alone for had I lived in a different society I would not be obsessed with my looks.*

Her looks mattered to her. When she was twenty-seven and taking anti-depressants and living with us at Greenacres, her skin reacted to medication by coming up in pimples. "I'm ugly," she complained. Right to the end of her life she was still plucking her eyebrows and waxing her legs.

From early childhood, Sarojini had been one of Zoë's role models. In her teens she added another - Florence Leader. She had four children in a similar age range to our own. First Tanya, then Zoë became friends of the family. Zoë admired Florence, a gentle Frenchwoman, married to an American professor of law, who has the lovely quality of really listening. (My daughters have always complained that I'm a poor listener.) Teenage girls often make a close friend of an older woman who acts as a substitute mother. I did so myself, at thirteen, with my elder brother's wife.

Habie and Tanya both had women friends, older than themselves, who were influential when they were growing up. It lessens the strains of the mother/daughter relationship to have a connection with another sympathetic older woman. Florence had become a born-again Christian and took Zoë to Evangelical church services. Florence gradually became her mentor. They enjoyed deep friendship and great love.

Florence's influence alone did not make Zoë religious; Zoë's already existing interest in spiritual matters gave them a common ground. When she was seven, she would ask me and Wal to come outside and look at the stars. Her appreciation of the natural world was intense, although it wasn't simply landscape that so enthralled her, as much as the figures captured within. She loved Constable's paintings. Zoë could look at a person, a child, a tree, a painting and really *see* them. The way in which she related to children had some of that quality – the ability to 'be-there'. You could, if you were feeling low be cheered up, simply by Zoë's presence or by the warmth in her voice on the telephone.

Wal and I were and are agnostic and our birth religion of Judaism has never been seriously practised at home so I do not believe that Zoë's spiritual side was something she learned from her parents.

Wednesday September 19th [1988, Zoe was sixteen]

*Before school I had the most beautiful experience and I
believe in God. I did the horses before school. The reservoir
was a colour I had never seen. I stood in the field. It was
completely tranquil and I fixed the view in my mind. The
water, the house, the grey pony in the field. Merry and
Sonya* [the Border collies] *who came running, the garden,
the pool, the autumn light through the trees, the manège and
stables. The feeling of peace knowing that Blue Boy and the
horses were having breakfast in the stables and that Mum,
Tanya and Zac were asleep in the house.*

Two nights after her suicide, we held a celebration of her
life around a bonfire on the lawn. Everyone said how much
Zoë would have enjoyed the impromptu party. Josh,
Florence's youngest son, now a six-footer, told the group
how Zoë had changed his life when he was a ten-year old
public school boy, "shy and a little snobby," Zoë insisted on
taking him out for a drink to *Roberto's* the smart café bar in
town. "I acted not scared. Zoë just took me along. We had a
great time; she treated me like an equal. First time a grown
up had ever done that."

After Zoë's death, Florence and I have often
comforted one another. I said that I thought Zoë had lost her
faith in God in her last depression.

"She hadn't," said Florence.

"That didn't stop her," I said.

Florence had no answer.

Were there clues in these years that Zoë would develop full-
blown depressive illness at the end of adolescence? We
never found any. In her retrospective account written in the
last months of her life, she marks *1988 a mild depression*.

52

All we remember from that summer is that she put on weight; used Goth makeup, which we thought hideous and she was very rude. "Typical teenage behaviour," we said. "She'll grow out of it," comforted friends. And by the following year Zoë was slim again and set for a brilliant school career. Being with Zoë was *fun.*

She shared other interests with me as well as horses. We both adored squeezing spots, especially other peoples'. For those who don't appreciate the exquisite sensation as the head of a pustule pops and a white worm yields to your fingertips' pressure and wriggles along the skin, this is a dirty habit. For those that enjoy it – it's bliss. Sadly for Zo and me, the Schwarz family are olive-skinned and rarely suffer from spots. Neither of Zoë's brothers had teenage spots and anyway both had steady girlfriends from the age of seventeen /eighteen and any rare spot was out of bounds to sister and mother. Wal had a couple of deep grease spots on his back that (very) rarely he would let Zo squeeze, "her fingers are lighter than yours." We'd both shriek as inches of goo slithered out and lay in minute coils on Wal's satiny skin. Antoine, Zac's godfather, who frequently lived with us, had fairer skin and a shoulder crop of pustules. He was less squeamish and we spent joyful minutes, stretched out on either side of him comparing the length of our "worms".

Some months after Zoë's death, Wal said: "You idealise her. Don't you? She had plenty of faults that weren't connected to her illness?" I thought about it. "No, I don't think she did." She was one of those rare people who when they're happy, brighten a room just being in it. Her charisma was joined to tenderness and I loved the way she didn't take herself too seriously.

The following was written in French. It translates as:

Tuesday January 10th [1988]

I am happy. I live a golden life of permanent holiday. I don't see a distinction between life and studies and the masses of activities I do out of school and with friends, I know for sure that I am super intelligent (and MODEST!!!]

She was proud of her successes. She wrote the following entry in French as well.

February 14th

A very special day. The morning was as usual. At 12.15 I had my interview with Mrs Jones. I had offended her a week ago. I apologised. I told her she was right and her scolding had done me good. I told her that all my activities outside school stimulated me and I adore my life. I told her I was top of the class in English, French, and one of the best with Kelly in History. Mrs J told me I was super-intelligent. That I had a combination of brilliant academic success and ambition and maturity!
I wanted to prove myself to my parents. Now it felt wonderful. Mrs J also said I would get excellent marks at my O Levels and I could easily get into Oxford. Miss Lane also told me I was very talented and that she was very impressed.
I came home. I chatted to Mum. I told her everything about Mrs Jones. I finished writing my essay. I went to work in the restaurant. I am really good at it now. I was alone on the top floor and I managed...

Our home life continued placidly. Late twentieth century middle-class professional life was easy; we had it good. Among other pleasures, Zoë discovered theatre with her two close school friends Sarah and Kelly.

Friday 3rd of November

We decided to go and queue for Othello after school. .... I saw Ian McKellan walk through to his dressing room. Othello was everything we had hoped. The sets were ingenious...at one point I was only inches away from Ian McKellan. It was the most stunning acting I have ever seen. But acting is the wrong word. McKellan lived the part ...

The three girls applied to Oxford but after their interviews only Sarah was offered a place. Zoë had been certain of an offer – her teachers had all told her what splendid Oxbridge material she was and she got 100% in a mock A-level examination on Chaucer. She wrote: *Oxbridge lesson with Miss Davidson. I was the only one to do all the questions. The lesson was really good.*

Her diary contains no details of her interviews in Oxford, although she had enjoyed her two-day stay and went to parties and met people. Her life continued absorbed with friends and family. She wrote for the weekend after the disappointment over Oxford.

Friday 15th ...

Rang Oxford. Magdelan was out but I didn't know about Lincoln and Jesus. Obviously really devastated at first but then thought clearly and I was fine ... I rode Najem for ten minutes and Dad took me to the Arts Centre and Mum made a lovely dinner. She's making such a big effort. So lovely.

Saturday 16th December

Caught train to national gallery. Saw Italian paintings. Tony arrived...we walked to Convent Garden. There was a fair; it was very beautiful. Tony was writing funny postcards. I said I couldn't go to Tony's flat. We caught the tube. It was a wonderful afternoon. Invited Tony to 'The Woman in Black' and Christmas because he can't get to

55

Ireland until Boxing Day. Grandma Lilly was still in pain but not complaining...

Sunday 17th December ...

Rode Najem. Marc came. Tony ran. Kelly rang up. She didn't get into Oxford. Tanya and I were mad about it and talked about it for a while. We walked at the Nature Reserve and we were in fits because it was pissing down and the wind was incredible. Tanya made a lovely dinner. Mylène - everything is fixed for her and Jean Guy coming 27th for a week. Mum arrived – read some poems to her! We watched some Narnia. Read Observer magazine. I'm shaken with the happiness I've been feeling.

Zoë wrote, "I'm shaken with the happiness I've been feeling." Whether that enthusiasm tinged over into mania, we will never know now. We do know that it was charismatic, that it drew people to her. Even now some years after her death you can't pass a photo of her smiling without returning such an infectious smile. This enthusiasm spread over other people. Kelly said at her funeral:

"A lot has been said over the last few days about Zoë's genius for friendship. For me, one of Zoë's most appealing traits has always been her unshakeable conviction that each and every one of her friends surpassed the combined assets of Albert Einstein, Marilyn Monroe and Mahatma Gandhi.

"The fact is, it is given to very few people to be as warm and wholeheartedly generous as Zoe; and it is one of the reasons she was loved by so many people."

CHAPTER THREE

"I had seen hell."

Zoë's first illness almost overwhelmed us. We'd been pleased with ourselves as a family – the clever, good-looking Schwarz children and their active parents. Wal's sister Marlene made a passing comment one summer in North Wales, she called us 'smug'. It took years before I understood what she meant. Now with humbler hindsight, Wal and I have tried to identify alarm signals Zoë might have sent out in her final year at high school, the year she became mentally ill…the first time that anyone noticed.

The signals in those months were not strong ones: she didn't immediately apply for her provisional driving licence on her seventeenth birthday. Our family, except for me, loves driving. We reminded her many times that we would pay for lessons as soon as she booked them, but she did nothing for six months and gave no reason. Then she gave up the piano. She had been a talented player, quickly overtaking her father who worked harder at it. Her playing showed musical understanding ahead of her years; her tunes sang out with her left hand in firm support. For a few months before she stopped altogether, she insisted on playing the same Chopin Nocturne in B flat minor over and over. She'd play no other piece. And then she stopped, and gave no reason.

Next the strange affair of the head girl election. Zoë was one of the favourite candidates, popular with girls and staff. On the morning of the election, Zoë refused to go to school and neither then nor later, did she give any explanation. Because she was not present her name did not make the ballot. We had been excited and proud of the idea of her being Head Girl to match her brother's achievement. Ben, who had never had such a shining school career as his sisters, had ended up Head Boy of his Lycée while we were still in France.

I made no link between these eccentricities and the memory I have of Zoë sitting on my lap, aged fifteen saying, "I never want to grow up." A mother less smug might have made a connection for she repeated that odd statement several times. I have wondered since whether Zoë ever felt some presentiment that a severe mental illness would strike her when she *did* grow up?

Our kids (apart from baby Nicola who died of the complications arising from Spina Bifida) were healthy with no more than expected childhood ailments. So when Zoë, just before she turned eighteen, developed a viral infection that kept her in bed on and off for three weeks, we didn't worry unduly. She was quite glum, as anyone with a fever might be. The family doctor muttered something about glandular fever, which a couple of other local teenage girls had contracted; a firm diagnosis was never confirmed. (Ten years later in several of the messages we received after writing about Zoë in *The Guardian,* correspondents said that *their* bout of manic depressive illness was triggered by glandular fever.) Zoë seemed neither ill nor well. She acted depressed and irritable, picking quarrels over trifles.

Still we refused to worry. In her early teens we had often quarrelled.

"She'll get over it. Everything comes out in the wash."

Our homely axioms weren't working. After one horrendous row, when she accused us of over-ambition for our children and we accused her of laziness because her school marks were slipping, Zoë announced, "I'm leaving," and slammed out of the house. She arrived safely at Florence Leader's but wouldn't come to the phone.

A sheet of yellow lined paper turned up in one of the cardboard boxes. When she was high on drugs or mania her writing became so scribbly and scrawled that it is almost illegible. The following note is neatly written, full of the bravura of the rebellious teenager with appropriate melodramatic flourishes (a habit that Zoë, like her Mum and elder sister Hab, sometimes indulged). Zoë must have written it the day after she left home for Florence Leader's house.

Yesterday I was walking down a path with a small bag. I remember that it held some fresh clothes, papers, passport and an address book.

And I asked myself why I was walking down that path away from a big property full of animals and people. I realised that regret is a component of my happiness as I recalled a pregnant animal whose foal I would not see, a brother whose adolescence I would not witness, a big cat whose purring I could no longer hear.

I still do not know whether I felt relief, bitterness or freedom. Perhaps I pushed a family to the edge. Perhaps in weakness and shock they rejected their own.

In my case Zugi has gone as has Daisy. So what remained was a group unprepared and incapable of accepting a person who threatened their values, their self esteem, their position in society, nevertheless a fragile ambitious person.

The going is rough. It's going to get rougher. And a man will come and money will be earned and friends will be supportive. And the house down Glebe lane will never be revisited, forgiven or loved again.

Goodbye. Do not remember me with too much bitterness.

Zaco, I suspect that you will hear much about me. Most of it is true. My departure has nothing to do with you. Mum and Dad are good to you. However, they and I can commune no longer.

I trust that you will continue to enjoy yourself with your old friends and achieve so magnificently at school.

Zoë

Although Habie and Tanya had never made similar scenes, Ben at a similar age had left home for three days after a row about his table manners. (I recall he threw a bowl of curry at the wall.) For myself, I felt more annoyed than alarmed and perhaps secretly jealous that Zoë had so readily decamped to the Leaders. She stayed with the Leaders for a couple of weeks before she came home again and we exchanged letters, all of which I found in Zoë's boxes.

Reading them years later with hindsight it's clear how much we loved one another and how little we could communicate. Our words formed a smokescreen behind which we could ignore what was really happening; that I was reluctant to give up the role of matriarch and that Zoë's symptoms of bi-polar disorder (neither recognised nor understood by anyone) were starting to emerge and hinder her life.

January, 1991

Dearest Zoë….

The horses have been put to bed and two things dominate my mind: that Najem will probably be sold tomorrow and that you've left home. Which is the more important?

The horse? Horses have been a major part of my life from six to sixteen and twenty-five until the present day. I always wanted to breed some marvellous horse which I did in Neuville Ferrieres but they had to be sold, Somehow I never thought Najem would be. Like Shah he would grow old in my family. But there you are. It's not practical to keep him and a good price has been agreed upon if he passes Ian Paton's vetting.

The daughter? Did I throw her out or did she leave of her own volition? I don't know….

I brood how pleasant it might have been to have you here for these last few months sharing the bores of housework and the tiny but very real pleasures of bourgeois domesticity. It was a fantasy. When you were here – you stayed in your room and me in mine. And you never helped or joined in except on your own terms. Your dad and I spent a long time trying to work out where it all went wrong. With your loss of a nanny in India? With my allowing you to be cheeky as a teenager? Your own theories of not wanting to be the clever, thin star? We don't agree that we are pushy parents. We have formed no conclusions – found no solutions.

Anger?

Zoë aged 16 and Dorothy her mother

A lot of anger in a family. Do you know who starts it – why it carries on? I don't. We were disappointed in you – not the failing or getting fat but with the withdrawal and the lack of communication.

...... How much of my reactions are hurt pride and loss of status as my little empire crumbles? No answer comes to mind.

It has been a strange week living without you and getting used to the idea of parting with Najem. A certain relief on both counts. Peace and lack of hassle. The physical beauty of this site continually entrances me.

I regret that people no longer correspond by letter. The telephone has an immediate intimacy but there is falsity built into the wires. You imagine that you are in close contact – actually you are not. It seems so artificial. There is something cold about a society that believes that a mother loves a child until the child is eighteen and then the child goes away as if it had never been. And no one thinks this is peculiar. I enjoyed the last weekend with the little new one in utero [Fredy, Ben's wife, was pregnant with her first child, Chloe] but nevertheless I have not adjusted to my new role. Will I ever? If I stopped existing tomorrow, I can't see much hardship for anyone.

... You have short changed me. But where and why your relationship with your parents had gone wrong I do not know. Nothing is ever anyone's FAULT in the end. It is merely the reaction of certain personalities together. As you so often say, you do not have problems with your friends. We certainly were wrong to make a fuss over your phoning Thomas that night but had you been on our side you would have understood.

Your loving Mum, Dot

All those rows while Zoë was with us, over costly phone calls to the new boy friend Thomas, over refusing to help with housework, we never thought of as more serious than growing up problems. Zoë replied:

Lexden, February, 91

Dear Mum,

...I do feel very sad for my own part in your unhappiness. Najem obviously is being sold because of me mainly and he

62

was one of the best things that you have ever produced. But on the other hand I don't think it necessarily a bad thing for him to go .....

I also think that you are dramatizing things. You want to be a drama queen. "If I stopped existing to morrow morning, I can't see much hardship for anyone."

Why should you be different to anyone else? That statement is simply banal and can be applied to any member of the family. NO one is God. The world doesn't stop because we do.

Your problem is that you are not internally at peace so that no matter what the external situation is it is hard for you to be happy ....

It seems to me that you have done many things others only dream of. Having produced quite literally this time – Zaco – surely one of the most stunning creations on God's earth – you should be ecstatically happy. But you are not .....

I could patronise you and say this is 'menopausal.
[Actually, I think it was!]

But I think it is something deeper.

You need to be re-pumped with love. Because you're full of hate which manifests itself in your daily negative remarks and thoughts such as "I feel bitter towards you because I feel that you have short-changed me." I've never heard that expression before. I guess that it means that you feel you've given more than you've got. If you can be that shallow then I do feel very sorry for you.

'... you used to go on about the theory of the jar being half empty or half full. At the moment all you focus on is the emptiness of the jar so you are not full of love. Turn the jar over Mum and you'll be happy. And remember that everyone has their own little jar. And they cope with it as best they can ... Only God has a completely full jar so our differences are negligible in comparison to him. This is why

all human beings are basically the same and why you are not alone in your struggles.

I did not leave home because I do not love you or because our relationship is a failure. I left to declare my independence ...

You have been a wonderful mother to me, You never made me unhappy and you made me realise what I could do, You used to say "You are pretty enough and clever enough to do whatever you want." Very few people are ever lucky enough to hear that at all let alone from their mother.

I think that my nanny in India could be a part of our problems. I do have the feeling of having been desperately loved. It is from me, from friends, family, Thomas. God but also, I am sure of it, from my nanny in India I'm sure that it could not have been easy for you to have to witness such a strong bond between my nanny and me. [Reading these words a dozen years later, I feel the poignancy of Zoë's repeating her parents' attempts to understand her problems in the light of pop-psychology].

I think of you all a lot.

Instinctive reactions are dead giveaways and the biggest giveaway was how excited and happy I was to get your letter...that must be the ultimate proof that I love you.

I miss Tigger and Daisy very painfully

See you soon

Zoë

In that exchange she showed more insight than I did. Of course she missed her cats, although she never spoke of them. I've written earlier how she lost nine cats in France. Daisy and Tigger were Zac's sixth birthday present. Daisy became Zoë's cat. A silver tabby, small and nervous. She had kittens with Tigger her brother. Three litters all in all before she was spayed. Zoë's diaries are full of references to the kittens. Daisy insisted on having her kittens on Zoë's bed.

A couple of years earlier at sixteen Zoë had written of her cat:

Daisy's kittens have climbed out of their basket today. The big grey one is so beautiful. The little girl is just like Daisy – same coat, same shape of face. And the other little girl is much quieter than the other two. She has a very round face.

In May 1991, Zoë and I took Daisy and Tigger to the vet for an annual flu booster. Zoë put Daisy back in the cat box and forgot to slip the nail through the wire loop that kept the carrier shut. As we walked towards the car, Daisy pushed against the loose grille; it fell out and she leapt through, jumped the vet's brick wall and vanished. After a couple of hours searching the nearby gardens and calling in vain, we went home. Daisy was never seen again. The next ten days passed with fly posting, leaflets and telephone calls. Two false alarms. A tabby cat was found but it wasn't Daisy. Zoë as usual never said much about it.

Zoë's poem found in the boxes:

Daisy

She drops wild animals at my feet.

She waits for me.

She lays a ball in my lap.

If she can love

As well as anyone

_ I've ever known,_

How dare they say

She has no soul?

The change in Zoë's behaviour crept upon us so insidiously that we were in the middle of it before anyone realised. But we were so busy pretending to ourselves that "this isn't happening." Any parent who has watched their happy teenager turn into a morose and lethargic lump of misery will understand. The anger you feel at their 'bad' behaviour is only a mask for the gut-wrenching grief that you cannot help your own child, nor can you tolerate watching the effects of clinical depression. I asked her once how she felt and she replied, "in a deep black pit with no way out."

Having been a brilliant student (for one of her mock exams on Chaucer she received 100%) her work deteriorated. Her A-levels were not the straight A's that had been predicted. However, after her interview, her place at Bristol was assured and Kelly, one of the three best friends was also going. Sarah took up a place at Oxford. The friendship between the three never faltered and Zoë's close relationship with Mylène continued with cross Channel visits both ways. Zoë's friendship with these three talented and loving young women misled me. How could I believe in the reality of her illness while she maintained such genuine intimate friends?

That summer Zoë became more and more withdrawn and listless. Relations between her and us were strained and scratchy. We persuaded the GP to send her to a psychiatrist. She agreed reluctantly. Unlike Habie, who has always considered therapy the answer to life's problems, Zoë's attitude was that therapy was a placebo for middle class, self-centred idiots who had nothing better to do.

Thirty months after her death, we asked for and were sent Zoë's medical records. The psychiatrist who saw her as an Out Patient, Dr Cahn Vasudevan, did not seem unduly perturbed with Zoë's mental state, nor considered her depressive illness too serious. He spoke of factors that might be precipitating it like her viral infection the winter before. 'Another possible factor could be the loss of her pet cat in May.'

In his letter to the GP he wrote:

She talks about a fairly close and supportive family. Her father is described as unemotional and "a distant person" whilst mother is said to be "very nervous" and generally over-involved with her children… She describes herself as a pleasant happy confident and rational and clear thinking person. She sets herself high standards and is often self-critical. (She feels that this is a family trait.)

He added: *her anxious preoccupation with her mood state is perhaps a family trait and, in particular, a reflection of mother's anxiety about her. I would think that she is coping adequately and is not at any risk of suicide and further deterioration.*

Since Cahn Vasudevan left the Health Service a couple of months after Zoë died, we haven't been able to find out whether, when he was the psychiatrist in charge in 2000, he recalled the articulate teenager he had seen nine years earlier and his wildly inaccurate forecast.

After that interview with Vasudevan, relations at home worsened. Zoë was by turn anxious or irritable and had too many casual boyfriends. We worried about the influence on eleven year old Zachary. We pride ourselves on being leftish and liberal but when it comes to the crunch, no parent likes a procession of men consorting with their daughter and (probably) having sex.

One morning she wasn't in the house. She left a note, addressed not to us but to my brother Mickey, her uncle, saying that she was going to Bristol to throw herself off the Severn Bridge. Four hours later a police car found her, scared and confused, at Colchester Station; she had not even got as far as London.

We took it rather calmly; we thought that we knew it all! We had read about 'cry for help' suicide attempts, which are not meant to succeed, even if sometimes they do. The community policeman, who brought her back, patted her knee and spoke with avuncular kindness: "What a silly thing that was to do. You'll never do such a silly thing again, will you?" She agreed bashfully; he meant well.

After that abortive effort to get to the Severn Bridge, Zoë's behaviour didn't improve. Wouldn't get up, wouldn't see her friends, wouldn't wash, and wouldn't talk. She was sullen; we were baffled.

"I can't deal with this," I told her. I could barely resist the damp fog of her sadness sucking me in along with her. Surely hospital MUST be the right place?

The GP agreed on a hospital admission.

The Lakes is an acute psychiatric unit in the grounds of the general hospital. Patients have their own rooms; most of wards are unlocked. Colours are light and pleasant. There is a garden. The staff said she had settled in and was speaking to them, which was more than she did to us.

Of one of her interviews the nurse's report stated:

She spoke about her feelings of wanting to jump off the bridge at Bristol University and why she didn't. Zoë said she had no energy and was also afraid that if she did kill herself that something worse would happen to her e.g. she would go to Hell … She asked many questions such as, "When you are feeling low how do you know that you are making the right decisions?" And she asked, "What stops people from committing suicide and what keeps them going." She feels guilty staying here as she feels she is taking up a bed which could be used for someone more ill than her."

Zoë hated being in hospital. She didn't WANT to be there. She visibly 'pulled herself together.'

Although the staff appeared reluctant to let her go home after only one week, she agreed to take anti-depressants and since she had come in as a voluntary patient, they had no right to detain her.

She must have written the following description of the Lakes around this time but typical Zo, she never showed anyone. Habie read out part of it at her funeral:

The Lakes

The Patronising nurse came into my bedroom. I couldn't be bothered to challenge her. I had to appear calm to get out of this place. My family and friends who had visited all commented on how incredibly comfortable the ward was, like a hotel with open spaces lawns flowers. Fucking imbeciles!

Last night a pig was brought in with a slit throat. My room mate had tried to top herself. With the exception of Pat, the staff sit around on their fat arses in the staff room. The patients sit around in the smokers' room. The crème of the patients smoke dope. Dave gives us the dope. He's in for heroin abuse. The patients are good people. None are violent. The only violence is self destruction. A beautiful young woman with two kids is being frantically sociable.

We're in this acute psychiatric ward because we've slipped a little too far from the norm of recognised 'sane' behaviour though fuck knows who decides what's sane. There's something here which makes me laugh. The only really crazy thing about this acute psychiatric ward is that it wouldn't matter if the staff and patients swapped places.

Family friends and other friends helped me get better. At first after the suicide attempt I was convinced that I was doomed to this hell forever.

A week later I was at home by the pool with friends. The experience of the depression was for me like dying. It

*was agony but the outcome was so great that I was grateful
for the illness. So much was put into perspective. I could see
my parents not as tyrants or gods but as real separate
people from me. I could begin to grow up.*

*I saw life as a building. You can have everything but
without a firm base happiness is very fragile.* [Then she
wrote about having a Buddhist philosophy]

Best, very good, close friends.

*Jean Guy, Mylène, Kelly, Sarah, Florence, Stephen, Henri,
Giselaine, Francis, Ludi Elodie, Helene, Dan, Dave, Zeph,
Mike, Sylvain, Denis, Nighat, Tariq, Richard, Sophie, Jean-
Marc, Paddy, Johnny, Betsey, Laurence, Cassie, Talitha,
Lizzy, Julia, Pen, Hab, Stephen, Zac, Sarojini, Fredy, Ben,
Grandma Lilly, Jamie.*

*Best memories. Daisy, Victoria Falls, running with
30 children across lawns.*

In that piece, she used intelligence and good sense
to help herself climb out of her depression. Or possibly the
chemical imbalance in her brain shifted by itself. I don't
know how many parents of mentally ill children make that
simple mistake of assuming that the young person CAN by
an effort of will 'pull themselves together'. It runs like a
refrain in everything we had to do with Zoë for the next
nine years. Although we 'knew' she had been ill, we
believed that she was a clever, self-aware person and we
were unable to reconcile these two attitudes. Had we done
so early enough at the onset of her illness second time
round, would Zoë have responded? That is one of the
unanswerable questions that lie at the heart of every suicide.

Dr Oyede commented when she was discharged:
*her parents complained that she is very active sexually and
has not taken their advice about this. She changes
boyfriends almost every 4-6 months.*

70

AIDS scared us more than depression.

For her first term, Wal drove her to Bristol. We were full of optimism, hopeful that once away from home, Zoë would find contentment again.

Our attitude throughout this crisis was one of irritated optimism. We felt it was a blip. The influence of our half-baked Freudian ideas blinded us; Zoë's erratic behaviour was a neurotic response to the problems of growing up; she was a middle child that causes problems. We did not consider that her illness might have more to do with physiological rather than just psychological – not something that Zoë could help by effort of will or heeding good advice.

Zoë was to study French Literature at Bristol. As she was almost bi-lingual, it seemed an excellent choice, although one we had to persuade her to make. She had a curious argument that she shouldn't study French because she was so good at it. As soon as she arrived, she switched to Religious Studies. Wal wondered whether it had anything to do with the fact that he was Religious Affairs Correspondent on *The Guardian*. Zoë had a passionate interest in religion and a growing love of Jesus, which she shared with Florence. They both went to services at the Evangelical church in Colchester. As a non-practising Jew myself, I didn't appreciate Jesus as saviour rather than prophet but didn't criticise her church-going.

Zoë and Kelly shared a room in Manor House, one the most sought-after halls of residence. Zoë made friends straightaway but then she always did. Within a few weeks, though, we sensed an uneasiness emanating from Bristol. None of the family could understand what was happening. The dis-ease showed up in exchanges of letters between Zoë and the family. Between us and the doctors and authorities.

I wrote:

Zoë,

We're so sorry that your depression has turned into a work block. All I can say to you is to try to do the minimum and gradually things will ease. I've found that out myself.

No one can do it for you – you must do it for yourself.

... Try to finish two of your four essays. You'll feel foolish if you don t. You have our support whatever you do. But don't you want a wider more exciting life than this constant childishness? See you very soon,

Love, Mum

PS. Courage/Honour are not buzz words but they would help you in this present predicament.

Wasn't her refusal to study simply wilfulness? Zoë came home for a family weekend. Her brothers and sisters and parents crowded around her, insisting, "of course you can read this chapter." "Just put your mind to it." "Wipe your eyes and blow your nose." "Concentrate." "Stop acting like a baby." We left her crying on the bed. An hour later; she had not read one single paragraph, her face smeared with tears. None of us were sympathetic; none of us was able to grasp that she simply could *not* assimilate the passage.

Wal, who himself had done poorly at Oxford (after an Open Exhibition, he only gained a Third) wrote suggesting work plans and offering help. In November he wrote from *The Guardian* office offering help with her essays. Although she kept his offers - there were several - she never asked his help.

Habie, who had got a first at LSE, was spending her twenties trying to become a filmmaker, sent loving elder-sister advice. Her view of mental illness was strictly Freudian. Her boyfriend Stephen, an older guy, had been in analysis for decades and she herself went through it for years. She wrote:

Dear Divine Zoë

.... When things are bad and there is emotional and internal pain and everything seems empty or black or unlovely or unloving the first reaction is a desire to escape. And ... the best route of escape is denial: convincing myself and then everyone else that the problem has gone away. I've been doing it all my life: I'm not unhappy. I don't talk too much; I don't behave in ways that upset people. I'm not fat.

...Your depression has left you on a high which makes everything seem wonderful but stops you asking yourself some real questions. ...

I know that you must be relieved to be out of the depths of depression but it doesn't mean you need to call yourself, "serene, stable and saintly". Don t you think that's a tiny bit OTT?

... God, you probably hate all this serious and humourless and sexless psychological stuff.

If Zoë kept any diaries at Bristol, they haven't surfaced in the cardboard boxes. From everything we've learned at the time and later, she veered between highs and lows. She kept odd mementos like letters from the warden of her college warning her she must behave less erratically. There are also many letters, sent and probably unsent. She wrote a pornographic letter to Thomas over whom we had quarrelled when she kept ringing him in France.

Early on in Bristol, Zoë began showing signs of mania. Zoë's great woman friend Florence had three sons, one a little older and two younger than Zoë. With Sam, the middle son, she developed a romantic affection that included sex. (She told me once with a lot of giggles that she'd seduced Sam in our local graveyard.) The Leader seniors rather sensibly asked their 16 year-old to wait until he was eighteen before committing his affections too seriously to Zoë.

Zoë saw herself as Sam's sexual mentor, as the following letter reveals:

Manor Hall

Dear Sam

Bristol is a fine city and I have some good friends here but sometimes I am a little bored as my course has not stimulated me and there are few people here like you.

As you know my feelings for you go beyond friendship. But I want to make it quite clear that, if you feel it necessary, you have my approval to discover other relationships.

I say this for two reasons. Your parents have told us to wait 1½ years and you are the last person I would want to entice in a suffocating situation.

To be blunt and patronising Sam I beg you to use condoms for both our sakes and now for the graphic details:

1)   Durex extra safe are best

2)   Use Duragel

3)   In case the rubber brakes [Zoë's spelling] *it is best for the girl to use a cap covered with spermicidal jelly.*

4) Always use protection. You cannot adequately judge who has HIV by age, sex, class, or personal background, hygiene, fitness, etc.

5) Try to sleep with as many virgins as possible in fact you could make it a rule. (It won't kill you and it's excellent for your street cred.)

6) Always carry condoms with you

7) Do not stay inside the woman after orgasm until you lose your erection and the condom falls off

8) Do not use any lubricants but Duragel. They rot the condoms

9) Learn this list by heart

You see having an older girl friend has its uses.

Sam, you are a brilliant lover. Uninhibited, confident, funny, passionate, absorbed etc. You have 1 ½ years to become perfect. This requires learning 2 skills which most men do not bother with: A making it last longer and B doing it more often.

You see I wont love you any less if you don't acquire these 2 skills. I want you to have them for purely selfish reasons… it will make me unbelievably satisfied.

Although of course if you are fit and sexy other aspects of your life will be effortless and pleasurable.

I apologise for this letter being like a lecture. But Sam I have no intention of letting your talent go to waste. Even the best talent in the world needs direction and exercise.

I will be back for you.

So keep growing up beautifully

I miss you more than you would believe, Z.

Sam himself ended the romance before the 18-months trial period with a letter to Zo which she kept; they remained close friends. Sam, now a happily married young writer living in California, remembers Zoë as the first romantic passion of his life.

A little later in the term her moods had become even more extravagant. The handwriting is more scrawled; the characters grow larger and wobbly.

She wrote to Kelly's sister:

God only knows how I have the energy to write. Kelly will tell you that I have been subjecting myself to far too much of you know what.

Anyway I saw the fish and reckoned that it belonged by your side. Your daughter will show you how to take it apart and put it back together again, if you ask her nicely.

My course is great though it is better suited to pre-toddler intellect. Most of the lecturers have negative IQs.

But with Kelly's fine example, I attend lectures and hand in EXTRA essays on time and give all my male lecturers daily blow jobs.

Your revolting little sister spends the majority of her time bleeding all over my bed through her nose. You should see the stains on the sleeping bag and sheets. So you can reach the blasted woman at the address above...

Write to us soon. Kelly has no friends and her lack of mail is becoming embarrassing, At least I have the odd letter from my family who are all completely in love with me, the incestuous bastards...

The letter was unfinished.

The university authorities, given Zoë's lack of written work and poor attendance in lectures, were supportive. After two terms she deferred and the authorities agreed she could resume in October 1992. In spite of her erratic behaviour, Zoë had impressed the college as a clever and charming girl. She came home. We lived in the same house alongside not *with* one another.

In the first week of June, 1991, I wrote to Rory, my friend in Australia:

My lovely Zoë is having a breakdown. A deep depression which keeps her in bed most of the day and we don't know what to do. She has deferred from Bristol until October 92 when her department (religious studies) will accept her back to read 1st year again. But we are now in June. She came back in March; she is not getting better. She doesn't want therapy, is reluctant to see a psychologist we found. She doesn't read or write, just stays in her self-imposed prison.

... the outlook appears gloomy. Wal and I are barely coping. At first he was harsh with her - undestandable - because in her manic phase she smashed his car and ran up a £500 phone bill. And she won't admit she is at fault, which drives him mad. Now she is just silent, passive, very thin and utterly sad. I feel there must be enormous anger there. Plenty of self loathing although what she has done is merely silly and not productive. Nothing to warrant such an abnegation of life. She was popular in Bristol with teachers and students and they want her back but how will she go when she cannot even pick up her dirty socks from the floor?

What I had neglected to tell Rory was that living with Zoë was making me sick, too, as if depression (or hers at any rate) was contagious. In early June, Zoë had been low for several weeks. She and I sat on the lawn in deckchairs, complaining about how awful the world was, how impossible it is to find happiness. We'd been talking for thirty minutes in the context of global misery. I explained *weltschwmerz* to her. The conversation became more and more surreal, forming its own weird logic. Zoë said in an uninflected tone, "I want to die."

I've always believed that if you were fully aware of the world's suffering, to feel even part of the pain, you couldn't carry on living. I entered her fantasy. "You're right. The world is too sad to live in." and said I'd join her and we talked about ways and means of how we could tidily kill ourselves. Then I sort of shuddered.

"I can't. Zac's too young. It'd ruin his life."

"I suppose so," said Zoë. I remember her listlessness. And our sick conversation carried on searching for ways and means for her alone, until another thought hit me.

"Zo, you can't! Zac couldn't take it."

Zoë thought about this. Without smiling, she agreed that I was right and she couldn't. I made her promise solemnly that she would never, NEVER even try. We kissed one another. The sun continued shining. Our unhappiness remained. The purple rock rose which grows against the corner of the bungalow, was in full bloom. I trusted Zoë's promise. I believe she believed it herself at that moment.

Most days, her depression kept her in bed. She wouldn't read or see her friends. She wouldn't even take a shower. (When I read Zoë's hospital notes thirteen years later, I read several times 'mother is anxious.' What a silly comment! Isn't every mother anxious when a daughter is ill?)

Seven days after our discussion on the lawn, Zac was staying overnight at a friend's place. It was also Habie's birthday. Wal had cooked pasta for dinner. Zoë had been in bed all day and didn't show up. Wal said leave her be, that had been the psychiatrist's advice.

I didn't care what the doctor had said. "I'm going into her room. She mustn't be left alone all day." The room smelled stale and musty, curtains half-drawn; her hair was stuck with sweat to her forehead.

"What's wrong?"

She wouldn't look at me. "I've taken something."

I ran to the kitchen and started laughing, "Wal, she says she's taken something, ha, ha, ha."

We had no idea what to do. We phoned the hospital, who told us to find out what she'd taken and bring her in without waiting for an ambulance. We hauled her out of bed. Quinine. She said she'd taken quinine. She began retching in the car but Wal would not stop or even slow down, so I just rolled down the car window and she vomited with her head out. When we arrived at Casualty, she was semi-conscious, the car door streaked with vomit.

At the hospital the nurses tried to slide a rubber pipe down her throat. She wouldn't open her mouth. The doctor in charge was Spanish. She spoke rudimentary English. She refused to *force* Zoë's mouth open. Zoë was over eighteen and an adult.

"But she might die."

The doctor shrugged. We stood like waxworks around the bed, willing her to open her mouth. Wal, in a sudden spurt of temper, leaned over the bed and pinched her

79

nostrils shut. Her mouth fish-gulped for air and the nurse rammed the rubber tube down her throat.

After the stomach pumping, Zoë lay asleep or unconscious. The vomiting in the car must have brought up a lot of the quinine already. The staff nurse said: "She's out of danger."

Zoë half-awoke, mumbling that she wanted Florence, who drove over immediately after we phoned. There was only one chair in the cubicle. We gave it to Florence. Wal and I leaned uncomfortably against the end of the bed, and the three of us waited, listening to Zoë's rasping breath, while Florence stroked her forehead. We stayed like this for three hours.

By 3 am, Wal had had enough. We had been in Casualty for seven hours. We went home. When I drove back to hospital at six a.m. Florence was still there. Zoë was half-awake.

"I wanna be an actress," she said in a slurred voice.

I went home for breakfast. When Wal and I returned, the staff had moved her to a ward but not cleaned her up; her hair was matted with vomit. We found her out of bed, trying to wash her hair in a hand basin. We sat and held her hand; she wanted to go home. Staff wanted to keep her for observation twenty-four hours more. A young houseman saw us the next morning. He was acutely embarrassed, as if he had never had any training of how to deal with a post-suicidal patient. We asked to take Zoë home. He discharged her.

Zoë rarely referred to that hospital stay, although she once flamed at me that I had left her alone and only Florence had stayed the night. Tanya had visited her in hospital the next afternoon. During Zoë's childhood, we had Schwarz-fashion glossed over Zoë's hero-worship of Tanya and Tanya's coolness towards her baby sister. We had not realised that Zoë was aware that Tanya was not as fond of her as she was of Tanya, until we read the poem she wrote in hospital after her first serious suicide attempt. A poem never shown to anyone and found in one of the cardboard boxes:

My sister has a huge shadow

 Looking over her shoulder

So I don't know if she could see me sitting in that big black space

She says that time heals

But she never shows me her repentance

I will try to pray

But my ego can barely contain the injustice of it

Nothing that I could ever do, that she has not already achieved

And the other one, she left when I was eight

And the first one, she died

What can I write to you my sister?

What are the words that melt a heart?

And raise the dead?

You brought me bad fruits

And said the room stank of sick and old age

How old I am

And the vomit matted my hair

I had seen hell

Nothing you could do could hurt me now

So why do I still yearn for you

Of all the people, why you?

I am liked by others

But not by you

I waited for her but she took forever

Your eyes are beautiful I know they are. But I never saw them right

Dear God, give me my sister back.

Tanya was shown this poem some days after Zoë died but has never since discussed it with us.

After her short stay in hospital after the suicide, Zoë seemed to recover with that astonishing rapidity of youth. She planned a trip to USA and persuaded the doctors that she was perfectly well enough. She was flying out to meet a guy she had briefly met at sixteen. He took her to St Olafs, his own college in Minnesota. Zoë never told us what actually happened. The retrospect of her life written in July 2000 contains the bare reference:

Summer 1992

Summer in the States – happy but very promiscuous,

That has to be somewhat of an understatement! She kept a cutting someone had sent her, a copy of St Olaf's college paper with the scrawled message 'Read this, dear.'

RADICAL RUMOURS DEMAND ADMINISTRATIVE ATTENTION.

....Towards the end of September a young Englishwoman named Zoie arrived on campus she stayed for two weeks

*and then left. These are the facts beyond that there are only
the rumours ... She was a nymphomaniac, she was a
prostitute. She had unprotected sex with fifteen students
.She was found masturbating in front of people...All
rumours. Mostly harmless ones at that...*

*The cover up of what Zoie was involved in was swift and
complete... the administration effectively denied ever
hearing any of the incidents in question.'*

I presume Zoë was in a manic state while she was
there and calmed down a bit before she came home,
apparently well, and happy. Nothing was ever said to us of
any manic behaviour in America or anything about St
Olaf's College. She left the boy she had gone to see almost
immediately. Like so many of Zoë's extravagant actions,
that could have a reasonable explanation. After all, she
hadn't seen him for four years; they must both have
changed in the interval. Zoë told me with great bravado that
she had sex with a stranger in an airport lavatory. Zoë could
do that, tell you something outrageous, give her little laugh,
her smile and you accepted. Now she was anxious to return
to Bristol.

The specialist from the mental health service, Dr
Thu, wrote to our GP, Paul Rasor:

*I saw Zoë again on September 30th, 1992 just before
she left for Bristol University. She had just returned from
her holiday in America the day before and claimed to have
remained on an even keel throughout. She has continued on
Lofepramine 20Mg bd and I have advised her to remain on
the same dose.*

*I understand that you will be transferring her care
to her new GP in Bristol. I will also arrange for her to be
seen by Dr Baloch at her Out Patient Clinic when Zoë
returns for her Christmas holidays.*

In the event 'an even keel' was a cruel deception,
not knowingly on Zoë's part, but through the doctors'

inability to see just how ill she was. You cannot blame them; she wished to present herself as a well woman.

She returned to Bristol and within weeks her behaviour became increasingly erratic. Her supervisor warned her that she was cutting too many lectures. One of the more bizarre incidents told us by the warden of her hall of residence was that she had written 'Fuck Off' in menstrual blood on the door of a student who had harassed her.

Zoë had come home for the weekend at a time when Ben and his wife Fredy were on a brief visit, Tanya and Habie as well. All the family were assembled. We had been anxious that she had obviously not been studying, had appeared very bizarre and secretive when we had visited her briefly, and had been in various sorts of trouble including episodes of violence. But none of us were prepared for the Zoë that appeared: coarsened in face, dress and speech, claiming to be earning sums of money in a nude modelling/filming project with hints that more went on than modelling/filming and that this new world was violent as well as opulent and glamorous.

We'd already received a worried phone call from her college warden, David Crossley-Evans that she was frequenting Bristol's red light district.

She asked Zac what kind of sports car he wanted because she had become rich enough to buy him one. Challenged by Wal over this, she said she had £10,000 in her current account. The two of them actually went the next morning to the cash point. The account was virtually empty: she claimed there had been some administrative delay of no importance. We never understood the nature of her manic delusions and kept trying to reason her out of them. Her brothers and sisters, who had been at home that weekend, were as puzzled as we were. She returned to Bristol after a disastrous visit. She had talked of resigning from the university and staying on with Kelly and doing her "modelling."

We were baffled; Wal tried and wrote the next day:

My dear Zoë,

> *I am deeply sorry that you arrived home on Friday apparently gay and bubbly and that an incessant inquisition from a disapproving family reduced you to misery humiliation, fury and finally to a precipitate departure. Could we not have been more charitable, less heavy as you put it to accept you on your own terms?*

> *We are heavy no doubt, as seen by a brilliant 20 year-old growing up in a faster more dangerous and unpredictable world. ...*

> *... None of us could make head or tail of your accounts of your life. One can make loving efforts to understand and help a daughter living in a way one might disapprove of, but first you need to know what's going on and it took until late Saturday night before we felt we had even a glimmer.*

> *Even that wasn't the real problem, which is this: the dominant impression left by your visit was that we weren't getting the real Zoë. The real Zoë is beautiful, full of affection, fun and laughter, sensitive, loving animals and children and music, bright but with no pretence of being free from any problems like your work blocks or the anxieties that go with growing up in an imperfect world.*

> *That Zoë has been ill, depressed and then over-the-top and perhaps never getting the balance right as yet. That same Zoë well or ill, successful or not, thin or fat, happy or miserable has the love and sympathy of a family and a wide circle beyond.*

> *What we got this weekend was a stranger, an impersonation. It was phoney; a hard-faced, calculating stranger presenting a vulgar front of money, sex and cynicism with a hint of violence and desperation.*

85

We all felt that you have come to hate yourself and we want to help you and if possible prevent emotional decisions in the spirit of self-hatred. In the immediate future is the question of you resigning. If you do resign we'll do anything we can to help you but are you really sure? The alternatives strike me as harder as and more problematic than staying on as you are and attempting a radical reform. ....

We all love you and so does Zac. It was grief at seeing the wrong phoney Zoe instead of the real one that made him unreasonable. He was trying to punish you for not showing him the Zoë he knows and adores... Love, Dad

What efforts Walter made - not easy for him - not a person who likes talking about his family to outsiders. But like me, he persisted in believing that rational persuasion would work eventually. After Zoë's disastrous December visit, he wrote to Dr Baloch, the chief psychiatrist in Colchester. A copy of this letter turned up in Zoë's hospital notes.

Dear Dr Baloch,

Dorothy and I are frightened and anxious about what the future holds for our daughter .....

Wal recounted Zoë's fantasies of being rich and successful.

In reality she is penniless, has run up debts and borrowed money on every occasion. She tells us that she is 'happy'.

We suggested that she move back home and offered to buy her a caravan for more privacy. She refused saying that she wants to live in Bristol. The story changes, sometimes she will be kept by a 'boy friend and 'modelling' in other versions she is to live on the dole.

....We want to pay for private psychotherapy and have given Zoë the name of a practitioner in Bristol. So far she has not taken this up.

We fear two possibilities: either a relapse into depression, or yet more extravagant behaviour resulting perhaps in drugs, AIDS venereal disease or crime....

We do not know what to do. Zoë appears to respect yourself and Dr Fu. She is of course an adult and we have no authority. I have written this letter because she is persuasive enough to tell you that nothing very much is wrong, that she left her studies because she had changed her mind about them, that she is quite happy about her future plans, etc.....

In the hospital notes, there is no record of any reply from Dr Baloch.

None of this helped. Zoe came home at the end of term. That was a dreadful Christmas. She arrived, presenting a vulgar image in leather skirt and bondage-type jewellery, and told us stories, elaborated in detail, of her working in a brothel. Her very expression had changed, becoming hard and glittery. The family were stunned.

I gave her an ultimatum, either give up the idea of living as a tart in Bristol or leave Greenacres. She said that she would leave.

The day after she left, I wrote in my journal.

29/12/92

I don't know how to pitch this. I'm so tired I can't think. It 2.30 am.

I told Zoë on Sunday morning either you give up the idea of being a tart in Bristol, stay here and go to Israel or else you are not welcome at home. So she went.

87

She said if love was conditional on my sharing the same values as her – it wasn't love. Love must be unconditional.

She never contacted us all Sunday or Monday and I have been torturing myself at the harshness of giving an ultimatum to a sick young woman.

I don't understand the dynamics of what she is doing. Last night spent from 1-3am puzzling over her behaviour and our behaviour.

.... an overwhelming sadness and a rage, how can this have happened to us?

Ben and his family went home to Paris, Ben grumbling that Christmas had been upset once again by 'the Zoë problem'. I wrote an unfair letter to Kelly in Bristol. Kelly was only a young girl herself. I was doing what the hurt and baffled often do, strike out in every direction.

...you appear to have accepted her decline from a promising student into one of society's outcasts. Why did you not warn us of these friends of Zoë's? Don't you realise that to fuck for money is degrading to both sides...? Prostitution is a no-win situation. Would YOU do the things Zo claims to have done? If you wouldn't – why did you accept her behaviour, condone it and thereby tacitly encourage her? Is this a friend?

In her heart Zoë hates herself. She turns her hate outward to her parents and family. She feels that you and Sarah support her. I have begged Zoë to remain at home and then go to Israel; she tells me she hates Jews and Arabs although she is one herself. Is it herself she hates?

Kelly never replied. Several years later she told me that she'd preferred to know that Zoë was working in the comparative safety of a brothel rather than have the constant anxiety that she was picking up men on the streets.

After my ultimatum, Zoe walked out. We didn't know where she had gone. We feared back to Bristol but she arrived at the Leaders' house in the middle of Anna Claire's birthday party. She appeared at ease and confident. She told Florence that she was on her way to Bristol, that her parents were simply bourgeois and she'd found a practicable, high-earning way of life. Florence was rendered speechless; she prayed in silence. Sheldon, who has always been fond of Zoë, broke into Zoë's monologue, tore into Zoë's arguments and reduced them to shreds. He wouldn't play her game. He didn't budge and logically unravelled all her statements as the excellent lawyer he is. It only took him ten minutes. "It was powerful to watch," said Florence. "She felt free after that." This incident made a great impression upon Sheldon; he would refer to it at Zoë's funeral nine years later.

Zoë allowed Sheldon to puncture her illusions; she herself didn't really want to continue working as a prostitute. She decided not to abandon Bristol and within a couple of days came home.

We were so focused on her disturbing behaviour while Zoë was coming and going from Bristol, we lost sight of the fact that she still kept that charisma which affected people so positively. Thirty months after she died, Wal and I wrote an article *Losing Zoë* in *The Guardian* and many people who'd known her, even slightly, responded. A fellow student at Bristol described an aspect of Zoë that we and the doctors so often forgot.

…… I knew Zoë during her time at Bristol - I was a mature student in theology and religious studies at the same time that she was there, and your loving elegy reminded me why she is one of those rare people I still remember with such vivid affection. In particular, I remember two occasions that I want to share with you, because they are so much stories about the Zoë you describe.

The first is of going to lunch with her one day, when she still seemed quite well. We were talking about faith, about her sense of Jewishness and also her interest in Christianity. Somehow we got on to the subject of the holocaust, probably because I was studying holocaust theology and finding it almost overwhelmingly difficult to cope with. I know she didn't say anything as clichéd as 'to know all is to forgive all', but that was the gist of what she was trying to explain to me. Even Hitler, she suggested, if we could know him as God must know him, couldn't be beyond forgiveness and redemption. It sounds too simplistic perhaps, when I put it like that, but it felt like a luminous observation full of hope. As you so beautifully describe her, Zoe had immediacy and a charismatic presence. It wasn't just the things she said but the way she said them, so I know that trying to capture that conversation in an e-mail is probably futile. But I wanted to share with you a sense of hope that she gave me that I've never forgotten. Particularly in view of the anguish you describe, I hope that her ability to believe in ultimate goodness didn't desert her.

The second story is about the last time I really spoke with her .... It was at the time when her breakdown was beginning, and with hindsight I realize that her situation was much more painful than I knew at the time. But again, it's a story about the Zoe who was 'seductive, hypnotic and all-consuming', and its sadness is shot through with the zaniest humour. I was sitting in the departmental common room one lunch time with another mature woman student - a Methodist minister who used to try hard to be radical and shocking, but who at heart was I suspect quite conservative. Zoe came sauntering in with a box of Ferro Rocher (I don't know why I remember that detail!), which she proceeded to share with us as she recounted very explicitly and with much laughter and flamboyant language, her sexual escapades with her man of the moment. I wasn't quite sure how much of it was true, but the situation was just full of wicked delight, as we two mature theology students sat there trying to seem open-minded at this glimpse into what we both assumed was ordinary student life!

I know things got worse for Zoe after that, but I also know from your article that the torment hasn't eclipsed your ability to recognize that dazzle that was the other side of her darkness, and sometimes it was hard to tell the two apart.

I have often thought about Zoe and wondered what became of her. ... She was an acutely memorable person - full of the most abundant life, who maybe just had too much abundance for one life to hold.

CHAPTER FOUR

"I've been to the bottom. I'm strong."

In the first few years after Zoë's first illness, she thought, we thought, her mental health was restored. Her plan to live in Bristol was quietly dropped and she never spoke another word about prostitution. So what next?

Until her final illness, whenever she had problems, Zoë had the knack of bumping into people who provided the solution. She knew how to seize opportunities. In this instance she met Jide - a Nigerian more than two metres tall, who wore flash suits and drove a BMW. He had a blonde wife Michelle and two little boys, Omar and Theo - somewhat of a film star couple, him so flamboyant and black, and her so voluptuous and fair. They made a majestic couple.

Jide recalled his first meeting with Zoë outside a Colchester wine bar: "I was winding down after a hard day's work, when my car alarm went off. I rushed outside not knowing what to expect."

He found Zoë, sitting on his bonnet, rifling through her handbag, ignoring the screaming car alarm. She apologised but went on searching for whatever it was she'd mislaid. Jide brought her a drink. "Once our chat began I realised here was no ordinary 'Essex' girl - not with *her* outlook and attitude towards life and others!"

Zoë became close friends with Jide and Michelle. He worked for an insurance company and found her a salesperson's job. It was a tough job, cold calling at building sites and persuading workers they needed personal insurance. We thought this wasn't an ideal occupation for someone just recovering from manic depression. How brave to attempt it. She needed a car; Wal gave her his old Renault 5 and bought himself a new one. Zoë drove well but often too fast. Sometimes she managed to sell insurance and other times she simply couldn't.

Although we knew that Bristol would not give her a third chance, we hoped she'd eventually return to college. Future plans were not spoken of. But Zoë returned to university far sooner than any of us imagined. Again, it happened though networking. At Jide and Michelle's house Zoë met Kingsley, who persuaded her to apply to Essex where he was studying Politics. For Essex University entry, her A-level grades were higher than asked for. She applied to the School of Government in which Kingsley was studying. After reading her medical reports, her application was turned down. The Head of Department advised her to wait a year to be sure that, "you have recovered from your breakdown." Anyone who has suffered from mental illness knows how much this type of rejection hurts. Zoë wouldn't talk about it. Chance intervened again. Or was it luck - the sort of luck that depends on the sort of person you are.

At the Girls High School, some years before, Zoë had been active in organising debates for the English Speaking Union. She'd arranged for her Dad to speak alongside a Professor of Physics. The event was badly advertised and only three people showed up. Walter suggested the two speakers and the audience spend the lecture time in the pub. The Physics professor, Shamim Siddiqui, invited them home to meet his wife Cora, and from that meeting the Siddiquis and Schwarz parents became friends, went to one another's dinner parties and theatres together.

When Shamim, a man of enormous charm and compassion, learnt about Zoë's rejection, he offered her a place in his own department – a sleight of hand to allow her into Essex University. Physics meant nothing to her; a GCSE subject she'd passed and never wanted to look at again. But, explained Shamin, once she was registered in one department she could switch to another.

And that's what she did - switched to Sociology – taking advantage of a chain of circumstances leading from her sitting unruffled on Jide's bonnet, meeting Kingsley, trying unsuccessfully to get back into college and then succeeding with the help of a sympathetic friend.

Wal and I remained dubious. Was she well enough for university so soon after Bristol? Although Zoë never again studied with the same intensity that she had in her first year of upper sixth, she kept up with coursework.

We grew wary of Kingsley, although grateful that he had persuaded her to return to college. He used to wear baggy check pantaloons and a baseball cap turned backwards. I thought he looked like a clown, He showed a violent streak and the pair of them fought during rows about his fidelity. This caused friction between us and Zoë, since she claimed we were being square as well as racist, when we complained about his treatment of her as well as his clothes.

I wrote to my friend Rory in Oz that December:

Zoë is much better. She has a Nigerian bloke whom I don't trust but she has completed first term at Essex uni in sociology. I think she may break through and get on top of herself. It's already a supreme achievement to finish a term if you recall the previous year she tried to kill herself. And altho' I think he's a macho pig - the bloke has helped her recovery.

Zoë moved into a flat with Kingsley. On campus she made friends as easily as she had at Bristol. We were increasingly pleased to be proved wrong as Zoë flourished, enjoying being a star. She dazzled in Essex. She developed a passion for playing and winning at pool. (In one of her boxes of souvenirs, she had keptthe records of her pool successes.)

In her second term she was given an option to write an essay on prostitution. Could she dare to use her own experience? She could and did - a brave thing to do for a twenty-one year old.

Part of her essay written in March, 1994 reads:

...I would like to make it clear that I am not writing this essay for the point of view of an intellectual who has never been in a brothel or the mind of a prostitute. ...

I am a twenty-one year old student at Essex. When I was nineteen I worked in brothels and hotels for several months as a prostitute. I believe this experience coupled with the wide range of prostitutes with whom I came into contact is relevant. So although I will analyse some classic texts relating to the subject my essay will focus on first-hand information I have acquired and my opinions on prostitution.

She went on to analyse some of these classic texts and then described her personal experience. Whether or not the 'work' was as easy as she describes, we have no way of knowing.

.... I would not work in these brothels again simply because I now enjoy monogamy. However, at the time, I, like the vast majority of women I worked with, did not find it regrettable. I actually thought that the work I was doing was fantastic. A typical day involved getting up late in the afternoon, splashing out on designer clothes I could afford thanks to the fact that I was earning hundreds of pounds a night, eating out with friends, chatting with the amusing friendly prostitutes at work, being paid hundreds of pounds in the space of a few hours to sit in a Jacuzzi with a regular client or to allow some client to practice oral sex on me. We were allowed to refuse a client we disliked and we were able to turn down work because our earnings were so high. Clients paid fifty pounds for straight sex, one hundred pounds for anal sex and if they wanted to be beaten the asking price was ten pounds a thrash. If a client wanted to

see us in a hotel the average price for an evening was £150 and £300 for the whole night.

I felt safe because the brothel was equipped with security cameras and locks. We were never alone with a client in the brothel as four girls worked a shift and most of the time the manager and her armed husband were also in the brothel. Each room was fitted with alarm buttons. I also felt safe in the hotels because the brothel knew where I was, whom I was with, as did the staff at the reception desk. I always went to and left the hotels in a separate taxi from the clients.

The hotels themselves were always the best in town and full of people. I also asked room service to call me every hour. I used condoms and spermicidal and only touched a client's penis with my mouth if he was wearing a condom.

I was also pleasantly surprised by the type of clients who visited these brothels and a few of them became friends. They were not the hideous unsexy men one might expect. For it takes a degree of confidence for a client to go to a prostitute who he knows will be beautiful, sexually experienced and might turn him down. The vast majority of my clients were attractive, professional men in their twenties and thirties with a good sense of humour. 95 % wanted straight sex and to go down on me. The others wanted anal sex or mild domination to which I had no objection. Whilst I was working I could not imagine a more pleasant easy way to earn a high salary. And if it were not for my year-old discovery of monogamy and my family's heartbreak when I told them of my job, I would probably still be a prostitute, at least part-time. Because for me, the type of prostitution I was involved in was different from casual promiscuous sex only in so far as I received money. And whilst I believed in casual promiscuous sex, it seemed more intelligent to get paid for it, especially as my clients tended to be more attractive and fun than the men I was sleeping with for free.

In conclusion, Zoë decides that ...*prostitution is regrettable only if one or all parties involved feel degraded or is in any form of psychological or physical danger ... and common sense tells us that there will always be someone prepared to pay for sex and someone willing to sell it.*

She argues persuasively but then, she always could. As far as we know for the rest of her life, although she went through bouts of promiscuity, she never returned to selling sex.

At this time of her life, her friendship with Florence and her attempts to find a spiritual basis for her life and belief in God were at their most intense.

She wrote to Florence:

We live in our world like bats upside down. We think that the nightmares are real and the well-being is a dream.

Devil is like a cigarette which only partially relieves the symptoms that it creates. The more we partake of the poison, the greater our tolerances to it until we reach a point of believing that it is actually of some benefit to us. We forget that we were happy and complete before the devil, before the poison entered us. We are led to believe that we are unable to cope without the trinkets that the devil gives us. We may know that abominations and disease lie behind the trinkets but the trinkets have become, or so we believe, our comforters.

The brainwashing is awesome. Even the strongest of us are vulnerable to it. With God we have no negative emotions only peace, joy, wisdom and strength. Devil feeds negative emotions into us. The devil is no more than a confidence trickster. Once the trick is exposed, the confidence trickster loses all power of persuasion. ... We fall into the trap of believing that our negative emotions are not so bad because sometimes an illusion of relief is created.

... The devil creates negative emotions. The longer that we stick with the devil, the greater the negative emotions become, and the smaller the periods of relief, as the devil wins us over. Hell is simply absolute negative emotions and sensations with no relief.

All we need to do is to return to God to positive emotions and sensations. The place of immunity is devoid of self-obsession, competition and insecurity.

Substitute the word 'addiction' for 'devil' in Zoë's letter and you find a foreshadowing of her torments in the following years. In her early twenties, these shadows remained at the fringes of her consciousness. She suppressed any references to her first episode, illness, depression or suicide attempts. And we, as her parents, who loved her, followed her lead; the easier path to follow and with hindsight one that adds to the useless regrets of another if-only.

At Essex the shadows retreated and Zoë was as happy a young woman as she had been as a child. As she wrote in her retrospective:

1993-96 Essex 2:1 Happy years. Lots of friends. Sociable.

In those years she sought love as most single young girls will. After her friendship with Matthew when she was fourteen and fifteen, Kingsley became the next most important man in her life. She wrote touchingly to him:

I would bring back Bob Marley for you if I could. I would take you to the bottom of the sea to see a whale rub its tummy over pebbles if I could, I would take away the memory of the boy who hurt you in school if I could. I wish I could do these things for you...

Most of Zoë's boyfriends came from a Nigerian or Afro-Caribbean background. Without denying her Jewish origins, on campus she made no Israeli or Jewish friends and many Palestinian and Arab ones. No social snob, she was nevertheless thrilled that Tariq's wife Nighat claimed descent from Timburlane. About her West Indian mates, she'd say that it was their warmth that drew her; she found the British "a cold, stuffy lot". She was drawn in to the glamour of the West Indian scene, the raffish running close to the wind aspect of clubs and parties with lots of pot smoking, rap and jazz. She also liked to laugh louder and longer than is correct in polite circles.

At the wake for Zo two days after her suicide, Zac said that of all his siblings, only Zoë treated him and his friends as equals, and spent time with them - happy, funny, dope-filled times. His friends all adored her. She used to take him out, not to museums or arty films but to rough pubs in Brixton and the East End, or taxi-driver's cafes. She would go to play pool, and she beat almost anyone she played with. Zac trusted her completely – with her he could visit those places and feel safe. She inspired both fear and attraction in the men around her; she amazed them. She was totally in control of the situation.

About this time, Zoë perfected the process of denial towards us, herself and her friends that lasted until her final illness. She'd say to us, "I've been to the bottom and now I am strong." One of the doctors at The Lakes had remarked casually after the suicide attempt, "This is an illness that can last years." I forgot what he said.

Watching our beautiful Zoë (yes, she had a violent temper but so did her Dad) I pushed niggling thoughts about mental illness away. I was being an ostrich. So, in spite of the amount of intimate talk in our family, her suicide attempt was never discussed, nor the reasons for it, either between ourselves or with her. A couple of years later, I asked her whether if I hadn't come in to fetch her for supper, would she have come out of the bedroom? She said no, she was too frightened that after taking the quinine tablets she would be maimed for life.

During the summer of her finals, something happened, which at the time appeared not especially important but had disastrous repercussions some years later. What happened was that one of my oldest friends, whom I see regularly, became strangely unavailable. I kept phoning; she kept stonewalling. Finally I asked what was wrong. With embarrassment and reluctance she told me that her daughter wanted nothing more to do with our family. Out of loyalty she felt obliged to do the same. I was nonplussed. What was the problem? No one had quarrelled or borrowed money. No, much worse. Fifteen years earlier this girl, I'll call her Margie, had spent a few weeks with us in Vaugenlieu - Tanya was eleven, Zoë three years younger. Wal had taken the three girls sightseeing in Paris; they'd spent the night in his office which doubled as an occasional place to stay. Margie, a year older than Tanya, seemed to enjoy her holiday and for some years after, she and Tanya remained close friends. In her late teens, Margie had a severe breakdown. She dropped her degree and rejected her family. She had a baby and rejected the baby. Eventually, she recovered enough to take charge of her little boy again and had another son. She lived with the father of the younger one. She has never returned to what we call 'normality' but she has never attempted suicide herself. Now in her late twenties, in the course of a violent row with her Mum, she accused Walter of sexual intercourse with *both* his daughters in the Paris office. She'd watched! My friend said that of course she didn't *believe* Margie but … I telephoned Margie, who retracted the accusation immediately, "maybe I've remembered it wrong," However, she maintained that Walter had masturbated in front of the three little girls. That she was sure of. This ridiculous accusation was so unfounded, so unlikely, that it could have been funny, only it wasn't. A year after Zoë's death, Margie's mother gave an explanation for her daughter's peculiar accusations. The

100

year following the eleven-year old girl's visit to us, her divorced father had taken her to Paris where they'd both stayed in the home of a friend. Margie's dad has himself never been particularly stable; his friend was a convicted paedophile. Margie's godmother, a clinical psychologist, believed that Margie had grafted memories of this Paris visit, too painful to accept, onto memories of that other earlier occasion.

We wouldn't find this out for some years and Zoë would never know what lay behind Margie's accusations. At the time, we gossiped about Margie being such a nutter. My reaction was anger; Wal was more tolerant, he knew how ill she had been. Tanya thought it unimportant and felt sorry for Margie's distress. Zoë appeared curious in a casual way and asked for details. Margie's accusations were forgotten as someone's silly fantasies, until they surfaced some years later from the mouth of Zoë, wild-eyed and raving, in the hotel lobby in Essouira. And their muddy footprints were smeared into Zoë's stoned ravings written in London before she even went to Morocco. Margie's sexual fantasies were incorporated into her own fragile grasp of reality. In her diaries she accused her father of abuse and by inference her mother of connivance. It was hard to read this and not be able to tell her what must have happened.

At Essex University, Zoë reached out to people. At the wake, one of her fellow students, Shireen, said that Zoe had been her "secret friend" at University. "We spent loads of time chatting, even though Zoe had lots of other friends. She used to talk about her little brother Zac and how much she adored him, and also her dad. She was so proud of him and his achievements. Most of all, Zoë liked to flirt. She wanted to teach me how. I kept on saying, 'I'm too fat.' Nonsense, she said. 'All you need to do is hold in your tummy, push out your breasts and smile.' We used to party together. If I can flirt now, I owe it to her."

Corinna, our German au pair, remembered how she and Zo drove into Colchester to find the first examples of this new marvel – the Wonder bra. "We spent a really girlish giggle day. Zoë and I picked out our size and started laughing about the difference as we went to try them on in *Dorothy Perkins*. I finished first and amazed, I called Zoë to come into my changing room to have a look. Wonder bras make your boobs look three sizes bigger and the result was that Zoë's chest was up under her chin. I bought one and the whole week when we went to Essex uni, she winked and made a gesture like - Corinna, stick 'em out!"

Zoë was ambivalent at how much help she wanted from us. On the one hand, she wanted us to finance her second university career. On the other, she wanted independence - financial and emotional. For financial independence she took a part-time job as French *assistante* in Philip Morant, a local comprehensive. She had to back up the French teacher in class and help the kids with pronunciation and grammar.

Coming home from work one day, she found a stray cat, whose story forms a bittersweet coda to Daisy's disappearance. The starving stray was in a lay by near the school; its collar so embedded into its neck that it had to be cut away. Zoë took it to the vet who treated it for worms, exhaustion, eczema and rotting teeth. Overjoyed, sure that it was Daisy coming home after a four-year disappearance, she compared photographs of Daisy with this small striped tabby. They looked similar but the vet said, "If it's Daisy, my dear, you ARE lucky; she's changed her sex. This is an elderly neutered tomcat."

Zoë accepted the disappointment and we provided a home for the ailing animal. Zoë was in her second year at Essex University, when the stray went missing. I found him next day, dead under the bush beside the back door.

I wrote to Tanya in Cambridge:

December 2nd 1994

Tanya,

Yesterday morning Zoë's cat was lying in its sand box looking bedraggled. The sand was full of pee and shit. I picked up the cat with one hand and a wodge of fur came away in my hand. It was very ill. It has been ill for a couple of weeks. About two weeks ago something bit it. Its leg swelled up and it went lame. We didn't take it to the vet. Zoe did. They drained the wound and prescribed antibiotics. The lameness was gradually dissappearing but something else must have gone terribly wrong. The cat had a swollen stomach. It slept all day on the towel-wrapped cushion.

This morning there was no sign of him. So I searched in the greenhouse where he lived most of the summer. The greenhouse was full of dying tomato plants we had forgotten to water.

I found the cat under the hedge beside the back door. I reckon he had been there since I put him outside the previous morning. He lay on his side - stiff and cold - his paws stretched out. ....

The body lies in a shoebox, a white cardboard box marked Fragile. I've dug a grave in the wild bit of front garden where we buried the terrier two years ago. I telephoned Zoë. I supposed she wants to see her cat for one last time. Zoe said that she didn't and asked if I would I bury him.

He died alone. In his final days I fed him but I never stroked him. I was never unkind to that cat nor was I ever anything other than self-centred....

I cried so much for the little stiff cat this morning. An autumn sun is shining and I suppose the last months of its life were happy.

The situation is complicated in the case of that cat because Zoë at present is going through a state of rage against herself and me because of her abortion. I begin to see what is important and what isn't. We try and never manage as well as we would like. Zoë's abortion had opened a deep and silent rift between us.

She kept a fairly complete diary when she was at Essex University. In the diary the pages for those dates around the time of the abortion, have been ripped out. She was finishing her second year. The affaire with Kingsley had already ended and we were glad. She had started another relationship.

<u>Monday 27th June</u> [1993]

I have felt strange all day. I want to do really well in Sociology next year and I am scared that I might not.

In the university diaries, Simon gradually makes an appearance. He was a quiet Welsh boy, dazzled by Zoë as so many people were. Her diary is an account people she met, had drinks with and went swimming.

<u>Tuesday 28th.</u>

Corinna, Paul and I went shopping for Zac's presents... Simon called I read him the parts of the diary about him.

They became lovers.

<u>Thursday 7th July</u>

Simon came over in the afternoon. ...Chatted to Mum and dad. We went to bed. It was incredible again.

<u>Friday 8th July</u>

Simon and I had a cigarette by Friday Woods. He picked me up after work. We did the shopping at Tescos. We had a mango at Wivenhoe sea front. We smoked. Went to bed for the rest of the day. Woke up to say goodnight to the others.

104

<u>*Saturday 9th July*</u>

Simon and I made love for the morning. He drove back to work…

We never met Simon, nor did Zoë ever introduce him to Kelly, Sarah or Mylène so they don't know him either. I don't believe he ever knew about her abortion, although she'd cared for him. I know that. Years later, I found this letter, torn out from the relevant notebook and stuffed into the pages of a children's book. I don't know whether she ever sent it.

Sunday 26th June [1993]

Simon

I miss you constantly. I want to take our relationship one step at a time because your friendship is so precious to me. And it is the friendship, as far as I am concerned which must always come first.

The night that we spent together was for me at least, the fuck of the century. And it was a lot more than fucking because of the way that I perceive you. The images and feelings of that night and the times we spent together preceding it, frequently wipe out the present.

I am afraid that this turns out to be too good to be true. I am afraid to be disappointed. I am afraid that it will not work out between us. I am afraid that you will run away from me. And I am very afraid of being a disappointment to you.

This fear shows one thing very clearly to me. That I deeply want our relationship to go well because it matters to me. It shows me that you matter to me very much.

I wish that you were here.

I can't wait to see you again.

Tonight, I have made a very conscious decision that I want to get involved with you.

I am proud of you.

Zoë came back to Greenacres for the summer holiday. She had done well in her exams. Nothing brilliant but then she didn't spend enough time studying to get first class results.

Thursday 21st July

Saw Nana at 10am. Met Simon at 1.30. Simon came with me to the dentist, John Bunyan who said I had perfect teeth and a perfect mouth.

John's verdict pleased Zoë enormously and she was proud of her perfect teeth. Along with her physical strength, it gave her a self-image that she cherished. Our photo albums contain many photos of Zoë picking people up ranging from Jonathan Porritt who must have weighed eighty kilos down to Ben's wife, Fredy who can't weigh more than forty-six.

July that year - a heat wave.

Friday 22nd

The weather is holding out.

Saturday 23rd July

We swam and sunbathed. Met Florence to go to the service at St Johns. Simon was horrified when half the congregation fainted wailed and giggled on command. Popped into the Students Union for a drink.... We went to bed early. I was switched off Simon because he got so angry over the service.

Sunday 24th July

We had really nice heavy sex all morning. We drove to
Stepney melting in the car from the heat.

<u>*Monday 25th July*</u>

 Woke up feeling ill.

She must have been in the first few weeks of pregnancy.
Because Mylène was feeling a bit miserable, Zoë planned a
week's visit to her in Marseilles where she was a student.

<u>*Wednesday 27th July*</u>

Train to Marseille. Mylène met me at the station. We had a
long chat about God. Back to her flat. It has views on the
sea and the mountains and is spacious. Had dinner and
drinks with some people from the business school who are
dead boring.

The rest of the week the girls spent on trips and
swimming and Zoë' 'chats' the content of which she rarely
notes. After visiting friends in Budapest, Zoë went to stay
with Corinna and her family in Germany.

Zoë and Sarojini her godmother and her mother

<u>*Monday 15th August*</u>

Corinna met me at the station. We had lunch with her family I like her mother a lot. Slept in the afternoon. After dinner Corinna and I went to a really nice beer hall where they make their own beer. Lost my rack with Corinna's boyfriend because he cheated at pool. Corinna and I came home and had a chat.

<u>*Tuesday 16th August*</u>

In the morning took the test Result purple!

Zoë now knew she was pregnant.

In the afternoon Corinna and I went to the stables. It's horrific the way they ride in Germany the horses are

108

over bent and the riders even the teachers are very rough and quick tempered. Not to mention piss arrogant.

Wednesday 17th August

_Had the scan. They offered Corinna a cognac!

We had a massive lunch with Corinna's family, a massive tea and a massive dinner.

Zoë had telephoned us the news from Germany so by the time she came home everyone in the family including Zac knew. Her elder sisters sent loving and supportive messages over her imminent return from Germany five weeks pregnant. Wal cut short his holiday in France to come home. The pregnancy was the result of a burst condom, she said.

Wednesday 24th August

Saw Dr Rasor. Arranged for Marie Stopes. [The clinic was in Buckhurst Hill about an hour's drive from Greenacres.]

Thursday 25th August

Played pool with Dave

Sarah came over for dinner. Zac had cooked a Chinese feast for Antoine

Friday ...still not feeling very well. Rested some more

Saturday 27th August

Consultation at lunchtime. Dad and I had lunch in Epping Forest.

The pages in the diary are ripped out for the next three weeks.

Her abortion took place in early September. She refused a general anaesthetic. On what must once have been the old village green in front of the Marie Stopes Clinic, a couple of Pro-Life protesters in raincoats were waving placards. I would have liked to wipe their sanctimonious expressions clear off their faces. We were ushered in the back entrance. I remember hugging my knees and crying on the green while the foetus was being destroyed. Wal and I had told Zoë we'd accept any decision of hers whether or not to keep the baby. She made the rational choice. After it was over, I wanted to rush home and mourn; Zoë wanted to stay and chat with the other women who had just had abortions.

"Can't you see I'm talking," she snapped.

Yes, I could but insisted that we drove home.

We drove home in silence, angry with one another.

I wrote: *What do I think about Zo's abortion? I know that it is all for the best. I feel that she is murdering my grandchild. Is there some hidden aggression against Zoë in this? Millions of babies. Why that one? The whole subject is terribly distasteful.*

I'm glad I never asked her whether she wanted to change her mind. I wonder if the spilt condom excuse is true.

Zoë had said with apparent calm just before the operation. "It's the right time for an abortion. The bundle of cells is just the right size." She's gone to visit Ben and Fredy in Paris before term starts. She remarked before she left: "I realise it must have been hard for you. It just clicked for me. It didn't for you."

Once Zoë had decided not to have the baby, she never even discussed the matter with Florence, who would have tried to dissuade her. Florence knew nothing of the abortion until she learned of it after Zoë's death. (*Another of the might-have-beens that haunted us after you died. If we had persuaded you to have that baby, might you have stayed alive to bring her up?*)

Zoë never mentioned the abortion again until the last summer of her life when she raved about "my baby in heaven."

The entries for September and October note nothing special. She mentions Simon. The last entry of the diary reads.

<u>Wednesday 12th October</u>.

Got back to campus in the afternoon. Played pool with Simon.

Met Francis [Winston] at 9 we went to the Hippo and then talked until 11.

With the resilience of youth Zoë pushed the bad time behind her and continued at university with a ceaseless round of social life punctuated with periods of study. Simon dropped out of her life and she began a new affaire with Francis Winston, a jazz musician, whom I liked a lot. He was a Jamaican cockney with dreadlocks and a smile as infectious as Zo's. He never showed much interest in any subject until music, especially jazz, was mentioned. (At Zo's funeral he was one of several young men who burst into tears, hugged me and said they wished that they had married her.)

We wanted her to get a First for a variety of reasons: Habie had found her First class honours from LSE opened many doors, employers take you seriously. We also believed a good degree would increase Zoë's self esteem.

111

Her social round never stopped for long enough for her to concentrate on studying. Her 2.1 was achieved by merit of intelligence rather than dilligence.

She grew more confident. She spent the summer temping in London and Colchester and felt competent enough to send her big brother advice.

After a visit to his family in Paris, she wrote: *I have to say I'm very impressed with your parenting. I'm still trying to work out how you managed to make a reasonably elaborate chocolate cake with a three and a six year old. Wow!' Part of her letter read:*

Living in London is a blast though the pace can get exhausting at times. ...

Anyway I hope that you are not overworking yourself. You seemed under a lot of pressure. A friend and I came up with a little philosophy about money and work

WORK isn't meant to be fun. If it was it would be called so; it isn't and it never will be.

MONEY: no matter how much you have, it is never enough because only financial geniuses can live within their incomes. It never was enough, it isn't and it never will be.

CONCLUSION: to worry about work or money is futile. This might all sound a bit simplistic but I have to say that attitude has helped me of late.

To refocus that true richness is family and friends. I am blessed with my friends and as for mum and dad. I guess that I must have got the bulk of my rage out when I went down the tubes. I remember in therapy, the beginning consisted of me literally cursing and swearing about how awful they can be, Once that violent rage was 'out' I realised that although I couldn't change Mum or dad, I could change my reactions to them, Once the rage is 'out' there is light at the end of the tunnel. Especially if humour can be used to diffuse tensions. I'm mentioning this because like I said, you seemed to me to be under some serious

pressure and from my own experience, I do recommend
therapy. With the right therapist of course. Personally I
could never do Habie's sort. My therapist just lets me blow
my top without dramatising but with full empathy.

After a lot of shilly-shallying, Zoë applied and was accepted
to study for an MSc at London School of Economics. We
were to finance her in part and she would take temporary
jobs as well. We were proud of her academic achievements.
Zoë was moving forward. If her plans were somewhat
vague, her fuse somewhat short, there was nothing in her
outward behaviour which we couldn't categorize as
'normal' problems of growing up. The therapist she had
seen for two and a half years agreed with her that she was
ready to 'move on.'

Her academic year at LSE was a success. She
financed herself in part by fundraising for the college. She
made as usual many friends. In the middle of the academic
year she wrote to Sarah. She had already met Francis
Npuedeche who was probably the greatest love of her life.

'11.03.97

Dearest Sarah,

... Amanda's younger brother Francis continues to be
utterly adorable. Can you believe that I am with a decent,
life-enhancing human being? I'm still patting myself on the
back.

'LSE is a blast. I could happily stay there for
years....

I've also started working for the LSE Foundation in
Promoting the School to Alumni. I won a prize today for
raising £2000 in one evening! I'm still buzzing from it. The
money will go to scholarships for the International
Relations Dept.

'Interestingly enough, since the 2 weeks I started
paid work; I've also started studying seriously. My

supervisor reckons I can get a distinction, which is a huge boost. But to be honest, with the amount (6 months) of catching up I have to do; I'll be over the moon if I pass. There was me thinking that an MSc would be a doddle but it's incredibly hard work. The standards are excellent.

God willing that I do well, I'd like to do a PhD at LSE, but as I say, at this point in time I still don't know how much I can catch up. So if I just do OK, I'll probably be going to India Jan '98 for a while to work on a project which Cares for 'untouchable' children.

...   'Et Dieu dans tout ça? Have come to the conclusion that praying is the only really worthwhile activity. Even if it's just a placebo, the positive outlook it creates makes things happen right.

...I'll be in England when you get back. Exams and writing up my dissertation, which is due in September. ...

Missing you terribly,

Lorra love, Zoë

After her death, in the days, weeks, months and now years of wondering, full of what-ifs and why-didn't-we's, one of our deepest regrets is that Zoë believed and so did we that her mental illness was OVER, Her erratic behaviour we simply ascribed to her personality. We believed (as we NOW know is wrong) that an attempt at suicide was rather like a case of measles. If you'd caught it once, you were immunised. But the facts are to the contrary; a successful suicide is more likely to have made earlier attempts.

We asked Paul Rasor, our family GP, recently why no one in the Health Service ever made sure that we knew that episodes of manic-depressive illness often reoccur. He said telling families about a patient's mental ill health was always problematic. "You tend to go lightly," he said.

114

"Many people would be devastated if you told them something like that."

CHAPTER FIVE

"It's time for me to grow up."

She left Essex University and went to live in London, initially with my mother and afterwards in a flat we bought in West Hampstead. Her moods switched from high to low, from loving to irritable. Visiting Greenacres most weekends, her outward behaviour was always upbeat. Her problems at work and the yo-yo state of her love life might have provided clues that her equilibrium was precarious. Would she have agreed to seek treatment, if anyone had suggested it? No one did.

Was it pride, reserve or some idea we'd transmitted to our kids that they must excel that prevented her from telling us about the mental states that tormented her, that she could describe in her diary but not to us. On her visits home, she never gave the slightest sign of unease. Only after reading her diaries did we realise what she showed in public was so different from what she felt alone.

That year, her love affair with Francis Ndupeuechi was flaming on and off. Two of Zoë's deepest loves were for the younger brothers of close girlfriends, Mylène's brother Jean-Guy and Amanda's brother Francis. I don't know whether this was more than a coincidence. She'd met Amanda at Essex University and through her, met her younger brother Francis.

Zoë wrote at the start of their love affaire:

The world is a better, brighter place, imbued with new meaning. The feeling, the recognition of the feeling began at a tangible moment in time - the night of the nineteenth leading into the twentieth of August, 1996. Unexpected and shattering. I see God in your eyes. I feel humbled and strengthened.'

116

And in another letter, she wrote: *'Life would be so much more peaceful without this passion. But calm waters are empty. I feel that I have embarked on a ride on which I am going to see and experience the unexpected, followed by the improbable, completed by the miraculous.*

Francis wrote to us after her death: ... *I dream of her a lot. ... now she can really see all the thoughts and feelings that were in my head that somehow I could not communicate.*

I have lots of memories from the time she would call me while on the motorway and hold her mobile to the engine, trying to let me hear the funny noises that she wanted me to diagnose, to driving straight into a pillar in Heathrow's Car Park after picking me up.

Deep down in my heart I always felt that regardless of our unresolved issues Zoë and I would eventually end up together.

Zoë and Francis were at Greenacres for Christmas 1997. A big family occasion with a lot of French spoken because of Ben and his French family. Zoë wrote:

Christmas Eve

Mum provided superb Christmas Eve dinner. Salad was extraordinary so were the mushroom ... Francis cross because of Frog talk. Me distraught because I felt that he did not like my family enough. Turns out that he does – just not especially when they are talking French.

Zoë and Francis set off for Southampton on Christmas day because Francis wanted to spend some of the holiday with his sister,

Tuesday 30*th* December

Francis and I woke up late. We sorted my car and shopped at ASDA. Francis is amazing with stuff like that. I was really touched that he took time off his studies. While he

*studied I read the job book Tanya gave me. This stuff with
Tanya, Mum and Dad is upsetting. I hope I can help.*

That was one of Zoë's warmest qualities; her
concern for family and friends. Tanya, having completed
the field work for her thesis, had come to write it up at
home; we were writing up our year of travels for *Living
Lightly*. Our book was not going well and the three of us
were scratching against each other's nerves. Tanya
complained that the house was filthy. It was. We countered
that if she found it dirty she should clean it. The row ended
with me yelling, "If you don't like it, get out," which she
did. Ben and Habie thought I had behaved abominably,
which I had. Eventually we made up and Tanya's thesis was
later published as, *Ethiopian Jewish Immigrants: The
Homeland Postponed.* Our book, *Living Lightly; travels in
post consumer society* was published the following summer.
Both Tanya's book and our book were well-received in the
specialist press but didn't get much attention from the
mainstream.

That winter, Wal and I were more concerned about
finishing our manuscript than about Zoë, who, although she
had no permanent job, seemed happy, radiant with her love
for Francis; it's good to remember that. She spent most of
her time either in Leeds with Francis or staying with him
and his sister Amanda in her Southampton flat.

Wednesday 31st December ...

*Francis and I fait l'amour with the boats tooting and
teenagers yelling from one block apartment to the other. We
fell asleep as we lay in the sitting room.*

Thursday 1ˢᵗ January .....

*Feeling a bit low with the job hunting business but it is
certainly good for my ego, Would be nice to be earning
some decent money to be able to help Francis. But I guess
that he will be fine. He is very good at managing stuff.
Thinking about my exceptionally nice friends and how I am
getting far with my family helps put the job thing in*

118

perspective. I guess this is a great opportunity for learning and persistence.

But I need to get more in tune and more in focus and less bloody melodramatic. Disappointed about smoking again this week but pleased about Callisthenics and eating better. The American job hunting book is good in parts but I have to inventory my past and list my transferable skills. Huh! Well it could be a laugh. It is amazing having time with Francis and the flat to ourselves.

<u>*Sunday 4th January*</u>

Very much in love with Francis. But I feel that my not having a permanent job is putting pressure on both of us. Also Francis is worried about his exams.

She made one of her lists on Thursday evening. Zo loved making lists (her papers are full of them) and was always trying to persuade her friends to do the same. "When the lists were about Zoë, so much the better," Kelly told me months after her death during one of our many 'afterwards' chats. "Zoë could always be enviously honest and analytical about both her weaknesses and her strengths, which is possibly the reason why her friends never took her erratic behaviour too seriously. It seemed presumptuous that you could do a better job of anaylsing Zoë than she could herself."

This particular list contains one of the rare references to her abortion:

- *My baby in heaven*
- *stewardship of gifts*
- *Loss of ego*
- *choice of attitude*
- *lack of melodrama*
- *jolliness*

- *positivity*

- *compassion*

- *questioning own assumptions*

- *confidence*

- *nothing to prove*

- *gratitude*

- *mind and body conditioning and maintenance*

- *patience*

- *repentance for own faults, not blame others*

- She ends the list with a group of friends and family.

Florence, Sarah, Kelly, Mylène

Zac and the family

Francis – best of the best God's Gift

For the first part of the year her love for Francis flourished.

... I'm so proud of him. Francis Nkonjika Ndupeuechi is the light of my life. There can be no one else but him because I am his in a way that I cannot describe in words. It's very practical and very peaceful. It's magical and real because I trust him and respect him with all my heart

-receiving phone messages is really one of my favourite rituals

- *feeling great about job situation because I know that with a lot of hard work it can still take some time.*

- *Thank you God for everything and especially Francis.*

-

Because Zoë visited us so often, so much more than the other kids, we gave her the nickname Cordelia. The other kids didn't see the joke.

Spent the day with Mum dad and Zac. Dad was nice. Mum just moaned and moaned.

At that period of my life, I *was* a terrible moaner. Zoë's judgements were harsh. She sent a long email, part of which reads:

I understand that even if mum can 'hear' this, old habits are hard to break. ... I don't know much but I do know that when you give pure love - that is love that is given graciously with no expectation of return, you receive it back tenfold and that is what strength is about.

Ask yourself some vital questions. For example, how do people feel when they hear an attractive, healthy, beloved, financially secure woman going on as though she needed pity? Ask yourself if you need to be the centre of attention by antagonising people around you?

You might say that your self-esteem is so low and you were so badly parented that you are doing the best you can.

Your children are grown up and don't 'need' to spend time with you unless they want to. Ask yourself why they would want to when they are going to be subjected to negativity and fantasies.

... I believe that deep down you know well enough what it is that you have to tackle. The simple truth is do you want to?

.... part of the problem is that you have been using your family as parental therapists for far too long and that is part of the vicious circle that has been created by us as a family. I do not want to facilitate that vicious circle any

more. I do not want to hear negativity and fantasy from you any more.

I will always love you unconditionally. I will always be thankful that you are my mother because I would choose you as my mother any day of the week and twice on Sundays. But my time is conditional. As you well know, I have many very close friendships and I am about to start a very demanding job. My time is therefore very precious to me. I am not a therapist who is paid to listen to your nonsense and I am not an emotional punching bag who has nothing better to do than to lap it up ...

Wal enjoyed quoting bits of this message back at me whenever I grumbled about the kids - they didn't visit or phone often enough or wouldn't tell me things. Zoë's angry analysis was perceptive because the less I demanded of the kids, the more responsive they became - a hard lesson to learn.

But where Zoë could criticise her Mum and her other family members, she idealized her lover - not that surprising. They were deeply in love.

Sunday 18th [1998]

I miss Tigger. I feel like a piece went out of me yesterday. I don't think I should be too attached to Mum and dad and Zaco. Just dinner once or twice a month. I think I should also move out of Nana's. Had a nice chat with mum and dad. Feeling very appropriate. It's fine to make a point when you have been hurt but then you must be nice. I miss Francis so, so much. I don't want to idealize him. I try to remind myself that he can be grumpy and insecure like other people but the difference with Francis is that it is rare for him to be grumpy. The other thing about Francis is that he is decent at all levels. He wouldn't just survive a war, he would help other people to survive it as well. Of his qualities two of my favourite are that he has got no time for bullshit and that he has got nothing to prove. Francis isn't just intelligent about his work, he's intelligent about people. There's so many things that he's done and said that make me think. He's powerful because he's strong and kind at the same time. Francis is the sexiest man I've ever met. I must have done something that made God very happy for me to deserve Francis. Being in this committed and exciting relationship with Francis is the sexiest and most stimulating thing that has happened to me.

Zoë wrote three prayers for herself and for Francis.

Please watch over Francis. Let him live with your love peace and wisdom inside of him. Protect his body and feed his mind. And please make me the best I can be for him. And for myself please take away my remaining insecurities so that I can enjoy Francis fully. Dear God I love this man truly. Please convey that message to him sealed with your faith, dear God. Thank you, Amen

The last prayer continues:

Father, I beg your forgiveness. I repent and thank you for giving me life. I rejoice to know that my baby, Zugi, Daisy and Tigger and Zac are safe in you. Watch over them father. And break me, my arrogance and conceit. Break me so that there is only good spirit left.

Father, I don't want me anymore things that are boring and futile. I want your spirit to replace my ego. In the name of my true love Francis, I beg you and authorise you to replace my ego with your spirit. Amen

As Kelly said at her funeral, Zoë always credited her friends with sparks of the divine fire - an attitude easily scorched by reality. Zoë loved and admired her friends but when someone was in a position of authority over her, this love and admiration was reversed. Zoë herself struggled with this neurosis in her diaries. We used to think her attitude to work and bosses peculiar, never suspecting it

123

could be a symptom of her bi-polar disorder. Helen Seaford was her direct superior at The Runymede Trust (her first proper job after university) and within a few weeks, Zoë was writing:

Monday 26th January [1998]...

Situation with HS has been a strain and I would like to make a grievance or try to talk to her again 'cos she could just carry on being psycho when she feels like it. After work made some job hunting phone calls which were good...I want to live in God's perspective.

Tuesday 27th January

Helen Seaford is affecting me badly. I am trying to be tolerant because she is unwell. She's having a stand-up psychotic breakdown. But you don't become a bitch just because you are ill. It's been very upsetting.

These comments are heart-wrenching because Zoë DID become a bitch herself when she was unwell.

For about two weeks work situation has been intolerable. Now that the launch is done I hope Helen gets removed and the help she needs. It's also unfair to anyone who works with her because she is so destabilising. Psychologically, I believe that she is dangerous. We are so belittled by her at work that it is affecting us even physically. ..

Chat with Francis, who is amazing. Everything is back in focus and perspective.

Francis had (and still has I suppose) a calm temperament; he found Zoë's volatile moods hard to cope with. He was also four years younger. They rowed a lot.

Sunday 8th February

Row with Francis was painful but we ended up learning a lot. Francis drove back. We had a gorgeous dinner at Pizza Express and kissed and made up.

Monday 9th Our love making has become quite mind-blowing. We grabbed a MacDonald's and swung on our branch at Kenwood.

> I loved reading that entry. Forty-three years earlier, Wal and I had swung on the same branch. I'd told Zoë where it was.

... We were tender. Francis drove back for classes in the morning.

I'm deeply impressed and in love with Francis

> She wrote a loving letter from Francis' flat in Leeds:

Feb 23

Dear Mum,

Today, I was reading this fascinating and thoroughly researched book on hypnosis and right and left-brains. The cover is deceptive but if you have a moment, it is well worth checking out. 'The Supernatural' by Colin Wilson published by Magpie books especially the chapter on 'the Powers of the Hidden self.' It blends history, science and poetry.

I've been thinking about you and I just wanted to say how touched I am that you really tried to hear what I wrote a while ago. You seen much happier and relaxed.

... I was very struck each time I walked into LSE via the Strand that while millions of pounds are spent widening the pavement, 100s of young people sleep on those pavements. And then the great rabbit- on about human rights violations abroad.

Your Mum is very sweet and quite dotty at the moment.

.... I hope you like this poem. ...

I am a playwright. I show

What I have seen.

In the man markets

I have seen how men are traded.

That I show.

I, the playwright.

I gave recognition marks to, so that they became like the sayings

Of impermanent men which are set down

So that they may not be forgotten

That a mother gave her child the breast

I reported like something no one would believe

That a porter slammed the door in a freezing man's face

Like something nobody had ever seen.

I'm back in London on Saturday. Give me a call when you fancy a chat

Lots of love, Zoë

That was Zoë at her best, with her demons at bay and full of awareness and loving kindness. When she swung into another state of mind, she managed to hide it from us (acting sulky or irritable). It got worse at Runymede; her workmates dissuaded her from making an official complaint.

Shocked at how others advised me not to make a fuss and were themselves petrified of stepping out of line. Lola particularly but then she has put up with nonsense at RT for years, they all seem trained to take bullshit and have had fear instilled in them –white and black alike.

Train to Oxford to have dinner with Sarah and Sylvain. [Sarah and Sylain, a French friend of Ben's, had begun a romantic friendship] Would *like to see her more often and for longer. Her lack of aggression is striking. Her work's going really well.*

I'm learning a lot of stuff through temping. About how people are controlled and how sick organisations can be. Especially how if you start to put up with some thing, it becomes harder and harder to put an end to it.

I have to keep reminding myself that I'm learning invaluable lessons because on another level working in a second rate place with colleagues who won't boo the goose and being intellectually boring is quite demoralising.

Must take Nana for a walk in the garden tomorrow.

Just woke up feeling utterly shite about the whole job thing. Maybe that is why we are all so compliant with bullshit.

If the job hunt is unpleasant enough when you actually get the job maybe you put up with just about anything. Can get over the lack of guts yesterday and there is no sun. It's enough to make me wonder what the fuck I am doing in London.

The majority of my friends are in and around London. I've got a free place to stay and although work is fucked up I am learning a lot. But just how much of this am I supposed to take?...

I can hardly stand looking at a grey sky when it's grey outside and inside as well. Couple of hours later: feeling fine.

Zoë nursed ambitions to set up her own charity or be a manager in the voluntary sector. What was holding her back was inner distress.

Mylène and I had a lovely chat .... Mylène is uniquely charming and warm. Thinking about Francis, I miss him. I feel very secure in our relationship and I don't mind us not seeing each other for a while. I think that we both need to focus, him on his studies and me on settling into permanent employment. I hope we don't grow apart. And I hope things work out for us, I think we've got a lot going for us as a couple but it's still too soon to know how we develop.

Writing this, I can still see the self-confident, snappy, affectionate Zoë who used to visit us at Greenacres, scoop up Tigger, her cat, and set the room buzzing. Her moods were always volatile and that was 'just Zoë'. Her fears - of change, of growing up - were never expressed aloud. As I wrote earlier, she used to say as a teenager, sitting on my lap, 'I don't want to grow up,' but it never seemed a prophecy of future problems.

... Feel quite panicky about growing up. Moving away from Colchester to London to work.

I need to be less afraid of change.

I'm sure that it can be relished.

I prefer the pace in Colchester to London. Everything is so close at hand. Maybe London is not the best place. At the moment I'm using a water bottle as an ashtray. I guess that is the problem – feeling anxious and lethargic cos I'm smoking, not exercising and eating badly.

The Gaia Foundation is a small environmental charity based in Hampstead. Tanya had fund-raised for them with brilliant success and made several trips to the Amazon on their behalf. (Wal and I have always hoped that one day Tanya will transcribe the notes she kept of her experiences living with the Yanomami tribe deep in the Amazon rainforest. Zoë, for whom envy formed no part of her personality, was terribly impressed with her sister's experience.) The directors of Gaia were looking for another staff person.

Zoë's qualifications were right. They were delighted to take another Schwarz, Tanya's sister on board; her responsibility would be coordinating their campaign against GM crops.

Sunday 1st March

F and I had unpleasant chat, He had got really upset that I had got stoned. I was upset that he was critical instead of being supportive. We made up and I jumped in his car to Leeds. Decided definitely on GAIA....

The new job started well.

Tuesday 3rd March....

Felt fortunate that Francis and my girl friends have been so supportive over job thing.

Mylène in particular was adorable.

Feeling pretty fucking terrified about starting work.

Wednesday 4th March

Feeling nervous about salary meeting at GAIA and lost keys. Ed Posey and Liz immediately put all my fears to rest and I felt completely reassured that GAIA was the right decision. Edited some papers.

Came home and read some more. Missing Francis like crazy.

Habie was very sweet.

Friday 6th

'Interesting' day at work. This is going to be character building.

Monday 9th March

Maya came in to brief me. Monday meeting went on forever. Lazed about at home.

After Zoë's death, Maya wrote about that briefing:
*Zoë took over my job at the Gaia Foundation as the press
person/networker/campaigner on the issues of Patents on
Life. I was called in to train her in the new post. A task
which took four days. I was amazed by Zoë's sharp mind,*

Zoë and Zac at Greenacres

*her ability to not just absorb a vast amount of information
but to make sense of it and structure it in her mind. She did
all this whilst looking like she was hardly paying attention.
On a few occasions I would check that she was taking it in,
as she asked so few questions and seemed to be somewhere*

else. I was always amazed at her response. She had taken in everything and more.

Zoë began showing familiar signs of disenchantment with her job. She'd complain, "I'm so much more intelligent than the others. Meetings are a complete waste of time. I fall asleep in them." Wal would respond, "Don't be silly." Why didn't we seek out deeper reasons for each rapid disillusion with new jobs and female bosses? I asked Kelly about it, a couple of years later. She explained that Zoë had trouble with all bosses not just female ones. "She would rail about being asked to do things like make the coffee or do the photocopying. You could not get it through to her that this was what she was being paid for. She used to claim that it was cheap ego-boosting titillation on behalf of those who asked her. Then if you couldn't see that - that showed how oppressed you'd allowed yourself to become in the corporate mentality. So everyone else was in denial apart from her."

Within a few weeks, Zoë's problems with Liz were as bad as or worse than those she'd had with Helen.

<u>*Monday 30th March*</u>

Bad day at work. Felt shitty. .... Went over to Mylène's and we had a good moan.

Zoë could not cope with the pressures of office politics. And she persisted in turning her female bosses into fantasy dragons. And as her reactions to her work went up and down and she and Francis quarrelled and made up.

<u>*Wednesday 1st April*</u>

Better day at work. Mylène phoned to say she was feeling better too. ... [Mylène had taken her first degree in Marseilles and now had come to London to study for an MBA and partly to be near Zoë.]

Vegged out with migraines. Not feeling very happy. I have to quit smoking, stop trying to impress Liz and Helen and re-energize.

Monday 6th April

Bad day at work. Good chat with Liz about it though which helped,

Horrible chat with Francis.

Tuesday 7th April

Woke up wretched about Francis situation.

Meeting Lutzenberger [a well-known ecologist] *at work was amazing. Mixture of vivid historical images and creative strategy. He's very old and I hope to get to meet him again before he dies.*

.... Came home feeling really positive at work and sad that Francis had not bothered to call. Feel insulted and humiliated by his behaviour recently.

Wednesday 8th April

Really nice day at work…. Came home and tried to work out Francis situation.

Nice time with Habie.

Feeling a bit better about Francis. He still hasn't called and I'm feeling very disappointed with him. He appears to be more immature and right wing than I had realised. I have no idea how this is going to pan out. His behaviour is denting my respect for him. I suppose we both need to be more tolerant of each other but I don't know if we are still in love with each other. I feel that he is being very casual about our relationship which makes me feel unsure about him.

Their relationship swung up and down. Zoë would complain bitterly that we didn't appreciate Francis enough but had he and Zoë stayed together, we'd have accepted him. Our misgivings were that he and Zoë shared few common interests.

Sunday 19th April

Francis sulking. Said he wanted to leave. .... When he sulked in the car something snapped in me. I was so bored. And told him that I didn't want to go out with him anymore.

I spent the evening with Henrik and his Mum. Slept with Henrik. We had sex which was no way near as good as I thought it would be.

Monday 20th April

Brilliant day at work. Realised that I had been transferring Francis- anxiety onto work. Feel free and fabulous.

Took musician Francis to dinner. We had a good chat. Stayed over his. Nice to wake up in his arms to Spanish music.

Tuesday 21st April

Another nice day at work. Crashed at Mylène's. Given up sleeping alone.

Were these cycles mild swings of bi-polar depression and elation? Zoë hid anxiety so well. That she would have other lovers when she was quarrelling with Francis didn't surprise me; she had always been capricious with men. She loved to gossip and tell hilarious stories about her amorous exploits. She was a baby femme fatale. She acted as if she were irresistible and so she was for almost every man she met. There were occasional exceptions.

In the weeks following her funeral, amongst the many callers were two men, one in his forties, the other a little older, neither of them members of Zoë's fan club. What traits had *they* sensed in Zo, that we, who loved her so much, were unaware of? Michael, an ex boyfriend of Tanya, and Rod, a playwright friend of mine, had both had mothers who suffered from mental illness and hospitalisation.

<u>*Monday 4th May*</u>

Feeling weird about Francis. Near Leeds and all. Drove back to London. Saw Kingsley and John. Did some dodgy coke.

This is the first mention of cocaine which we now think was one of the factors that led to Zoë's psychotic episode in Morocco.

<u>*Tuesday 5th May*</u>

Worked well. Had dinner with Henrik and some of his friends. Did some smack. Really lovely evening. Crashed.

Zoë's affaire with Francis rocked from side to side.

<u>*Friday 8th May*</u>

Francis came over after work. I was pleased to see him. It confirmed that it was right to break it off.

<u>*Saturday 9th May*</u>

Francis and I had a nice day vegging. Sex was nice but not uplifting and was in pain.

<u>*Monday 11th May*</u>

After work saw Kingsley and John. Lovely evening. Quoted twice in FT!

This was the campaign run by Gaia Trust against patents enforced by global trade rules which harm the interests of third world economies. Zoë assimilated the pro and anti arguments so swiftly and so thoroughly that Liz and Ed chose her as Gaia spokesperson in the national media. It was the high point of Zoë's work at Gaia but her relations with Liz her boss, were steadily deteriorating.

<u>*Wednesday 13th May*</u>

Good day at work. Gave a sound bite for News Night and did a live debate for News 24.

Considering she had only mastered the subject in the last few months, she spoke with confidence and charm. We watched her on News night, looking poised and confident with her hair swept back. We listened to her husky voice on Radio Four; she spoke without hesitation without ums and errs. Everyone was proud of her.

<u>*Wednesday 13th May*</u>

Gaia meeting. Liz was back. We had stories on the front pages of Independent and FT .... Went over to Henrik. Stunning evening. We played pool.... Smoked. While Henrik was making love to me there was thunder and lightning for three hours.

<u>*Friday 15th May.*</u>

Mylène and I drove to Colchester. Nice birthday dinner with Mum and Dad.

Mylène and I went over to see Tolis and Eleni and other friends. Tolis and I made love. It was cosmic. Magical.

<u>*Sunday 17th May*</u>

135

After dinner, had a row with Zac, Mum and Dad and changed the way I feel about home.

That row was about our criticising Zoë for her reactions to Liz at Gaia. As the summer continued so her moods swung more wildly.

<u>*Sunday 24th May*</u>

Stoned again. Back to Henrik.

I might see a doctor.

Feel weird. Probably just the demands of starting new job.

Not ready to be an adult. Rushing around scared: work, friends, little bit of sleep, work, friends, etc.

Not appreciating things properly. Although Kenwood today was amazing. Sad about Francis. I hope he is OK. Don't know if I'm falling in love with Tolis or I'm just transferring my love for Francis onto him because I can't love myself.

Feel dissatisfied and bored and very scared and ashamed.

Zoë asked no one for help. The frenetic activity hid such fear; none of us perceived her internal distress. This summer must have marked the start of the torment that slid to suicide.

<u>*Monday 25th May*</u>

Sarah came over and I went from flat to peaceful. Spoke to Tolis. I feel a spark for him but not head over heels or anything. Positive thoughts. Stillness.

<u>*Tuesday 26th May*</u>

I love the answer phone. It's good to hear the voice of loved ones. Like yesterday while Mylène and Henrik were chatting while I dozed.

136

Wednesday 27th May ...

All day meeting at GAIA Liz *went on and on in the afternoon. Very boring.*

Thursday 28th May

Horrible day at work. Liz *is really silly. Got better later.*

She concocted lists, as she had done since she was a small girl.

What I don't like

Nana being self-obsessed

Mum being self-obsessed.

Liz *being dim*

Being frightened

Not getting laid properly

What I do like

Friends

Nice weather. Playing pool. Being slightly stoned. Tolis.

Foot massages. Being slim and fit

Pizza Express, Cheese Pizza, Maria's chocolate cake

What I love

God and compassion

      Tragic glimmers of realisation that it might be herself who was misreading the situation. This irrational dislike that Zoë felt for Liz, for Helen earlier (and for Su the following year) was the opposite of her usual reaction to people. Sometimes she bundles these women together as awful mother figures. Yet I know that along with a frightening anger she felt towards me, she loved me as much as I loved, and still do, love her. Her mind divided, a part of it realises that her attitudes to Liz and Helen (and later on in her next job) to Su are unreasonable.

Monday 1ˢᵗ June

Stuck in traffic late for work. Almost burst into tears. Liz and I had a word. Maybe it is actually my problem. I get all worked up over criticism instead of learning gracefully but still think Liz and maybe Helen a bitch.

Wednesday 3ʳᵈ June

Did a Radio Four programme debate in the morning. Appraisal with Helen and Liz. H was sweet. Liz her usual twatty self. ...I hate Liz more than anything or anyone. I think that maybe I should resign. I'm so bored at work and disgusted with Liz. It's a bit of a nightmare.

Thursday 4ᵗʰ June

Meditation about work and paranoia.

Why do I hate and despise and loathe Liz so much?

Why am I so suspicious of Helena?

   a)   Liz is horrid and Helena is envious

   b)   I'm off my head

   c)   The three of us have major character faults and so it is hard to adjust to working together.

   d)   Answer is c)

   e)   But I now realise that I have to be the one to give deep down. I have a BETTER CHARACTER THAN THEM SO IT'S EASIER FOR ME.

That month, Zoë saw her local GP. Paul Rasor no longer recalls the visit. But he says when someone like Zoë presents themselves, apparently showing insight; you do not tell them they are ill. And he didn't. He reassured her instead of suggesting she see a therapist. One of the great if-onlys in Zoë's story. Had he suggested further treatment, would she have complied?

138

Dr Rasor was great and very reassuring not to be mad after all.

Zoë began to sleep with James whom she'd known at Essex University. She'd recount details of the fabulous sex they had together and giggle. I met James - a nice boy but like so many of Zoë's boyfriends - too much in awe of her. The family used to wonder why Zoë's boyfriends were often a bit younger than she was or apparently less confident.

Saturday 4th July

Jamie and I smoked made love and had a fabulous dinner at Mum and Dad. Found out no funds for position at Gaia.

Effectively Zoë had been sacked but no one actually admitted it aloud, so Zoë never had to acknowledge this in public.

That summer, my book, *Simple Stories about Women,* was published by Iron Press and *Living Lightly: travels in Post-consumer Society,* the book Wal and I co-authored was published by Jon Carpenter. The Colchester branch of Waterstones gave a launch for my short story book. Zoë jobless but in good spirits, was at Greenacres and offered to help with the party.

Wednesday 23rd July

Came home to help Mum with the party.

We made canapés and Zoë folded napkins into roses, one of her party skills.

Book launch was a great occasion with a mixture of Mum's old friends, local friends and students. Tammy, Andy,

*Jamie, Jack, Charlotte, Jide, Michelle and Mum's friends
Peter and Helen and I had a dopey truth session at home.*

Helen Shay, who'd been a student in my creative
writing classes and is now herself a published poet and
writer, described her memories of that night at Greenacres
after Wal and I had gone to bed at midnight.

*Zoë was vivacious, lovely, warm, surprising,
controversial, provocative (towards getting a truthful
reaction), vibrant, sensuous, appreciative, perceptive. I felt
that if you dared be honest with her, then she would be your
friend. It was absolute honesty which she demanded.*

*...I think sexuality was an enormous part of her,
and enthralling ... and none of it was lewd or distasteful. ...
I suppose my life isn't as full of interesting people as yours,
so the evening sticks with me; I enjoyed the Bohemianism of
it.*

'Won't bore you with much of the scene-setting and
periphery – your house, meeting Peter Mortimer [publisher
of Iron Press] whose company I quickly got to like, vaguely
fancying Darren the actor bod (yes, I know you told me he's
very provincial), then upsetting him because I told him he
looked like a Stuart king (suppose there isn't much of any
answer to that). He went home early (being provincial).
Peter and I joined the fun in the back room – Zoë , the
French girl, a young Swiss lad with slightly strange eyes (a
bit like David Bowie), an Algerian boy, a soldier (who also
went home early) and Zoë's friend (David?). Zoë was
wearing dark colours, low-cut casual dress with her hair
tied back ... a 'sex-goddess type'. Her 'friend' (she
wouldn't say 'boyfriend') was a pretty-faced young boy,
who came across as very sweet and probably besotted if
only she'd allow him to admit it. She introduced him with
"we've been shagging each other for three months, but
we're not in a relationship," to which Peter challenged,
"Well, that is a relationship, isn't it?" Through the evening,
I got the impression she did feel very fond of this friend,
because she kept teasing him as to how soon he'd have*

another girl, once she'd left for Australia (which was imminent).

We were smoking joints. Zoë pronounced it 'good skunk'. Led by Zoë, we ended up playing a sort of truth game, all to do with asking questions on sex and individual habits (like what to do if you get the 'munchies'). It reminded me a bit of something similar in 'Darling', the 1960s' Julie Christie film, only we stayed sitting down (having moved to the kitchen by then, because of some smoke problem with the stove in the other room). The Swiss guy got show-offy and intellectual (though he was quite nice really, despite being a bit fascist). Zoë was having no pretensions. She shut him up by mentioning some well-known philosopher or theologian she'd studied under, and then insisted the conversation switch from God to sex. She felt sex was something more real for people to talk about. I can't remember her exact words, but to the effect that sex grounded people in something tangible, which they could then compare life through.

...I think Zoë wanted us to open up, so people were being real to each other. The questions she posed were quite fierce ones. Zoë asked Peter for his most intense sexual encounter, and he told her it was when he first got together with Kitty Fitzgerald ... his partner, at age 45 years. Zoë thought this was 'sweet', and seemed quite moved that it was a mature romantic experience, as opposed to anything racy. I remember, at one point, she also said that she felt friendship was an all-important thing in life, and I told her that she was astute to realise this at her age. ... Zoë asked me my fantasy and when I answered, "My eighteen year-old babysitter," Zoë also asked me whom I'd most like to sleep with round the table, and then excluded the men. She did seem to like to get people up against the wall to see how they'd react. I gave some weak answer about being purely heterosexual (though I know nothing's that clear-cut). She also asked if my orgasms were clitoral or vaginal. I said mainly the latter and she said, "You bitch. I hate you." This led to the Swiss guy wanting

141

to know if the 'G' spot really existed. Zoë was very sympathetic about this. She said she could understand how male confusion arose and provoked such a question. Her friend said it definitely did exist and mentioned a time when he'd been a bit worried about the neighbours and her screams. Zoë also mentioned about the coloured guy she'd broken up with (hadn't they been engaged?), and how she'd felt he himself was deeply prejudiced. I got the impression that he'd hurt her a lot, but she was over him.

The talk continued well past 4 am. At one point, your son came in and made us all a cup of tea, but didn't even want one himself. When Zoë realised that, she said something like, "See my problem! How am I ever going to find a man to match my own brother?"

She briefly talked about you. She worried that sometimes you got down and needed chivvying up. She'd asked you who you most wanted to impress that night of the book launch and you'd said, "Walter." She seemed to take delight in that

... She seemed happy that night, confident and knowing where she was going in life. She also seemed proud of her family and very much part of it. It would have been nice to have met her again and talked, the two of us, though I'm not sure what about. There was something very forceful about her, though in a purely good way and with something gentle beneath, like some wild cat shielding its kitten. I wish I had better words.

Her affaire with Jamie petered out. So did the idea of going to Australia to study Aikido.

July 28th It's weird how it seems to have ended with Jamie. He got Saki's complete works and I got 3 multiple orgasms.

I think about Francis quite a lot. I'm not over him yet. I'm also a bit attached to Jamie.

Feeling emotional plus petrified that Aikido plan turn out to be too soul-searching and I'll have to rethink.

I feel really sick about how I behaved at Gaia. I sucked up to Liz and Helen. At the end of the day I humiliated myself more than they did, but it's still hard to let go. Hopefully, I'm better qualified to spot wankers in future.

I don't think I'll have sex for a very long time. I know I hurt Francis, Jamie and others but it hurts me too and I'm getting sick of it.

Zoë's affaire with Francis restarted.

Met up with Francis. Fell in love with him. It felt like old times. We drove to Southampton. We stopped at Tescos at 2.30 a.m. The flat was lovely. Sex was o.k. Weak orgasm.

Sunday 2nd August

We started talking about whether we had sex with other people since we separated. I thought Francis lied to me and asked him to drive me back to London. During the drive I found out that he hadn't lied. He told me how self-centred I'd been and how much I hurt him. He asked me point blank how many people I'd slept with and I told him 6 - he freaked out. He had only tried to sleep with one person and hadn't been able to go through with it. I tried to explain to him not to be broken hearted because I didn't have the same attitude to sex as him. We went to Hampstead Heath. Francis was adorable and tried to keep his sense of humour. We went for a coffee and got some videos out.

Monday 3rd August

The atmosphere between Francis and I was awful. Driving back to Colchester, I realised what a complete bitch I've been. Dumping him brutally and then sticking the knife in by giving him mixed signals. I love him very much. His strength, his competence and his decency but I haven't enjoyed sex with him that much and I don't know if our lives could mix really. If he could enjoy my friends and family. Maybe Francis is the man for me. Maybe if I had given him more, sex would have been more enjoyable and he would have felt good around my friends and family.

Tuesday, 4th August

Woke up really pissed off to have crashed. Decided to stop smoking dope.

Came home and did some housework with Dad. Cleaned my car.

Francis phoned. He was really kind. He's taking up my offer to stay with me while I look after Nana. I told him how sorry I was for the way I treated him. I hope that over the next few evenings, Francis and I can be really honest with each other.

I've decided to stop sleeping around and leading men on. I want to stop being so self-centred and be more gentle and giving.

Whatever happens between Francis and me, he deserves me to be a really kind girl friend and a really kind friend.

Wednesday 5th August

Really hot weather. Pissed off to be at Nana's. Lazed about all day. Asked Nana to be more pleasant.

Francis and I rowed in the garden. We had a really long chat about what to do with our relationship. Dad came for dinner. He was unbelievably self-centred but I appreciated him coming. Francis and I finished our chat and we decided to give our relationship another go.

Friday 6th August

Met Mylène at work. Went into a state of shock at her new haircut. It looks really nice - it's just the change.

Friday 13th August ...

Drove to Oxford to see Sarah. Kon is coming and about as appetising as a boiled beetroot. God knows why Sarah can't stand on her own two feet without a man in tow. She made a nice curry and she was sweet. But a little strained 'cos obvious that I don't approve of her relationship with Kon.

Sarah still regrets that Zoë didn't live long enough to become friends with Kon. She is sure that they would have liked one another. On initial meetings, Zoë never found her girl friends' boyfriends good enough.

Her character contained many contradictions. She wanted to be 'at home' yet she resented living at Greenacres. Had she lived and managed to stabilise her mood swings, maybe she would have found the right person and made a home for herself and her family? It was her deepest desire. Meanwhile she lived in Nana's house and my mother's growing senile dementia affected Zoë badly...

Tuesday 17th August

Another lovely day at Greenacres. Drove to London to look after Nana. She's starting to change, which is really heart-warming. To understand that it's time to get her strength and dignity back. Dear God, help me to be patient.

Mylène came over and we had a lovely evening - we watched a video.

Tuesday 24th August

Handled Nana badly in the night.

Unnoticed by any of us, Zoë was suffering from mild swings of mania. It emerged many months later that she had hit Nana that night. At this stage Nana's dementia was in its early stages. She was immensely irritating, repeating herself and acting as if she did not recognise you. Zoë in her normal state could not possibly have hit her. Zoë was convinced that sympathy and prayer would enable Nana to accept her growing frailty. None of us recognised that Nana was becoming demented.

The diary then has a puzzling change of style. Zoë might have been on drugs. The text reads like a draft for a book or a sketch for a philosophy of life. A key sentence emerges: "Live your life as a celebration of it not an apology for it." The following was written in wild, swerving, almost undecipherable handwriting.

145

I take free will back it was a mistake. That's it - finally out in the open. And we would all end the pretence and the agony. We can all go back to the source. The reality. The ramblings of someone who thinks (may think wrongly ah, hah) that they are more intelligent/enlightened than they are always - oh dear, this is not going well. Rather embarrassing really - would-be artist. Or is it the art that is embarrassing? Oh dear - is it Chapter one!

Chapter II

You're not mad - you're boring and you worry about things that aren't worth worrying about on my plane. We're on different planes. And I don't know why your plane or is it my plane is boring to me.

> *Why are we bored? Or are we boring?*

> *Are you lovable really and I can't feel it? Or are you not lovable to me in the way that ants are not lovable to me in a lesser species kind of way. ....*

> *Is that why Kelly and I like David Attenborough? Footnote: D.A. is a mature man - does wacky documentaries on ants with the same conviction as he does on arctic bears, emperor penguins or tiger seals.*

> *...Why do we spend most of our energy convincing ourselves that different ways of thinking put people on different planes, which are mutually exclusive? Obviously they're different but maybe a more enlightened/intelligent person will see beyond the mutual exclusivity to the oneness of the universe. But first, Judaeo-Christians have to apologise without over-emphasising the <u>nonsense</u> around free will. Simply does not make sense that a genius/all-loving/all-wise God will not have come up with a better system.*

> *Innocents suffer - with the end result that some end up happy forever and others suffer forever.*

If God loves us all equally how can God bear a system where some people suffer for ever simply because he didn't equip them with a better system than having free will which can lead to some choosing lasting agony....

The fact that people suffer is not your fault: the fact that you suffer is your fault.

Do something about it and make as many people as possible happy because if you are happy you will have the energy and possibility to contribute to theirs and they will be as happy for you too. <u>Mutuality</u> not <u>mutual exclusivity!</u>

...Do we 'love' our kids because it is socially acceptable or is that we 'love' is a genetic urge to protect the carriers of our genes to take them to the future.

Celebration of life. Live your life as a celebration of it not an apology for it.

That's a fine aphorism - live your life as a celebration of it not an apology for it. It sums up her struggle. This bizarre, appealing, disconnected writing foreshadowed her manic outbursts in Essaouira the following year. After that interlude the diary goes back to August and resumes in normal handwriting.

Zoë now decided she needed a job to earn a lot of money. She applied to a city recruitment agency and once she'd decided on a course of action, if she was in a stable mood, she got what she wanted. Rusby's was a recruitment agency in the city which promised extremely high salaries once you had got the hang of it.

<u>*Friday 28th August.*</u>

Interview in the morning with Greg. Marc told me I had the job at 4.

Zoë decided to camp in Dave Bigsby's sitting room in Stepney. Dave was one of Zoë's many admirers. I'd never really forgiven him for having sex with her when she was suffering from her first episode of manic depression. He was fifteen years older and I thought he was taking

147

advantage. Maybe I was wrong. They maintained an uneven friendship, Dave always lusting after and admiring Zoë far more than she did him. We didn't like her staying in his flat because he was a heavy pot smoker and drinker. But Dave, as so many of her friends, mourned her deeply and came to Greenacres to join in the family mourning. With no beds free, he camped in the garden.

Tuesday 8th Sept.

Job is mad. Excruciatingly boring and feels silly. The people are really nice though. Over to Mylène's. We decided I should quit. It's frying my brains and my morals.

The Rusby job only lasted a few weeks in September. We never questioned these rapid job changes. But Zoë rapidly became bored. She wanted not only a high salary but also a job that benefited society. She was still in debt from her student loans. She decided to apply to the School of Social Entrepreneurs where Tanya had recently worked and also do some voluntary work for Friends of The Earth. Tanya who had had little time for her baby sister when they were children now helped Zoë with introductions and help in finding suitable jobs.

Thursday 17th September

Jamie a bit of a wanker.

Think about Francis a lot. He's still in me......

My faith in God is returning but the struggle is still painful.

I'm very very scared of winding up an old bag who talks about doing good and does bugger all beyond self-pity, fear and rage.

Feel like I could lose my mind if I'm not careful.

But also feel a lot of good stuff and getting stronger. Need to be peaceful and positive. All feels so melodramatic. Francis leaving the way he did has knocked my stuffing out. Having no home of my own and no job is making me feel more insecure than usual.

My fantasy is that all the people I love are in walking distance and we all have meaningful roles. And I'm too cross to accept the fact that some of the people I love are growing fast and moving especially Zac, and that it's time for me to grow up and find an occupation and create a lovely home to share with loved ones. But I want to be careful to be doing an occupation which is worthwhile for me and others........

I want to stop feeling sorry for myself and be positive. Very angry with Mum: my nanny in India, Zugi, Francis. Need to relate to Mum how she is not how I would like her to be.

Realised what an insecure prat I can be.

Drove to Colchester and found the meaning of my life in the sitting room and put him on my bed. [Her cat Tigger]

Exercise, yoga and fitness training were activities that Zoë picked up from me and kept up for herself almost to the end. Her diaries reiterate her wish to exercise, eat moderately, and stop smoking and drug taking. The healthy part of her mind struggled with the ill part and this expressed itself in physical exercises, learning karate and in the self-improvement lists.

<u>Saturday 19th September</u>

Callisthenics with Mum, Sheena and Trixie. Always so nice to see Sheena. Finished SSE application. Drove with Trixie to London. Nice chat.

Mylène, and I drove to Oxford. We had a really good giggle. Picked up Sarah, who was on fabulous serene form. ...

<u>Tuesday 22nd September ....</u>

I'm having panic attacks.

Zoë never mentioned these attacks to us or anyone else that I know of; I wish that she had; I wish I could have helped her through them.

Monday 28th September

*Drive to Colchester. Lovely evening with Mum and Dad.
Dad angry about the idea of me leaving FoE but Mum
supportive of book idea.*

It's so beautiful at Mum and Dad's. [And she repeats her
wish of some days earlier.] *My dream is that everyone I love
is in walking distance in a beautiful place.*

Zoë was the most persuasive person I've ever
known. As she said herself, she could have sold swimsuits
to Inuits. She persuaded me, although Wal was more
sceptical, that she could write a book about environmental
ideas for young people. On the strength of her needing time
to do research I lent her £2000. Hoodwinked? Yes, I
suppose so; she meant me to take her seriously.

Wednesday 30th September

*The work I'm doing at FoE is very, very boring.......... I get
down sometimes about not having a stable fulfilling
occupation and the state of the world. Though I'm far more
upset about my state.*

*I love seeing my friends. But I am very unsettled and
insecure.*

*I'm getting back in shape though which is good and being
creative about thinking about how I can do my bit.*

*I feel sorry for myself which is pathetic and makes me
afraid..*

Friday 2nd October .....

*Spent the day with Florence. We talked and prayed and she
was very supportive of my project and so loving ...*

Saturday 3rd October......

We met Sarah and Rachel in Birmingham to see Michael McAbe in Hamlet. Sarah was fabulous and Rachel very sweet. I didn't think much of the play but the others liked it. Drove to Oxford....

Sunday 4th October....

Kelly and I dropped Rachel off at the tube and had dinner with Mylène, Dad, Zac and Maria. Zac is starting at LCF tomorrow!

Zac started his degree in Fashion Promotion at The London College of Fashion. Zoë was tremendously proud of him.

I'm panicky about following my instincts instead of status quo.

I wrote to Francis that I had to <u>do</u> it more and worry about it less. Feels like a deep strengthening process.

Must use my car less<u>.</u>

Zoë at twenty-five had achieved her MSc from LSE, had had several short term jobs and one profound on/off love affair. We felt she was succeeding but she had no inner confidence and hid her insecurities from everyone.

Wednesday 2nd December

Procrastinated. Stop smoking Get up at 7am and exercise. Discipline. Faith............

I've been unhappy for a long time. The legacy from my Mum especially and my Dad and siblings. How do you detach from the legacy, recognise it and identify the areas in which it is affecting you. I have a huge emptiness inside me, which makes me insecure and frightened and weak.

Legacy:

Dad: Pushing / Brashness / Self-centredness / lecturing / Insensitivity /

Not getting on with office politics

Addictive

Willing to learn, dynamic

Good at solitude

Mum: low self-esteem, guilt machine, negativity, lack of grooming,

Procrastination, fussing, winging / Gutless, lost, moaning no job, dependent (bit of a joke)

Sense of humour, open,

Dishonest to self, inaccurate, inappropriate,

Selfish, self-centred, grasping, snobby, antagonistic, frenetic, sexist   Elitist

Habie: Exhausting, antagonistic, frenetic, jealous, envious, snobby, elitist,

Creative, quite perceptive, quite talented.

Ben: neurotic, depressed, boring, mean.

Quite good father, quite trustworthy

Tanya: emotionally dim, desperate, cold, insecure, dependable, civilised,

Quite secret.

Zac: self-absorbed, insecure, low self-confidence,

Lovely, sorted, sweet, kind, quite strong.

Zoë: self-absorbed, very insecure, low self-confidence, procrastinator,

Big, perceptive, intelligent, warm, bubbly, eager to please, clear mind,

Boring, beloved, quite strong, potential, fun, charismatic, quite sexy,

Pompous, quite down to earth, tiring.

This savage character assassination of her family members pinpoints our weak spots. Although I would love to bring up with her in heaven - if she and I ever meet there – that she's given herself considerably more plus points than anyone else.

Friday 4th Dec

Felt frantic.

Eurostar Mylène met me. We had a good giggle on the train to Compiegne. Amazing to see Henri [Mylène's dad] *again. Mylène and I talked about sex with him. Jean Guy told me about Descartes...*

Saturday 5th December

Lazed in be. Champagne lunch from Giselaine, Henri and Jean Guy, Mylène and Giselaine gave me lovely card and presents.

Giselaine talks about herself a lot.

Zoë had gone to France to spend her birthday with Mylène and her family. This was her 26th.

Sunday 6th December

Woke up blissed to be in Giramont.

Mylène. Jean Guy and I went for a long amazing walk up the Mont Galpin. We ate like horses when we got back..... The three of us giggled for hours.

Monday 7th December

Came home to a list of messages and mail which I always love. Drove to Colchester. Chatted with Mum and dad.

Wednesday 9th December

Row with Mum. Not nice time in town she got her stuff done but not mine. Took dogs for a walk.

Callanetics

153

Lovely evening with Michelle and Jide. Michelle is so warm and loving.

Finally sinking in that being unemployed not fully occupied is soul destroying. Specifically in a cold country there is not much incentive to get up. Because there is less going on everything gets out of proportion because it seems more significant than it really is. I am so looking forward to working full time in the New Year and always.

I need structure. I don't have enough discipline to do it myself in a cold country.

Movement diversity growth change

Legacy –must not throw out the baby with the bathwater fear → contentment

Inertia → growth

Monday 14TH December....

Feel quite settled re job and accommodation. Very bored and embarrassed with myself. Fed up being overweight and lazy. Fed up being weak and fearful.

Slender dynamic strong brave

Wednesday 16th December.

Spent the day getting room ready for Francis.....

From then until Christmas, Zoë and Francis were together. She picked him up from Heathrow on his return from work experience in Canada. He mentions this drive in his letter to us. They were happy together but the relationship had fractured again by the New Year.

Sunday 20th December

Francis fixed up Amanda's car.... We drove back to London. The weather has been nice. Cold but sunny. Chatted and did coke with Penny and Simon until 4. Francis and I made love.

She never told Wal or me that she taken cocaine. She knew that we were totally against hard drugs. After her death I brought the subject up with Zoë's cousin Jamey, Penny's brother. Jamey laughed and said that everyone in London took coke. Maybe they do - but I'm sure now that Zoë's final breakdown was precipitated by hard drugs.

In the photographs of this family Christmas at Greenacres, Zoë and Sarah look happy and relaxed. But the rapprochement with Francis did not last. This time he rejected her. I don't know whether he knew about Zoë taking cocaine; he was very anti-drug, even pot smoking. As the year ended Zoë tried to sum up and say what she wanted for her future. What she never admits was that her mood swings were making her life more and more impossible.

Sunday 27th December

Feeling wretched over Francis. Migraines. Badly cut up. Hurt and humiliated. That he was so casual on the phone after the intimate lovely week we have had. Maria, Sarah and Fredy say that he is just protecting himself. It is hard knowing that he is spending so much time with his ex and that it seems that he has slept with all the people in his flat which is hypocritical after going ballistic for me doing it when we were separated. Makes me very angry and lose respect for him. I don't think he loves me like I need/deserve whatever. And we seem locked in an incredible vicious circle.

... Feel rejected by Francis and not nurtured by family.

Focus on lovely friends and promising work. But I am not happy... I feel the need to create my self esteem, personal space and health.

I want to grow up and not have to write this kind of babble anymore.

Zoë finished the year with one of her many lists of what she was trying to achieve.

<u>*1999 will be My Year of growth and consolidation.*</u>

Grow: express anger in an adult manner and achieve personal space. Consolidate physical and mental health,

I'm really hurt by Francis.

Will NOT make a scene

Will ENJOY his company

Will NOT take the initiative

Will NOT expect anything from him will REMEMBER that he is young and he has been very badly hurt by me and is afraid.

I think that I am very fond of Francis because he is good in bed and sweet. But he doesn't empower me to grow and I don't seem to be helpful to him either. As Sarah says, we don't seem to bring out the best in each other. I guess that I should just try to accept that and enjoy his company without trying to make more out of the situation than what it actually is.

<u>*1998*</u> *The year I discovered my needs*

<u>*1998*</u> *Low points*

Mum's behaviour

Unpleasant sexual relationships

Inactivity, lack of self-esteem, immaturity

Florence's dogma

Nana's bitchiness and crudity.

<u>High points</u>

Meeting Charlotte. Oral sex in a thunderstorm. one/two weeks drug binge affair

Getting to grips with Callanetics

Nice rooms in Golders Green/Colchester.

Tigger

Times with Mylène, Sarah and Kelly

Time with Tolis, Eleni....

Getting through to Antoine, Dad.

The diary ended with:

<u>1999</u> *The year in which I feel ready to grow and become grown up.*

CHAPTER SIX

"The only thing to fear is fear itself."

After her death, we found her laptop, most of its folders
were work-related, some diary entries and some folders
contained the emails she and Francis sent one another, the
silly loving emails of a couple in love. The rest of the
entries from December '97 to March '98 were sombre. Zoë
was living a double life, appearing happy and carefree and
writing pages to herself full of anger, fear and confusion.
Reading them after her death opens up one of the dreadful
if-onlys that every suicide survivor knows about. If only she
had expressed some of this anguish to those who loved her,
could we have heard or helped?

She came to Greenacres for Christmas, apparently
happy, carefree and loving. I only learned from the
computer diary that she had felt rejected by Francis and
neglected by her family:

*They've spent three days discussing Josh and Tanya and
no-one has noticed that I have migraine because I'm so
unhappy about Francis. I guess it's less glamorous because
Francis is 'boring' and not a multi-millionaire and I'm in
pain. I do not have nurturing parents. Of my four siblings
only one cares - at least about my career - Tanya.*

We were not overly sympathetic to Zo, since we
thought that she created problems with Francis by being
promiscuous. Yet her criticism was not unjust; the idea of a
multi-millionaire in the family WAS enticing – even if Josh
himself wasn't.

Zoë battled with her demons, trying to solve
problems with lists, more lists, and then rejecting her own
advice for silly promiscuity fuelled by drugs.

January 4th

Spliff and Charlie with Simon.

Wednesday 6th January

Mum and Dad doing me head in. Still feeling kacky over Francis: Feel really fat and bumpy and loud and horrible. Feeling so kacky over fucking Francis, I am easily irritated. I still 'love' him. But now it's great. I can stop all the faking and really be me, on my terms. I want to make myself really happy. Fall in love with myself. I basically want to be more like Kelly. I want to get to the point where I don't need to write silly diaries like this anymore. Must remember to enjoy getting there and all that stuff. God, I'm sick of being stupid and doing stupid stuff with stupid people. Really should be more tolerant. Guess that's why Kelly's tolerant because she's so much more intelligent. Like you'd be tolerant of sheep bleating or something.

Really, really insecure about the SSE on some levels. I wish Tanya was still there to have her perspective. I miss her. Tomorrow, I want to put Francis in his box and not let my emotional life overspill. It's hurt pride and mismanagement not true love, so there's no point getting wound up.

...I want my own space.

That's what she wrote in January 1999, the year she hoped to make her own with plans and lists so reasonable.

- *I'll have dinner with Mum and Dad once a month. Be sympathetic to them and enjoy Tigger.*

- *Then spend a day or two with friends in Colchester.*

- *The rest of the time, I'll be in London, with the odd week-end in Liverpool and the odd evening in Oxford.*

- *Holiday time: three extended week-ends, one week with Flo's [Florence Leader's] family in south of France and a one week treat somewhere.*

159

- *Healthy eating and Callenetics and fly machine on Saturdays and Sundays*

- *Try to quit smoking fags or at least smoke much less.*

Ironically, she finally succeeded in giving up smoking in the last summer of her life. I thought she'd overcome her nicotine addiction; I think now she was simply too depressed to smoke.

In this New Year, Zoë fantasised her ideal husband. [A year later she believed she had found him in Morocco.]

Sunday 10th January.

Happy but empty. I need to get fit for my husband as fast as possible. Will make that my priority because I am getting impatient.

I am still hurting over Francis. And I feel polluted by drugs. Invaded by certain family pressures from mum and dad not being honest, anxious about Duncan – don't want to sleep with and scared I will for a cheap thrill. Don't want to lead him on. I like him as a friend. Maybe I should flirt with him less. Stop smoking dope and doing Charlie. Spend more time alone by getting a studio flat in Fulham. Must phone student loan company.

Give away all unnecessary possessions. Put all precious stuff from loft at Greenacres in two or three boxes. Want to end up with minimum of clothes, and my photo album, lap top and phone and exercise machine. It will be a wonderful feeling. Essentials only. I am making space for my husband to be ready to welcome him into my life because there will be enough room for him in my heart, soul, mind and body.

Zoë repacked her stuff for OXFAM, giving away most of her books, and souvenirs, the bits and pieces collected from a middle class childhood. After her death few possessions were found in her room apart from clothes

160

and the cardboard boxes. It was not the first time she had done this. Once in her late teens, she had given all her possessions away. I understand her wish not to let our possessions choke us. None of her siblings ever felt this urge to strip away belongings which I believe belongs with the desire for a sort of spiritual purity. Years after they have left Greenacres, our loft bulges with an exuberance of bin liners and cartons labelled with their names.

We knew nothing about the terrible migraines over Francis. She admonishes herself constantly to stop drugs, stop cocaine and learn to be on her own. The lists contain many repetitions. I've left them in this chapter because they show Zo's lonely struggle to match reality with her expectations.

Do spend time alone with self

Do eat moderately

Do be serene

Do be chilled

Do spend time on body maintenance

Do save up money from smoking - save 100 pounds a month

Wait and see what happens with accommodation. Let it sort itself out.

Send letter to bank re overdraft tomorrow without fail.

Do see mum and dad a couple of times a month

Do respond to outstanding invitations – catch up with those

Don't generate too much socialising – Respond to the essential stuff warmly, but remember to keep personal free time to be alone

Do maintain scrupulous cleanliness

Do constant maintenance. Priority

Do learn always. Be humble and receptive and generous

Don't be loud. Be a soothing and inspiring influence with smooth energy. Be ultra feminine. Not demure. That's mildly entertaining. Physically attractive and in great shape. Wholesome, fun to be around and sophisticated. That's what is aimed for! Three out of five ain't bad!! Priority therefore to get fit and healthy.

It was about this time that Zoë and I argued often about her smoking so much pot. A sixties relic myself I had no objection to a joint as the end of a day to relax. But Zoë was smoking joints all day long. I couldn't stop her and I couldn't stop her being angry with my interference. She sought transcendence, to rise to a loftier plane, to leave her *self* behind.

I am desperate to feel a genuine buzz. A natural high. I want to be lifted up. I believe that I have experienced it before. I want to live with that feeling more. I want to fulfil my need to be fit and healthy. I want to enjoy the process as well without fretting. I want to stop using my sex appeal as a weapon and relax knowing that it is to be preserved for my husband. To be used only with him.

You're not going to have sex before the spring at least. You're going to discuss need for sexual partner to be tested before anything happens and to use condoms too. Going to discuss that this is sexual friendship / open relationship whatever. Not commitment or monogamy. That is for husband only. Indeed may end up not having sex until meet husband because of wanting that more than anything else and not wanting any clutter. Life can be simple.

Must not be afraid. A great deal of life is pain. It is only damaging when there is fear. Fear makes the pain destructive instead of constructive.

THE ONLY THING TO FEAR IS FEAR ITSELF

She repeats this insight several times in her diaries. A clue perhaps? Along with her wish to be a success in worldly terms, Zoë felt fear that she was too proud to show.

Must have a ciggie and get some sleep. Must get some sleep and start to work out another possibility for stopping smoking. Seek advice. So many wonderful things to gain. Health, fitness, vitality, confidence, comfort, respect and strength.

You are loved and cared for. Don't take that for granted.

Mother figures: Florence, Giselaine, Kelly

Father figures: Grandma Lilly, Dad, Henri

Sister figures: Habie, Tanya, Antoine, Mylène, Sarah

Brother figure: Zac

Uncle: Mickey

Aunt: Sarojini

Cousins: Simon

Friends: Fifty solid broad friendships

Higher than average: Education, Socio-economic background, and Strength

Exceptional: IQ, Sophistication, Looks, Compassion, Popularity

Weaknesses: unresolved issues of abuse, control and power, lack of faith and confidence

I want to dare to feel more real. I want to dare to meet myself at sunrise. I want to dare to shower myself with compassion, understanding and patience. I want to dare to expect discipline, faith and patience from myself in my behaviour. I want to dare to detach myself from my neediness of family and friends to have emotional space and physical time for my husband whom I long for. I am waiting. I know that he is getting nearer. He will not rush his arrival. Nor will he dawdle. He himself is also growing

163

and fine-tuning. For example, learning how to speak French, or ride effortlessly again. He is already fully-grown. He is just fine-tuning.

I have to achieve the fundamental goal of health and fitness.

My husband, for example, is already fit, healthy and independent. He, for example, is learning French. We're at different stages, but we're going to arrive at our meeting ground or place together.

I believe in love at first sight. I believe in certitude. I believe in change. I believe in growth and movement as the meaning of life. Growth should be considered and movement should be peaceful. I am so fucking stoned. I am happy and empty at the same time. I am stressed, under pressure, fearful, insecure, bored, lonesome, and self-ashamed-destructive. I am ashamed because of my own terror: Attempted suicide and abortion. I am ashamed because I am ashamed of my weakness.

"I am ashamed because I am ashamed of my weakness." After Zoë's 'successful' suicide, Mylène, Sarah and Kelly spent a week at Greenacres and one of Mylène's remarks resonated both then and later, "Her pride killed her." Zoë's terrible pride that would not allow her to ask for help.

At this stage of her life, she hoped that faith would slay the demons for her:

If you have faith, you are serene, which means you are dynamic which means you have confidence, which means you have compassion, which means you have forgiveness, which means you have humility. Faith is the first step to humility. The order then is to experience serenity followed by dynamism, confidence, compassion and forgiveness.

That is the path to joy and courage. Love is joyful and courageous. By being faithful, serene, dynamic, confident, compassion, forgiving and humble to or in the presence of others, one is able to love oneself and be at peace with the world. Faith is the hardest step because one has to choose to have faith before having experienced humility, which is the tangible expression of faith. That is why faith is a choice. Why it can also appear to be bollocks. The starting point is nonsensical. So is the time before the big bang. That does not mean that the sequence of events that we believe to have occurred and to be real after the big bang are bollocks. Zoë, you are stoned and fretting, go to sleep. Bad things will not happen while you sleep. If bad things did happen when you slept, it was a long time ago and it was not your fault.

"If bad things did happen when you slept." It is painful to read those words. Zoë had incorporated another person's bad experience into her own mind. In Essaouira, the following year, she would accuse her father of sexual abuse and accuse her mother of conniving and condoning. False memories from her but nonetheless wounding, both to Zoë and to her parents. Margie's memories not her own - traumatised her.

Must face these issues. But not try to solve them in a black and white swipe. Must take my time. One step at a time. The steps can be strategic, but nevertheless must be taken with thought for all the others involved. Proceed with courage and caution.

...Long term is part of consciousness. But feeling experience must be focused in the present. Otherwise life becomes a projection, which is imagined rather than an experienced reality. I want to be there during my lifetime. Think of now. The computer. The room. The thoughts you are writing.

Had Zoë lived, she might have written excellent self help and how to books. She achieved excellent results in helping her friends. If only she could have helped herself!

Think of today. Restful sleep. Time in the morning to rise and stretch.

Hear interesting talks. Enjoy classmates company. Enjoy either flirting and playing pool with classmates or renting a fun video. Time to unwind and reflect and rest alone.

Can always be resting by blocking the clutter. At first will be a conscious activity until it becomes second nature and unconscious automatically blocks clutter. Discipline is my priority. Be firm with yourself. When you feel the teensiest piece of fear, tell it to piss off. You are tired of getting trapped by fear. You have sussed its clever little trick. 26 is not old. Nor are you a spring chicken. So you're getting bored with fear and are about to grow out of my fear. You are extreme. You must fulfil the stages of your nature. Your stages are:

Popularity, sexuality, intelligence, love

You were first popular, then sexy, then bright. When you allow love, you will be whole. And as a whole person, you will experience humility as second nature rather than just as privileged moments.

I'm trying to formulate my future instead of experiencing my life.

PEACE PREDECESSES TRUE UNDERSTANDING

The Dalai Lama would get away with that. I need to be more like Kelly and more subtle. Or at least, when I'm not being subtle be aware of it, and know why I'm using a particular pitch or communication.

What had always impressed Zoë about Kelly was that Kelly, coming from a far less 'privileged' background, always managed to keep grounded. Kelly never had patience for what our family calls New Age eco la-la.

Kelly's personality is a powerful guide, because my husband will have a similar outlook as Kelly. If I am in harmony with her, I will be in harmony with my husband. Kelly is a key. Damian is a key. My work is a key. My health and fitness goal is a key. Reading good books is a key. Taking my time and enjoying my space is a key.

> *Action is a key. I am in the vicious circle of not daring to take the plunge because I am not at peace with the past. I feel that I have suffered too much. And that there is no point launching oneself into happiness when it is short lived. The attitude makes no sense but appears deep-rooted. It is not logical, but maybe quite common. I am very angry at my parents, Habie and Ben and any notion of God. It all seems like abusing positions of power and influence. I am so angry I came dangerously close to killing myself once. I am going to have to express that anger. I am going to have to face these issues with Tanya and Hab at least. I am going to have to get fit and healthy and take up a martial art in a very determined manner. I have to acquire a motivated training partner. That has to become a part of my life. I am angry, angry, angry, angry, betrayed, scared, angry, angry, angry, angry. Fucking pricks. Most men should be castrated and most mothers drowned at birth. Zoë's solution for population control. Ashamed to be human. Just hope that enough humans are capable of saving the Earth and all life sustained on Earth.*

Her violence is terrifying to read about now. I understand her meaning in spite of her twisted logic. Swept away by ideas, she longs for love, unable to find it. Fear drives her into the silly pointless relationships with so many guys who often treat her badly.

I am so fucking stoned. I am going to unclutter every pore in my body. My husband will walk into a gleaming dazzling shrine. Purification has become my raison d'être. I will receive my husband into my temple. Why only one person? Because the exchange is rooted in sex and it is more potent when concentrated between just two people and not dissipated among many. Some energy can be shared. For example entertaining together, being in public places but not the energy source, which is sex and sensual intimacy. That is the energy source. I have to be ready to receive that. I am going to make room. Once received, that energy reproduces itself: Procreation. That is how we achieve immortality. Sharing with the right man is heaven. I believe in my heaven. Actually, we are already immortal. Procreation is growth. Since the big bang we have been 'growing'. Maybe it will shrink at some stages. The processes appear to be immortal. Energy, spirit, matter, growth, decay, regeneration, birth, death, rebirth, reincarnation, pain, love, light, earth, moon, sun, stars, planers, galaxies, universe.

Puzzle. Need to rest. Need to simplify. Need to unclutter. Unclutter. 1999: Clean by the spring of 1999. ...

Being willing to die makes life safe.

Being willing to repent the deepest horrors is to gain the greatest honour.

Rest now, Zoë.

Yield Zoë. Yield to the secrets of the universe. Yield to your spirit communication. Yield to your memory. Yield to your knowledge and belief. Yield to the power of love. Yield to the truth of faith. Yield, Zoë. Recognise the signs and symbols. Be receptive. Be protective. Be strong. Be compassionate. Be intelligent. Be dignified. Be dignified. Be unpretentious. Be unpretentious. Be humble. Be humble. Be forgiving. Repent yourself, to the Spirit and to yourself. Forgive others. Enjoy your rest now. Sleep peacefully. All is well. It is safe for me to change and grow. Always scared of growing. Bad things happen when you are big. Bad things happen to big people, and bad people do bad things. Bad things happen to strong, responsible people. Do not want to be independent or responsible.

And this thought harks back to her remarking at fifteen, "I don't want to grow up." Did she have presentiments of the horrors that would descend upon her at twenty-five?

Zoë both loved and hated living in Nana's house with its shifting population of grandchildren and the eccentricities of Maria the Portuguese housekeeper. The tone of her diary entries grows frantic with its desire for calm:

Feel much stronger and happier about sex and work. Last night, I really wound myself up. I want to empty myself of clutter. I'm stoned and high again so I better stop writing now. Need more sleep than I've been getting.

And then she lists again her priorities to stop drugs and smoking. *I love myself. I am learning about Zoë. And I like her very much.*

Stopping the smoking trap is a fundamentally right decision and is non-negotiable.

A few things are not negotiable. This is one of them.

LEARNING, GROWING/CHANGING. NEW PHASE:

And then Zoë had to start her placement at United Response. She had had a week's briefing at SSE and had enjoyed being a star in the seminars and flirting.

Monday 18th January

Really nervous about starting at United Response. Su [Su Sayer, one of the directors] *told me that I had to get wearing suits. Everyone was really nice to me. Dad and I went to a nice concert – Berlin Quartet adorable. We had a lovely dinner and atmosphere at Sitar restaurant.*

Tuesday 19th January

Another nice day at UR. Nice flirty, productive meeting and then drink with Tony Deeds. I like the attention from Tony, but I'm really fancying Duncan. I want to sleep with them both and I intend to. But I want to be honest with myself and not on an ego trip. This is sex, not true love-making and connection with my soul mate.

I feel really sad because I'm so impatient and insecure.

I don't like Su or Tania Michell. Is there a connection? I've never had a problem being liked. I've got heaps of friends. So why do I take such violent, insecure dislikes to people I work with, who – the three of them – have in common: female, authority over me (two of them), very attractive, anxious, insecure.

> *I could be describing my mother. Maybe that is the link. Women, who remind me of my mother, remind me of how much I dislike her, because like my mother they make me feel insecure and impatient most of the time I'm under their influence.*

Harsh to read such comments about yourself. Zoë was not 'wrong'. Wal and I often made her feel insecure. I kept nagging that she was using men and dope "instead of" living her life rather than "as well as". We represented a certain way of behaviour. We represented living in society. That was why Wal believed her manic behaviour grew so much worse when we met in Morocco, the following year.

So: the challenge is, to not relate to Su and Tania like I did to Liz. Which involves:

-Keeping a healthy distance

-Not trying to impress them

-Not flatter them

-Be sensitive to their insecurity (i.e. do not make them feel like they are not being taken into account or are having their role usurped.... Su wants to feel like she is boss, which is in many ways she is. So show her some respect.

-How can I be nice? i.e. how can I think that my mother does not like me?

Actually, it's not mum, it's Tanya. But now that Tanya likes me better, I need not have the same problem with Su as I had with Liz. Also Su is not in my face. If she gets in my face, I have Helen, James, Duncan, Linda, Tony and possibly even Bob to get her out of my face.

To us at Greenacres, Zoë seemed volatile in her moods. Reading the diaries is like watching a swing go up and down. On the upswing the thoughts grow angrier and wilder on the downswing they become more settled and sensible.

The fact is that nobody is hurting me or cramping me. The fact is that I am free, and I am so not used to it, that I can't see the wood for the trees. Well, it feels like I've finally let go of my fear and become my own grown up. Welcome to the rest of your life, Zo.

The problems with female bosses (or anyone in authority over her) that had so bedevilled Zoë's earlier work experiences were to surface even more violently in regard to her female bosses at United Response. And Zoë herself has flashes of insight into why she found these relationships so difficult.

Identify links and distractions. E.g. link, authority, women and mum. See Su for what she is, not as symbol of your mum. Treat like an individual, not a member of some ghastly sect. Accept her as she is. You don't have to shrink yourself for her.

DON'T BE WORRIED ABOUT REJECTION FROM MOTHER FIGURES. YOU ARE IN THE DRIVING SEAT NOW, BECAUSE YOU ARE GROWN UP. YOU ARE YOUR OWN MOTHER. YOU CAN ONLY BE HURT IF YOU DON'T NURTURE AND PROTECT YOURSELF. IT'S MY CHOICE. IN THAT SENSE, WE ARE THE DIRECTORS OF OUR OWN LIVES / PLAYS. IN THAT SENSE, WE WRITE THE SCRIPT AND DIRECT OUR ACTORS.

It's ok to me. What happens to me is ok. What I do is ok

She was unable to sustain those insights and embarked on several love affaires at the same time that left her confused and unhappy.

After a particularly difficult affaire she had with a colleague, on whom she rather forced her attentions, she writes:

I want to prove my spirituality to myself. My husband will value that above everything.

Actually, I think that Kelly and I are spiritual. The word's got dead naff vibes, but I know what I mean. Kelly doesn't spout on about it, like Florence and I do. I think maybe it's time for action. Maybe that's why Florence can be irritating to people. Spouting instead of doing.

Less spouting. More Action.

My excellent communicating ability is picking up on the need to lead others to spirituality without spouting. The answer is to lead by example. The further answer is to forget about leadership. Be the master of your own bloody life.

Otherwise, it's dead pompous. I don't want to be pompous. Do I want to be a mother? Accepted? Is that why people have kids? So that they can feel grown up.

I won't have a kid until I'm not pompous.

And then the swing rises so high that Zoë loses her ability to think straight and she blames those she loves.

Time is weird. Always changing, and reacting. Nothing really is. Nano-seconds. Infinities of nano-seconds. I feel like I'm losing my mind. I am ashamed. I hate myself because I'm afraid that Kelly thinks I'm a twit. Part of me thinks that maybe I can keep it a secret from her. Part of me thinks that she doesn't, and another that she does but she doesn't mind. Yeah, I like that. Kelly thinks that among other things, I am a twit but she doesn't mind. I guess that freaks me out because my mum is among other things a twit. Bingo. I related to Kelly relating to me how I relate to my

172

*mum. Inverse mothering. Kelly does not see me, as I see my
mum. Thank God for that.*

And then Zoë becomes full of fear and turns the fear to
anger.

*I'm scared to be happy because I've been unhappy. Don't
know if I believe in happiness. Fuck God. Fuck Florence.
Fuck it all. Because innocents suffer and it's just pain, pain,
pain. I'm sick to death of these roller coaster emotions. It's
all so amazing and such a crap design in some ways. Fuck
it. Sometimes, I wish I'd never been born. I am so angry. I
hate myself because I profoundly loathe my parents. OR at
least I profoundly loathe the parts of them that I fear are
evil. I hate all of us for being so perverted by mum and
dad's sexuality that there were times when I thought it was
'normal' to be a prostitute, when Habie thinks it was
normal to sleep with men who used her and when Tanya is
even considering trying to fall in love with a fat sweaty
boring man. It makes me sick to the pit of my stomach. We
have been robbed and nobody is doing anything about it. I
want compensation. And I will never get it because of the
need to protect Zac and the risk of us just getting more hurt
by bringing this stuff up with mum and Dad and fucking
Ben. I HATE BEN I HATE HIM I HATE HIM AND I HATE
HIS WIFE I HATE BOTH OF THEM I hate so much I
could die. I am completely poisoned and I continue to
poison myself with drugs. I hate dad mum Ben and Habie
and Fredy so profoundly for the pain they have inflicted on
me. And I hate or am afraid of anyone who reminds me of
them or of how they make me feel.*

*I am beginning to understand links of emotional
behaviour and why I relate to some people the way I do. It
explains a lot about why we like and don't like people. I
guess we like people who remind of us those we like and
things we like and dislike, etc.*

I could explode.

*...Why shouldn't I have to prove myself? I guess
I'm scared of growing up because mum has rammed down*

*our throats all our lives that she sees herself as a failure.
That's why we can't stand it when she moans. Stupid
fucking bitch.*

*Self-importance is a lack of self worth. When you
have to puff yourself up. Mum has horrible parts, which are
self-important. That is weakness. Which is not the same as
fragility. Like a leaf which is beautiful. There are parts of
mum that are horrible and detestable. And there are parts
of mum – or even of a monster – which are lovely. There are
parts of me, which are detestable. And parts of me which
are lovely. I am in a position of privilege and self-
awareness to make the detestable parts of me lovely. I must
stop being influenced by mum. Mum is not me. Mum has
free will. I have free will. And I want to change and grow
up. I am safe. I can't be hurt if I don't allow it. I can
condition my mind. I am still young enough. And I believe
that I have enough self-awareness, experience and support
to grow into a beautiful person.*

How much of this rage was due to the family she
grew up in; the inevitable mistakes parents make; how
much due to faulty chemical firing messages in her brain
that shook her out of reasoned behaviour? I wish that she
could have used her brilliance to see how fragmented her
thinking was. I wish that she could have asked for help. She
used sex as a tool to clear her mind of demons. She wanted
to be promiscuous and celibate both at once.

She wrote later that month.

*I wonder if I'll get girly and play hard to get. ... Or
maybe it's not that cool. Because Mitch who is totally cool
about fucking doesn't turn me on as much as them. I really
fancy Kev Moore. Actually I would like to sleep with him the
most. But it's risky because he's Fulham plus he's married.
Maybe if I was super discreet. In any case, unless we took a
day off work, it would probably be logistically impossible.
He's got a lovely way of carrying himself and he's really
down to earth. Plus I was very happy hanging out with him
even without smoking.*

174

I've just finished having sex with Mitch and it was the best so far.

Zoë brought Mitch to Greenacres a couple of times. He seemed a pleasant, ambitious young Nigerian businessman sharing none of Zoë's real interests. And so the usual bickering occurred with Wal and I saying "Mitch isn't right for you, darling." And she accused us of racism.

But I know that I wouldn't stay interested with Mitch for too long. I'm really looking forward to meeting the man who can make me feel like that long-term. Plus I get fed up of worrying about pregnancy and other stuff. We used condoms but not after he came. Stupid.

Zoë now had a pregnancy scare that we were never told of at the time.

She continued with this phase of promiscuity never seeming to see how it didn't fit with her ideals of 'dazzling purity.'

Sex with Mitch once or twice a week. Sex with Kevin Moore. Sex with Tony Deeds. Yum. With Tony at his place and stay overnight. With Kev in his car. With Duncan? With Giuseppe in Ibiza on the third night. Must stay four nights. With Duncan, I'm not sure if I'm going off him or just haven't really got a chance. Do you know when you are bullshitting yourself? Definitely sex with Duncan. But I like him a lot, so not till the spring. Not sure when or how. Let it go for now. It's not the right time, as he keeps saying. There's other stuff to do in the meantime. Duncan could well be one of my last before my husband. Must be celibate for over a year before my husband. Could be with my husband for 15 years before kids. Be about 42. Twins.

I want to live secure and have fun. Be happy, Zoë.

I was distinctly under whelmed by her stated intention to have an affaire with Damien, whom she described as a handsome and charming Jamaican musician. The downside was that he was without a job, married and a heroin addict. She got on terribly well with his sister.

175

Yet Zoë was trying so hard to clear her mind, not admitting to herself or anyone else that her mind was shaking, that the violence of her feelings appalled her.

Wednesday 27th January

Life is fab, friends and family as ever are well, flat is fab work and training and now these glam lovers...

Right now, if I could choose one of the four to sleep with, it would be Giuseppe, Duncan, Francis and Mitch in that order. I'm really looking forward to Giuseppe's body.

REALITY check: I've been lax in terms of safety. Must not only use condoms, but also get the guy to withdraw before he comes in case the condom breaks. Also HIV test in May just to be completely sure.

Friday 1st February

So turned on by Duncan, I jumped around so much last night; I twisted my ankle carrying Mick down the stairs.

Came home and chilled out by myself, thinking about Duncan. I am learning patience.

And humility.

I want to ask Helen Cope about my career strategy on Thursday. And continue trying to give up drugs and undertaking exercise regularly....

Want to sort out a few things for moving into the flat next week.

Next weekend can pick up what I need from home.

I'm crazy about Duncan. He fills me up....

God I hope I get my period next week. And I pray to be really safe.

Sometimes little remarks creep in and I sense the Zoë I used to know, lucid and gentle.

Saturday 2nd February

I am very nervous about what I will be up to next year and about kids. I'm really hoping that I get a period soon. Once I know what sort of employment I will be doing next year and once I know that I am not pregnant, I will be more relaxed. ..

Tomorrow will make a stew; buy fruit and veg, bread, rice pudding, salad stuff, and food for the office: bread, bananas, ready made salad dressing, salad, tomatoes, cheddar and feta, cereal, powdered milk.

Actually, I do want to be in a relationship and living with someone I envisage being close to forever. Therefore, having admitted that, I'm going to do what it takes to be ready for that. So it's back to patience, timing and humility. And of course, job security and fitness.

For the first time, my state appears to be more up to me than outside circumstances. It feels like I have more of a choice.

But she was wrong; she did not have the power to choose.

* Some names are changed

CHAPTER SEVEN

"I need a bigger challenge."

Zoë's emotions continued to seesaw between exhilaration and fear. Exhilaration we saw; fear she hid, until we found it in the cardboard boxes and in the computer files.

Wednesday 3rd February

Good meetings at work. Made progress with the procedures manual.

Nice drink after work. Nice chat with Tanya.

Mum and Dad came over. Mum said she had a present for me. I was very surprised because I didn't know for what occasion. She handed me the keys to my flat!

Wal and I used my Dad's legacy and our savings to buy a basement flat in West Hampstead. It was too good an opportunity to pass over, to provide a home at a reduced rent for Zo and somewhere that her brother Zac could eventually share.

Turns out that Mum's been very organised about the flat, and she's going to sort the garden out at the weekend.

I'm very happy. Also Tanya reckons I'm not pregnant. Will have to wait up the ten days to be sure though....

I'm going to be amused by the bonkerness of society, and be very disciplined and focused with myself. Will not sleep with Mitch because I don't fancy him. Will not sleep with Winston because his track record is poor. Will not even consider sleeping with X [a work colleague] *because he's caused me considerable distress. Will consider sleeping with Tony in time because I've enjoyed his company and I can test out my new girliness with him and he seems to enjoy it.*

I feel as if I've just done fat Charlie lines.

I miss canine Charlie [her Cousin Simon's collie] *big time. I'm looking forward to seeing ma Tigger this weekend.*

I feel all grown up.

This girlie shit is cool. I'm quite interested in Tony now.

<u>*Thursday 4th February*</u>

I'm off to bed. Looking forward to spending time with Helen. [Helen Cope was Zoë's mentor from SSE] *And bracing myself for presentation to Su. I don't want to be crawly like Mum with people in authority. Just polite and natural. ...*

With Helen Cope, as with so many others in UR, Zoë hid her inner anguish and charmed and delighted them. Helen told me how beautifully Zoë played the piano when Zo came for tea. But Zoë had stopped playing five years before and only knew the one piece.

Very nice meeting with Helen Cope in her sweet house. Learned not to babble in response to a question, but to answer briefly and await or pose the next question.

Presentation to Su and Bob. Must keep the fact that Su gets on my wick in some ways in proportion. Much prefer Bob.

Su is like a high powered Liz Hosken *in some ways.*

Did a pregnancy test. Negative. But will have to wait a couple of weeks to be 100%

Feeling desperate about relationships and work.

Relationships: I've cheapened myself with casual sex recently and I still have strong feelings of loss towards Francis and rage for the fact that he's torn me apart emotionally while parading as the victim. Like Mum. Yes Freud.

179

*Work: Really like all the staff at UR, apart from Su. I felt
really undermined by the way she managed me today. It was
a one-way street. Her preferences were non-negotiable.*

*Just unburdened myself to Tanya, which was a big mistake,
as she doesn't have the scope to deal with it.*

*Maybe it is good to learn with someone you don't respect
having power over you. Maybe Su doesn't have power over
me actually. I learned from my conversation with Francis
just now, that you can 'reclaim' you rights as it were.*

*Unlike the trap with Liz , to deal with Su, there is a
network of support. Mentor, SSE, ALS.*

*I should try and be calm, and if the situation with Su
becomes untenable, call an emergency meeting with
someone in authority who can help. Like Gerard or Helen.*

*Actually, talking to Tanya was good, because she didn't
give in to me.*

*Negatives can be turned into positives, as long as one as not
crossed irreversible boundaries like bitching, or cruelty,
etc.*

Feel much better.

Tanya disapproved of Zoë's promiscuity and
punctured her wild ideas about her boss at UR, but like us,
did not see Zoë as being unwell, simply exaggerated in her
responses. Zoë could always convince me that what she
was doing was acceptable; Tanya was harder to fool.

Could Zoë ever have accepted that her reactions to
a female boss like Su Sawyer were inappropriate? Fit that
question in with so many if-onlys and what-ifs! If Zoë had
ever been able to accept her illness, would she over time
accepted how unjust she could be to women like Su Sawyer
or Liz Hosken or even me? She used her intelligence to
bamboozle herself as well as others.

I should have asked Su why she asked me to do a presentation for Richard W. And then after I had put considerable work into it, told me not to. Is it because she thought it wasn't good enough? All this it well and good, but at a deeper level, I feel that I am actually learning to make myself smaller, to play the demeaning games. What I mean is that actually, left to my own devices, my style would be very different but as valid as and probably far more powerful than Su's. It's like being put into a smaller mould. How can I escape, and really fly with my limitations and brilliance?

Maybe one does have to prove that one can make oneself small before one gets a break to be truly big. Shit, I don't know. I just know that I am deeply unhappy and desperate....

Some powerful stuff is going on.

... I should be compassionate and strong in myself. Not demean myself. Mandela had to prove that he could put up with crap before flying for decades.

I guess that a year isn't so bad.

I just wish that I could get to use my brain.

I am going to treat this as an apprenticeship.

Now, I am 26 in London with great friends, a lovely flat, a good family, and opportunity to learn heaps at work and at the school. I should be truly grateful for that.

Fear is debilitating. The fear of loss.

The only thing to fear is fear itself. Have no fear.

Tune into positivity. Non-verbal communication is the most powerful tool.

Zoë could realize these insights but she could not sustain her awareness. She wrote herself a short memo:

Be positive about Su. She was right today. I rely on charisma and looks to get what I want. That is not right. It is not duplicable by someone with less charisma and looks.

Wrote Francis a long letter which when I read on the tube was very helpful.

I found this letter, drafted in February, in one of the boxes. I don't know whether it was an original or a copy. [Francis never told us after Zoë died, whether he received it.] That letter hints of suicide; one of the rare occasions Zoë

Zoë aged 27 at her Dad's 70th birthday party

ever mentions it or refers to her earlier episode. And also one of even rarer occasions when Zoë hints that she needs help.

Francis,

I am trying to keep a handle on things. I showed up at work today. Thanks for encouraging that and had a very good day. I'm keeping it together with family and friends …

But there is a part of me that is in acute pain. The migraines have stopped but there are now other symptoms and my behaviour has been dangerous and erratic at times - some of it you wouldn't believe unless I told you face to face. I am so glad to have been able to share this with you. It's nice to be able to be honest and you were the only person I could talk to about this. The fact is, though, that I am in a very fragile state and do not want to take any risks. I think of myself as a strong person but that idea does not mean that I should tempt fate.

Also, to be honest, I have so much rage towards you; I would not trust myself not to hurt you. In fact, there are things I have done recently that would make you cry or shiver. I think the most pathetic was walking around the back of Golders Green barefoot with a sprained ankle in freezing temperature at night.

I'm lucky so far that my emotional state has not interfered with work, but it came dangerously close last night. After we spoke, I started screaming at Tanya that I couldn't work any more and was going to have a nightmare year. Thanks partly to your phone call in the morning, I managed to calm down and regained some sort of 'normal' perspective.

But also, with my history, I can't afford to let myself go. If I took a week off for emotional reasons, my family would flip. Because when I present anything less than a fully functioning self, they get reminded of the horror of my past illness and Zac completely shuts down.

My desk is by the window and the immediate buildings are in grey. The horizon buildings are bathed in light. It's actually how I feel sometimes. Even though there are times when it weren't for the people I love and feel obliged to, I could easily jump - I do still have hope.

... I believe in miracles, I may be 'cured' fast, but I'm not holding my breath.....

I am still in love with you, but I am offended at the deepest level by you. My disappointment is practically unbelievable. I would rather hurt myself than you because I love you that much. All the rage against you is turned on me, and so I am busy abusing myself in all the ways that I can get away with without my family finding out.

I was happy before I met you. I was happy with you. I have been unhappy since we broke up. But I don't reckon that I can find happiness again through you. I don't have enough respect for your integrity any more to place my happiness in your hands. That is something I have to do for myself and by myself. And while I lay the demons of our relationship to rest, I might as well work at laying my old ones to rest too. I would like to develop enough deep self-esteem, and then when I am unhappy, I don't turn to life-threatening drugs and the sort of sex that make me physically ill and ashamed.

I am not being blunt with you just to guilt-trip you. But I think that you should be aware of what you have done here. You will be a husband and father one day, and you will open your eyes. If you can't be real about yourself, you will never treat your wife like a real person.

I had hoped to be your wife. But the way you have treated me and casually disregarded your love for me, makes me afraid for my unborn children. I wonder how easily your children could fall out of favour with you and be denied access to you as I was and how easily you might disown them.

My clock is not ticking, but I do not have time to waste either. I don't want to get involved in any sort of meaningful relationship with someone whom I would not feel comfortable fathering my children. You asked if I believed in fate. In many ways I do. If you are destined to grow into a self-aware, strong, active and forgiving man, then maybe one day, who knows we will be a couple again.

Please don't feel bad, and don't worry about me. I have incredible powers of recovery which is partly why I abuse myself so easily because deep down I know that I pull through. But that is not a way to carry on, when I want to build a stable adult future.

I love you, I miss you. I want to make love with you. I want everything to be like it was. I want the ugliness to go away. To be honest, I believe that you still love me as ever, you are just not in touch with those feelings right now. I could get on the next plane, I really could. But I have to deal with my tatty ego and my self-esteem in order to be free, first and foremost. I don't want illusions any more. I want to be connected. I want to keep my life very simple and I want to become whole again.

I feel that what I am like now is not really me. It's like all the shit from my childhood coming to the surface, and I have to filter it all out. Before I became aware and started remembering, I was the healthiest, most disciplined, pure young woman. This is not me, Francis, and I can't stand it any more. I want to process all this shit that is not mine but of others. It's not a question of discovering myself. I know what I am like deep inside, as my closest friends do and some very subtle people who have x-ray emotional vision. I don't know if you ever did really. My emotional inheritance is mixed. Until I was 17, only the good things were apparent. From the age of 17, I have been processing the bad bits out of me. Now is the time for me really to break free and become my own person. I love you, I do. But I have to get well. Really become myself again.

What were the 'bad bits' that haunted Zoë and would explode in what she called a 'primal scream' one year later in Morocco? We ransacked our memories to no avail, trying to recall any traumatic episodes from Zoë's childhood. The only explanation that fits is that Zoë adopted Margie's fantasies. Those fantasies of a very sick young woman were discussed and brushed aside when brought up into the humdrum light of daily life; not so easily dismissed when Zoë was struggling with her own sanity. Margie's fantasies of Walter having sex with his daughters became a focus for her despair, much as the death of Tigger became a focus for her rage. At the same time she admits her pain and fear to Francis, she admonishes herself in her diary: *I'm going to use this weekend to get rid of all the stuff I don't use. And that physical cleansing should make it easier to cleanse my body.*

Maybe writing such a letter suppressed the demons for a couple of weeks. At that time, we in the family found her impossible to live with. She was moving her stuff from Nana's house to the new flat and arguing with me, her sisters and eventually even Zachary.

Sunday (Monday morning early) 1.30 am, 21/22nd February

Quite pleased that I haven't written in diary for a couple of weeks. Been a busy bee at work and with the move to the new flat. Feel very stimulated and stable at work, and very peaceful in the flat. Habie is a bit of a thorn. The way she makes me feel guilty for grieving when she's monstrous to me. You can tell she's seething that I'm not being chatty. But why should I want to be close to her straight away when she's been so beastly. But I'm not going to write to her about this. Because it's embarrassing, and she knows it anyway, she's just full of shit. I'll send her copies of the photos though as arranged, and I'm looking forward to looking at the photos from Nana's when I go to bed. Typical Habie, she's upstairs taking photos not just of her, but of

186

*everyone else too - baby and childhood photos of ourselves,
before anyone apart from Mum and Jan have seen them. I
managed to pick from her clutches a photo for Tanya of her
looking identical to Chloe. Chloe's gonna love it too* ... [The
sisters quarrelled bitterly over who was to keep the family
photos in my mother's house. Among Zoë's papers is a
handwritten note from Hab about the row that Zo had ripped
in half and then stuck back together with Sellotape.]

*Think about Francis quite rarely. I'm quite pleased to have
finally admitted to myself how bored I was of him and my
lovers.*

A strange comment in the light of the letter which
she'd written him a couple of weeks earlier. She gave much
louder signals of a rocking mental state during the final
illness of her cat. But none of us heard them, drowned out
by our own preoccupations. One of my dearest friends
Sheena with whom Zoë and I used to do Callisthenics said
to me some months after her death, "Didn't you see how
peculiarly she behaved over the cat's illness." No, I hadn't.
Sheena said, "I was giving her and Mylène a lift into
Colchester and she told me that it felt the same as if her
brother was dying. When I said she exaggerated, she
jumped out of the car. Mylène was with us."

"What did Mylène do?"

"Got out and followed Zoë."

February 28th

Tigger is dying. Maybe he has a few weeks of good life left.

*I love him and will miss him, but knowing that he will not
suffer is the greatest comfort.*

March 10th

*Tigger is still comfortable, but will have to speak to vet in
the morning about his bleeding.* [The vet had advised us to
put the cat to sleep; Zoë wouldn't hear of it.]

187

... Feel really dulled. I guess it's a mixture of Tigger, work anxiety, sexual loneliness, and irritation with Thomas, fear about Francis, worry about Zac, etc, etc.

... Drugs are getting me down. I've become dependent on weed. I don't often have it, and I miss it badly like now. I can't seem to stop smoking.

I don't like living in a bad weather country, travelling on dingy trains with bad connections.

Working in a prefab office with very straight people. Bob is great and overall I'm very lucky, but something is missing. Also Sarah is being a bit of a cow.

Physically, I'm a mess. Eating badly and not exercising. Haven't moved my muscles properly in weeks, or is it months now. ...

I have to stop fretting and get physically well again.

Tigger, I love you. I hate not being with you. I hate leaving you. I hate you going away. Heaven had better exist. Tigger, Tigger, Tigger. I love you Tigger.

<u>*Monday 15th March*</u>

Tigger is comfortable. It was lovely to spend the weekend with him. It's a real blessing to know that he's enjoying his life.

Francis and I got back together this evening. I feel very happy about that.

A family incident showed how she'd lost touch with 'normal' behaviour but we couldn't or wouldn't allow ourselves to see it.

Zac was visiting his sisters in Golders Green. Zoë, already moved into the West End Lane flat had come to Golders Green to collect some stuff. She'd left so much junk piled up in her old room that everyone was cross with her, as we were trying to clean the house ready for sale. I'd come to London to visit my mother in the old people's home and dropped in for supper afterwards with Habie and Tanya. There was a zany atmosphere, the housekeeper kept wandering around wringing her hands, more for dramatic impact than for reality, as she was about to return to Portugal with a golden handshake. Various grandchildren were camped in the bedrooms, gradually stripping the house of its china and silver. That evening, Zac told Zoë off for forgetting to send Maria, his girlfriend, a birthday card. Zoë snapped that she couldn't be expected to remember birthdays when Tigger was dying. Zac said yes she could. Zoë slapped him. He has a hot Schwarz temper, too, and hit her back. The fight escalated, ending on the kitchen tiles with her biting him through his sweater, her teeth closing on his chest. Habie tried to defuse the situation. Zoë broke the kitchen broom handle over her sister's head. Tanya and I huddled in the back room, awed by the yells and shouting, laughing nervously, the way you do when you're slightly scared and embarrassed. Zoë slammed outside to drive off but her car was blocked by mine, which I refused to move; she was in no fit state to drive. The row simmered down and by the end of the evening we were all on teeth-gritted speaking terms.

We told each other, 'Zoë's being Zoë again.' Worried, I phoned Mylène a day or so later to talk about the row and she remarked that she and her brother Jean-Guy used to fight when they were teenagers. But Zoë wasn't a teenager. Why did none of us stop to question such uncontrolled rage?

The flat in West Hampstead had two small bedrooms, a tiny garden and a kitchen/ living room. Zoë was thrilled at the idea of living with her little brother. The flat sharing turned into a disaster. Zoë was smoking pot all day long and not doing her share of flat cleaning and grocery buying. Maria stayed over most nights and would be using the bathroom when Zoë wanted it before going to work. Zoë and Zac rowed continually over who should buy

189

the lavatory paper or how long Maria should stay in the bathroom.

One Friday I drove to the flat to give Zoë and Mylène a lift to Greenacres for the weekend. The two dogs, Leah and Dac, had come along for the ride and sat in the back of the Peugeot station wagon. The flat needing hoovering and there were mugs and plates in the sink. I did a parental nag about the dirty state the flat was in. She replied: "it's my flat and none of your business."

That was true. We set off for Colchester in a slight drizzle with Zoë driving. I felt apologetic for nagging. Zoë was in an elevated mood; work was going well. She began to drive. Faster and faster. Abashed by the earlier row, I didn't dare say slow down.

On the M25 she reached over 80 miles an hour. The rain grew heavier. She switched on the back windscreen wipers and kept her foot down. The speedometer was 84 mph and rising. The last thought I remembered was we'll have an accident. The car went into an almighty skid. Zoë lost control. The car zigzagged, rocking from side to side, for several hundred metres before crashing backwards against the central barriers. The boot sprung open with the impact.

None of us were hurt only shocked. The dogs had vanished, thrown out by the impact. We had been driving ahead of a line of heavy trucks, which now drove past. We were lucky that none of them hit us. I said to Zoë, "you've killed my dogs." But she hadn't. Mylène had seen, in the blazing headlights of a truck, the dogs crossing the motorway. We found them in amongst some bushes on top of the verge, Dac unhurt, Leah shaking in some sort of fit. On Mylène's mobile we raised the AA, who loaded up the smashed car on a trailer and drove us home in the front cab. The car was a write-off.

Zoë never mentioned the accident again. In her diary she notes laconically:

Mylène, mum and I and Leah and Dac had a near fatal accident on Friday. Miracle that we're alive.

Mylène and I also, so relieved at being uninjured, made no reproaches to Zo and were philosophical about what we had lost. Everything in the boot had been thrown out. Mylène lost her attaché case containing files and address book; I lost a suitcase I'd fetched from Nana's house with the photographs of my grandparents and great grandparents.

<u>March 17th</u>

Feeling quite happy. Especially because Tigger is comfortable.

Be the master of your own bloody life.

Otherwise ...

That was the last entry Zoë made in her computer diary. The only other records that she has left of that summer are her work notes and memos. Most are written in tiny almost undecipherable handwriting.

In March, 1999, Tigger's jaw cancer had spread round his face. Drugs had given him a few weeks more life in less pain. The jaw was now permanently open, the abscess bleeding. Wal was away. Femke a friend who practises Reiki came to see the cat. She laid her hands over his body and said, "He wants to go." Zoë agreed that I call the emergency vet. It was already Sunday evening and Zoë had to drive back to London that night. The vet gave Tigger the lethal injection. But it was Zoë, brave enough to hold him in her arms and me who ran out of the room. The young vet comforted us both, as we sobbed in his arms. In the front garden, in a March drizzle, he dug a hole. Zoë was pleased that we buried the cat wrapped in white muslin instead of a bin bag. A large stone covered in moss that the vet could just move, was laid over the grave. Eighteen months later, we put Zoë's ashes under the same stone.

Zoë spent the New Year in France and in early January started at the School of Social Entrepreneurs (SSE) one of Michael Young's brainchildren. This most recent of the many institutions he had started (amongst them the Open University and the Consumer Council) trained young post graduates in how to start enterprises that would be beneficial to society. As I write, there are over 150 graduates. Students attended lectures and seminars at the school and were also were placed with companies for which they ran socially beneficial projects. Zoë's placement was with United Response, a medium-sized charity for people with mental and physical handicaps. She was to join a project that had just begun, encouraging football clubs to award cleaning contracts to people with learning difficulties. Zoë's charm, charisma and talents for empathy were to find full outlet. It was almost the perfect job for her.

One of her fellow employees, Sandra recalls:

"Zoë was one of the first people to chat to me. Five minutes later she walked away and I felt like I'd known her for years. She had that effect she had on people. Career-wise she was fantastic at her job and a great inspiration, sometimes it was hard not to be envious."

The football cleaning contract project eventually became part of United Response in Business. The chairman of UR in Business (obviously taken with Zoë's charm) wrote after her death, *I am a rather dry business man and not so good at writing a letter of condolence. But I am happy to tell you that if my daughter achieves even half of what Zoë did, I would be a very proud father indeed.*

I shall never forget Zoë. She made an incredible impression: dedicated, effective, imaginative and charming. When I discovered that she was half-French we started to communicate in French. ... She was a wonderful young lady.

Zoë was bi-lingual; she didn't have a drop of French blood. I'm pretty sure she didn't tell the chairman a fib; she simply charmed and dazzled him.

It was thanks to her that we could get UR in business up and running and she would be very pleased to see what her work had created, a thriving company with close to one hundred employees, a company that was the best new charity in 2000. I am determined that the company should continue to grow and offer work to people with learning disabilities. This will be a permanent memorial to Zoë and what she did.

As I write, three and a half years after Zoë's death, the program she set up still functions with two football clubs and two sports centres currently operating the scheme. Sadly, the program's expansion has been checked by the cut-throat competition in this business and inadequate wages often paid to these workers.

But while she triumphed at work (she was so proud of the £500 bonus she received) her private life floundered. Nana had already been taken to the old people's home where she would die two years later. Her house not yet sold, several grandchildren made the Golders Green house their London base. Habie lived there and Tanya from time to time. And Mickey's daughter, Penny, divorced with four kids also stayed when she visited London. Zoë never told us she was taking cocaine (Charlie) with Simon, my divorced nephew, another resident.

When we met Su Sawyer and Bob Tindall, two years after her death, we asked if either of them had realised that Zoë was suffering from bi-polar disorder and neither of them had. Su admitted there had been difficulties with managing Zoë and had found her manipulative in office politics. Bob said, "If you had asked me out who, of our 50 possible employees who might commit suicide I would never have picked Zoë."

He wrote to us:

Along with Su, I was responsible for monitoring Zoë's work during her time at United Response. ... When people die, others often tend ...to make the most of the positive aspects... However, virtually at any point over the last 18 months, I would have told you that Zoe was one of the most thoughtful, positive and warm people I have had the privilege of meeting. She had a particular ability to see the good in everyone. When she negotiated with some hard-bitten stadium managers over UR in Business, I privately nurtured a doubt that her ability to see good everywhere would mean that she would be naïve. At the launch of UR in Business, which came later than some of the negotiations, I saw the same managers – having travelled considerable distances to be there – eating out of her hand. So, almost by lacking artifice, it was successful in its own right. ... My image of her is sitting on the telephone – within my view as I came out of the office – looking very much like the photo you have sent out, talking enthusiastically to someone, sometimes catching me to tell me something good that had happened. She had a strong belief in providing opportunities for people with learning difficulties, and she has left a legacy which is actively benefiting people every day. I have some more personal recollections of Zoë giving me a sticker from Derby County for my son, and arranging for me and him to attend a game ... bringing me a smoked salmon bagel from one of your family parties, coming back from football clubs with various amusing stories.... You will be aware by now that Zoe was very popular here. This was because she could relate to literally everyone on a personal basis. I do remember her causing regular amusement at her updates on her work to the whole of the office (we meet every Friday) by assessing the willingness of each football club to enter into a contract with us on the basis of whether they were "hot to trot" or otherwise. ...She was the sort of person I would have always been watching

194

out for, willing her to do well. I will miss her and I will certainly never forget her.

In September 1999, Zoë's life reached a hiatus. Her year's placement with United Response was soon to end in apparent triumph, with ringing endorsements from her employers who had offered her another job. But Zoë, now increasingly agitated, filled with somewhat grandiose ideas of her achievements and potential, smoking more and more pot, had other ideas. These were encouraged by Michael Young who had taken Zoë up as the star ex-student of his School for Social Entrepreneurs.

Lord Young told Zoë (he told us too) she was the most brilliant pupil to have passed through the school and wanted her to start out on a socially useful venture of her own – to run her own show, which, after all, was the basic purpose of SSE.

She was now convinced that she was going to be a businesswoman – a social entrepreneur but she had no experience of management, no capital, minimal contacts in the business world did not keep up with current affairs and thus had little likelihood of identifying new openings. She talked vaguely of going into ethical investment but lacked all knowledge of investment and would have been legally barred from setting up as an investment advisor. She replied defiantly: "I'll hire someone."

I tried to support these plans, believing that Zoë could do anything she wanted once she was fully engaged: Wal and Ben could not suppress doubts. Ben visited her in the West End Lane flat and advised her to get another job to gain more experience before venturing on her own: her track record had too many short stints. Zoë told her brother he was a stuffy bourgeois with no vision. Wal made great efforts to support her, giving her his own contacts in the voluntary and "green" action fields she was exploring, ringing and writing to a few old friends who might help her. But she sensed his underlying scepticism and grew deeply resentful.

She emailed us both: *I wouldn't call my behaviour unbalanced. In fact I think my behaviour was remarkably calm on the day that Dad poo-poohed my plans and achievements. Neither of you have referred to this incident but it wasn't exactly supportive or nice.*

And both of you have been weird about my smoking. I would very much appreciate expressions of concern and offers of help, but to be told that I'm an especially silly smoker, etc. etc. is not how to help an addict.

I don't have any hardcore skills like accounting, architecture or IT. What I have is my ability to combine my intelligence and integrity to motivate people to support organisations like the one I set up this year which now employs 70 adults with learning disabilities in the biggest football Clubs around the country. The company was launched at the House of Commons and is used as an example of good practice - 3 workers are now managers.

I need my confidence to do this. Please don't try to undermine it. I need even more to go on to my next challenge. The reason I have been successful this year was because I was on a huge learning curve. I knew nothing about disability or business. Now that the company is successful and sustainable, my learning curve is petering out and I need a bigger challenge. I need to be encouraged not talked down at...

I have had enough traumas in my young life. I have had to work really hard and be very humble to have the opportunities that are before me now. I actually believe that I deserve to be happy. So please, you are either with me or against me. Either support me and have faith in me, and keep your problems to yourself (I don't think that family members are automatic punch bags - and you will have noticed that I have not burdened you with mine - and let's face it: the problems that spoiled people like us have are mostly in the more unpleasant realms of our negative emotions), or not: The ball is in your court. I think I've made myself clear.

196

Zoë seemed so rational. Only much later did we realise the fragility of her house of cards. She planned to hold a brainstorming in the flat about starting her own company, to which she invited various mentors, including Nicolas Albery [an entrepreneur in many fields] and Michael Young. Wal, too, was invited. He told Zoë he intended to ask the group whether her ideas were viable. She flared up, "Don't bother to come if that's your stuffy attitude. You're disinvited." I sided with her and told Wal he wasn't being supportive.

She planned the event meticulously, preparing a meal for her guests. But she was stoned throughout the meeting. Afterwards Nicholas Albery told us that he'd warned her that she wouldn't inspire confidence in her backers if she smoked pot so continuously.

Zoë was irritable whenever met. About the project of which Wal was so critical, she emailed Habie in early October.

Subject: Good news:

My current project is going so well that James Cornford – government advisor in the treasury, Lord Young and others are backing me to set up a new project in the New Year in ethical investment. The chief executive of the Co-op bank set up meetings for me to ensure I get the assistance I need. As you can imagine, I need a lot! As you can also imagine, I'm on a high. This is a tremendous boost for me and the research into my new project, as I always find the first steps the biggest and the most challenging.

Zoë wasn't lying but she wasn't presenting the whole truth either. I'd supported her over the idea of her setting up in business. Her plans were grandiose but she showed such enthusiasm and why couldn't we have faith in her, she repeated. Then we had my own flaming row about the amount of pot she smoked. She must stop. My attitude infuriated her. We stopped speaking. Habie tried, as she so often did, to calm the situation.

She emailed me:

Re Zoe, it's up to you how you react but I do think that 'standing your ground' is not the Mum-like thing to do, given that she is not proud to have become addicted to pot, and needs more support than criticism if she is to have the guts to face up to it, don't you think? Basically what she needs from all of us, especially you is to say "I know you are addicted, how can I help?" rather than to point out the obvious failing which she knows better than anyone.

It's much harder to admit one's problems when under attack, and you know how easily Zoe feels under attack, so why not just support her as you do with Tanya, and enjoy the resultant renewal of the friendship you and she usually have? No?

And she emailed her sister:

I don't know the latest re you and Mum, but I do hope both of you will be able to move towards each other at least enough for it not to hurt any more, so you can enjoy your trip to Morocco and Mum can stop moaning for five minutes. God, it's so crazy the way this family carries on, considering how much we love each other!

Zoë was now planning to take a short holiday before she left United Response in December. None of her friends was free. We worried about her going alone and Wal volunteered to accompany her. Michael Young suggested Morocco and they both decided on that.

Wal wrote: *an adventure for both of us, we were closer than we had been for many years. It was alarming that first night in Marrakech, as we stumbled with a suitcase in the dark through narrow, crowded lanes (my suitcase: Zoë travelled light with only a small rucksack). We*

198

were a team: she was noticed and admired for her youth, beauty and quick mind, but she was disorientated and needed me for protection and for my experience of travel.

In a dirt-poor mountain village she became intimate, or so she thought, with every member, young and old, of the family we stayed with, promising to keep in touch with them when she was back home, to send them medicines they needed. She'd inherited this gift for instant communication from her mother. (I tend to err the other way, reserved and a little brusque with people I meet, always too ready to move on rather than linger.)

Everywhere she attracted attention, especially from young men. One older man told me to look after my daughter well, "or someone will snap her up."

We two with our different ages and temperaments were sharing an adventure and we talked endlessly about everything and everyone. Yet I must have been worried about her, without formulating my fears even to myself. If she was crossed in any way, her mood could change.

In the seaside resort of Essaouira, we would walk out each morning to have breakfast at an open-air street café. One morning she kept me waiting, refusing to hurry, so I went ahead. When she did not appear I was worried: I didn't want her alone in the town. Why be worried? She was old enough and physically strong enough to take care of herself. Deep down I feared that she was ill again but I didn't let those fears surface.

After the holiday, Zoë tried to resume her preparations for business life but sensing a lack of enthusiasm from her friends and contacts; she, too, lost interest. She prepared to leave the flat in West End Lane and talked of moving in with her friend Mylène, who was flat sharing in Brixton. She was aware of everyone's disapproval of her lifestyle, her irritability, her having too many friends to stay. She must have felt her life was in a cul de sac – and decided to return to Morocco. She wanted a "time out to find my space." She intended to learn Arabic, study Islam and a new culture." Wacky but rational at the same time. She would conduct a business there, she said – perhaps with a charity, perhaps going into equitable carpet trading. Her brother Ben tried to dissuade her. Her sisters urged caution but she listened to no one.

At United Response she had succeeded brilliantly, in spite of her inner turbulence. She had earned a £500 bonus. Bob and Su had suggested she apply for a permanent job. She discussed it with us excitedly but changed her mind and turned it down; she wanted her own business.

Her grandmother had given her an upright Bechstein piano which she proposed to sell. Fearing that she would sell it for a fraction of its value, we bought it from her for £2000, arranging to sell our own piano to make room for it. So she was set up for Morocco, where she imagined she would find relief from unbearable tensions, frustrations and, above all, criticism. When she left on December 15th, we didn't drive her to Heathrow.

*some names have been changed

200

CHAPTER EIGHT

"Hicham, my angel 'pon the earth."

She was in Morocco where she had chosen to be. She had removed herself from the family tensions and quarrels of the end of 1999. She sounded deliriously happy in messages and phone calls, full of extravagant love for everyone, especially her parents and siblings.

Zoë and her siblings in the garden at Greenacres in the summer of 1996

She sent a long SOL email (Schwarz on Line) to the whole family. We had started sending SOLS a couple of years earlier, when Wal and I were abroad researching

Living Lightly. A good way to keep in touch. Zoë's SOL was warm but you sensed an underlying oddness. Why did she describe herself with such hyperbole? She sent the following message.

For Schwarzes at Greenacres, London, France, Scotland, Jo'burg and please print/post copy to Marlene. Love you all – Zoë

    My name is Zoë. But most people in Marrakech call me Zourans.

I have just spent four days with the Zahrissi family in a strict Moslem neighbourhood. I am treated like a decadent, minor celebrity. Most people have a mixture of respect, love, contempt and genuine affection for me. I am very curious to discover how deep my friendships here are and can become. I love friendship. I have wonderful friends of long standing in England. And a large, amazing family. I feel a bit homesick.

... Mum & Dad fly out on the 13th of April. Inch Allah I will still be here.

    I am 27 years old. I enjoy being beautiful and admired. I am medium height, olive skin, slender and very shapely. I have incredibly good teeth. Although being a relatively well-off European tourist, I would probably get as much cosseting, though maybe a little less male attention. I enjoy the attention. I have put myself in a very safe and reasonably respectable situation here. There is an extraordinary and delicious innocence around relationships here. Even with Hicham, my "copain" who is known among the family and some of their friends as an admirer, we would not even kiss. We meet like adolescents, exchange a few jokes, listen to the walkman and part. ...

    The leisurely pace, the tenderness in even the simplest human interactions, the quality and freshness of the food, the love of children, the sharing of objects.

But I don't know how I will handle the segregation in the main square and the Medina. Moroccans who are not very rich need permits to socialise with tourists - if I can get a visa to stay a few months or if I will have to use my return ticket on the 7th March.

I am in a little hotel room with marble floors and pretty mosaics. The terrace is nice and the hotel keepers are very funny. I think of my room at home and my parents' house which would be seen as a millionaire's pad here, and which even by English standards is breathtaking. I miss the cotton sheets and my double bed, the hot water on tap and the animals. Especially Leah and Shah who I feel very connected to. As I do to Mum and Dad.

I feel very "real" here. Maybe because I am on such a steep learning curve - so much to assimilate - that my mind is switched on and I feel like I am celebrating.

I feel a special kind of freedom here. As long as I make an effort to be respectful - which is a pleasure anyway; and maintain adequate boundaries - nobody gets at me. I feel free in my soul and so very stimulated - it's kind of religious because I feel a very nice energy - and it feels personal, like I have a choice on how happy I want to be.

I respect happiness. There are still some very deep community values, even among the most tourist rip-off parts of town. Although money can buy a certain kind of freedom like everywhere, I have the feeling that people take greater notice of peoples' warmth and happiness as manifested in their faces and body language and gestures - in beggars the same as in rich people. That is what I like best.

Also I like how I have to be honest here - because Marrakechis can smell bullshit a mile off and also because I feel connected to my parents and grandma and friends back home - especially Mylène, so I am secure in myself. I can still be me and enjoy the best aspects of Marrakech without being crushed by the alien and sometimes very complex nature of things.

I think of my sister Tanya a lot here and how she will help me decode and integrate into the culture. I hope she can come - 'inch Allah.

I think a lot of Noe and how lucky he is to be born into the family of Ben, Fredy, Chloe and Max with all its extensions. I am so touched by Ben's concern for me before I left and it helps me to stay focused and encourages me to stay in touch with all my work colleagues and contacts so as not to close any doors.

I'm not quite sure what will happen in Marrakech but it feels potent and good. An opening which does not jeopardise but strengthens me.

I think of Aunties Tanya and Marlene and Habie and my other girlfriends Lola, Sayuri, Helen, Judith, and young friends like Arie, Thomas, Anne-Laure, and intimates like Sarah and Kelly and Lindsay and my treasure of treasures - Florence who all gave me so much confidence and energy when I was in England for three weeks.

I think a lot of the work I did last year - how work is like duty. And I wonder what my next work/duty will be?

I am picking up Arabic much faster than I had dreamed because it has become a main mission among the people I know here to help me learn. They pick up languages at the drop of a hat. Their enthusiasm and ease is contagious.

... I am writing this to all of you hoping that it will put some fears at rest, to share my growing strength and faith in the power of love, to say thanks to my family.

Especially to Zac and Maria who were both so kind to me in London and who I thank in my heart for being there as my brother and my dear friend. Their love is inspiring.

I think of my godmother Sarojini who taught me not to be a victim, which made the journey possible. This may sound sententious and melodramatic, but I am opening my eyes, seeing people as they are with their selfishness, their complexities and our need for love and acceptance. I am becoming a grown-up. And I am a late developer so it's blowing my little mind. ...

I didn't allow myself to reflect about what she was saying. Her sisters sent her friendly messages in reply. We hid our disquiet from one another. Tanya was more realistic and wrote to Habie that Zoë had gone OTT.

Some of the emails were normal, chatty and pleasant. She found a sympathetic Moroccan family and started a love affair with Hicham, the youngest son.

Zac would like it here. The brothers are all trendy because of the middle sister's job. She's always sending amazing stuff for them. A bit of a fashion parade. I'm keeping my end up and have started to take a great pleasure in clothes.....

I can swear, greet and make love in Arabic now but past tense is difficult. Plural is a nightmare because there is no grammatical rule. You have to learn the plural of each word as you learn the singular.

A few days before we were due to leave, we were shocked by a sudden phone call, saying she proposed to marry Hicham the following day. After the call, I rang Mylène and asked her to phone Zoë. "Persuade her not to do anything rash." Mylène obliged. But this marriage plan was fantasy because marrying a foreigner in Morocco needed immense amounts of bureaucratic red tape.

Zoë emailed next day:

I miss you both so much. My life in this muddled, backward, enlightened place is a novel which you understand better than anyone. I am half of each of you but not as intelligent or wise because my experience of life is still small..... I see you both for the first time. And I thank God from the bottom of my heart, my soul and my mind that my parents are Walter and Dorothy.

I am so proud to be your daughter and to have the freedom you have given me both materially and spiritually.

I would be a fool to throw it away. I miss you both and am looking forward to your coming..... I am honoured that you love me enough to care so much about my future: because I don't make it easy for you to love me. I am very selfish and silly – it's not the first time I have caused my family pain by being such a baby. Please continue to help me to grow up.... What you said to me on the phone is the sweetest thing you have said – about how what you want most is my happiness, husband and kids, but that you want to be sure I have chosen carefully with Hicham ......

Shouldn't we have guessed that she was losing touch with reality? Yes, with hindsight. From his photograph, Hicham had a loving expression but looked far too young for her.

Hicham sends lots of love and says I'm lucky to have such loving, sensible parents.

The postcard that he sent us was written in semi-literate French.

Then Zoë's messages grew irregular, more and more exaggerated:

First of all Mum: you would be proud of me: I have started writing copiously and it's uninhibited (I remember what you said)

.....My mind is firing in potent cylinders and my body is finely tuned. Combination of being stretched intellectually (by the culture shock and complexity of Moroccan daily life) and deeply in love with Hicham. He proves himself each day to be honest, tender, funny and strong.

I would never have dreamed that I would fall in love with a man who is the same size as me (identical body weight.) and younger - but his presence enthrals me. His body is lean, almost thin, and muscular.... We are living as a married couple and are perceived as such. Discreet and passionate. Being together in Essaouira in a dilapidated exquisite hotel in a magical fishing town in unspoilt country is heaven - is the most poetic and romantic time in my life. I feel like a grown woman at long last, responsible, in control and cherished.

I love you both so much.

After the months of strain and recrimination, we enjoyed the extravagant praise and love, of course; however, even before we reached Morocco and met him; it was obvious that her plans for Hicham coming to Britain were worthless. Without a passport and with none of the qualifications he would need to make any sort of a life here, he could barely speak French, let alone English and had left school before taking the baccalaureate. Zoë was the first girl friend he'd ever had. Clearly he adored her.

Before our arrival, Zoë had sent detailed plans:

Hicham and I are not planning on living in Morocco. Not until we're much older and tougher that's for sure. Even in honey moon mode, it's quite tough here.

We want to come back with you and Dad. I think it's better with customs because we're not that experienced. Dad in particular is a world class expert on all that. From a practical point of view, I appreciate your help, but also I don't want to bring Hicham to England without your blessing. You haven't met him yet, but the four of us will have over two weeks together. Hopefully you'll have enough of an idea by then to make a decision. As you know we consider ourselves to be married already in our hearts. I know what Dad means now when he says that Zac and M are married. I think like a married person now and thankfully act like one too.

Zac would approve!

I hope you will too. But this is also a decision for our children, your grandchildren, and I would like your input. Logistically, we are in the final stage of validating Hicham's passport so that he can travel and extending my Visa to cover your holiday period here and a few weeks extra if necessary.

207

We offered no criticism of these dreams; none of which turned out to be realisable. (Hicham told us when we arrived that he had never wanted to go to UK.)

I don't know how to write about the feelings Hicham and I have for each other. You will see and sense for yourselves when we are all in Essaouira soon. It will be a doddle and a giggle for Dad to get his daughter and her beloved out of Morocco in peace time bearing in mind that the political system here is mega-pro West. Dad's track record is as a brilliant family man who risked his life for truth and to help protect the planet and future generations. He is a free agent in a place like this to move Hicham and me out as he wishes.

Wal was taken aback at being described as a world class expert in getting people across frontiers – and wrote asking Zoë to modify her extravagant opinion, advising them to go to the British Embassy in Rabat. She took no notice.

I will fill you in with more of the detailed and amusing political contexts here when you arrive. I also don't want to brainwash you. It has been pointed out that I can sell freezers to the Eskimos, but I want you to help me objectively because it isn't just my happiness, but my children, your grandchildren, too. Hicham and I want to start a family in a few years and his coming to England is a very big step closer to that, especially if it turns out that Dad has to sign a marriage contract to allow Hicham to leave Morocco with me / us.

...I NEED your help.

I don't want to be melodramatic because we are going to have a lovely holiday and Hicham and I are not the first couple to fall in love and want a family together.

Our flight to Marrakech was booked for April 13th. My new pet Arthur the West African grey parrot went home to his breeder for three weeks. Rachel would look after the dogs and cats and old Shah. Wal and I were looking forward to a Moroccan holiday; Zoë sent elaborate instructions of presents to bring for every one of her acquaintances. We had to bring - cactus (enough for ten big pots) and rose seeds for adorning the ancient hotel courtyard a walkman as a present for a young artist who was also the watchman at the hotel, various cosmetics and prescription medicines. We bought barely one tenth of what she asked for. And when we arrived none of it was needed.

Then these almost daily emails dried up. Eight days before we were to leave came the last one:

Dear Mum and Dad,

I adored your messages. And I am blissfully well and wise. But right now I am a tad agitated because I've just spent three hours writing a SOL message and private messages for you which were wiped out by mistake - fucking unfamiliar fucking fucked-up fuck systems. The heat is sweltering so I'm going to go to the hotel, take a shower and write it out again tomorrow.

Quickly though: I love you to bits.

Parrot in Arab is babagha - pronounced babara. Arthur sounds a total scream.

Re the hotel, it's all fixed. Breathtaking views and private bathroom for the grand sum of five and half quid a day...

And Wal replied:

It was lovely to hear you in such good spirits the other morning and I hope your idyll is holding up in every way. Do send us an e-mail every few days with all your news. We think about you and thoughts, like pets, need to be fed.

209

At first Zoë's exaggerated response to everything in Morocco could be still glossed over as 'Zoë being Zoë.' We were not unduly alarmed.

At 1.30 am on the night of the 11th, we were both asleep. The phone rang. Someone speaking broken English said, "Ring quick to this number. I have news of your daughter."

Wal was more awake than me. The caller was the owner of the Hotel des Ramparts, where Zoë and Hicham were staying. He handed over to Hicham who spoke pidgin French. Zoë was ill.

"Ill – how?"

For the last four days. She had smashed furniture, a telephone and slapped the hotel receptionist. Sounded like some sort of breakdown. Wal tried to find out whether drugs were involved. Hicham's French wasn't fluent enough. He spoke of "un petard" which can be a firework or a spliff. Hicham wasn't phoning to tell us that she was ill but to explain why he wouldn't be coming to meet us at Marrakech; he must stay with her.

The next morning, we called back. Hicham said Zoë was "better" but would not come to the phone because she was "nerveuse". We wondered whether she was under some sort of room arrest. We spent a gloomy Thursday trying to guess what might have happened. Wal decided to email the other children.

Tanya rang up, her voice full of smiles. Her desk carried a vase of white roses from Niall, her new admirer. Habie rang. She had already told cousin Julia, who wasn't surprised. Julia had said than when she met Zoë last year working for United Response she was like a child wearing her mother's shoes. Her younger brother Zac remarked: "if she is in love how come she's attacking furniture?"

The day passed.

In eight or ten hours we would see her and know what had happened. From Marrakech, we took a three-hour taxi to Essaouira and arrived at three in the morning. Zoë and Hicham had waited up. Our room was next to theirs on the third of four floors. The rooms of the Hotel des Remparts were arranged around an interior courtyard open to the sky rooms with a cold water tap and a western-style loo.

Zoë, berry brown and affectionate, hugged us hard, grown so thin that her shoulder blades were sharp to touch. Within three minutes, she was rambling, her words wild and disjointed. Hicham, even smaller than in his photos, appeared traumatized. He asked in a bewildered aside, "Are all English girls like this?"

Zoë had decorated our bathroom in a manner which shocked us. Each shelf and ledge was covered with small piles of broken shells and pebbles, empty boxes of shampoo and bath oil. It looked crazy and chilling, reminding me of Miss Faversham's cobwebbed banquet in *Great Expectations*. To her father she offered a "birthday present" - six weeks before his 70th birthday. "Treasure it. It will be immensely valuable one day." The black ledger was half-wrapped in torn brown paper. A first glance scrawled and partly illegible writing was arranged at different angles across the page, with many cryptic drawings and diagrams. Later, when we set our minds to decipher this book, we discovered much beauty, love and poetry as well as bizarre ravings: we called it her "mad" diary.

We had brought a bottle of duty free whisky and, although it was now nearly 4 am, Zoë insisted we must have a drink. Hicham looked on, his lower lip drooping.

We'd uttered no word of criticism but Zoë could read our expressions of dismay. "You're being negative," she spat like a young tigress. Our presence seemed hostile, our silence a threat. She had been rising in a delicious exaltation towards a peak of mania. In such a state, anyone

211

who potentially brings you down has to be an enemy - and what is more dispiriting than the silent, grave faces of mum and dad?

Hicham told us that she'd been in this exalted state for ten days, hardly eating or sleeping. She grabbed the black diary from Wal's hand, "you don't deserve it."

We arranged to have breakfast together at ten but by ten-thirty, neither she nor Hicham had appeared. We spent an anxious morning wandering around the pretty fishing port with the sun smiling on our bewildered misery. When we returned to our room, Hicham hovered in the doorway; he didn't know where Zoë had gone. Maybe she was walking with the people who kept horses and camels on the beach. They had become her friends.

Two English girl tourists, both Oxford undergraduates, came to our room; they wanted to tell us about Zoë. At first, they'd found her delightful and charismatic. She had stood in front of Charlotte and said, "I can see that you're a poet." For ten days or so, the two girls became members of a group surrounding Zoë. Then the scene darkened. Louise said the attempted rape of a tourist on the beach, some days earlier, had upset her. She had told them fabulous tales: that she worked for the FBI; that she had married Hicham in UK; that she had 8 million dollars. Most disturbing of all - her elder sister had been "raped for twenty years." They knew she was smoking a lot of dope. The day before our arrival she had been crawling around the parapet of the roof and shouting that she was ridding the hotel of snakes. Staff and guests had been terrified she would fall four flights to her death.

Zoë had assembled a group of supporters "to catch the beach rapist". The students told us that as she became wilder everyone began to avoid her. She and Hicham were left alone. From this isolation, she became hostile and abusive to her former friends, smashing the telephone, slapping the receptionist.

When the students left, we looked for Zoë and found her on the hotel roof terrace, crouched against a buttress, wearing sunglasses. Returning from the beach, she had seen a blind cat and she was praying for it. She accused us of showing disrespect for Hicham. "Go and talk nicely to him," she ordered.

Later that afternoon, she was in her room. We tried to talk to her through the window opening onto the courtyard; she went on cursing and complaining. "Come off it, Zo." I gave her a light slap. She reacted with fury, punching me in the face; the lens fell out of my glasses.

"Zoë, how can you live here without money?" her dad asked, hoping to steer her towards the idea of a homecoming. She kept repeating she didn't need money because she had eight million dollars. The hotel was a sacred temple which had become a brothel. She had rid it of snakes and she and Hicham had purified it. "I won't speak to you." She locked herself in her room, leaving Hicham outside with us. From within we heard her chanting in English, French and snatches of Arabic.

Hicham said we must send for the *sapeurs pompiers*. Apparently in Morocco, it is the fire brigade who cart off deranged persons to hospitals.

Louise suggested we contact the British Embassy. Walter had travelled the world as a journalist for thirty years without asking for diplomatic protection but now recognised we needed help. The embassy gave it; they told him Essaouira only had one general hospital but that Marrakech had a reputable asylum. We should contact the British Consul there.

I didn't want Zoë admitted to a hospital; I knew she feared them. We'd try and get medical help locally. With Hicham we walked to the local hospital - a colonial-style set of buildings set among trees. At 6 pm everyone was going home. Tactlessly, I asked one of the women wearing a black headscarf, "Does anyone speak French?"

"We all do."

We were directed to the psychiatrist's home, a squat bungalow in the hospital grounds with an unkempt garden of palm trees leaning at angles. We were kept waiting outside the gate for ten minutes until a serious young man in his thirties came to speak to us. He agreed to see Zoë, posing as an acquaintance we had met in the town.

Walking back with us towards the hotel, the psychiatrist asked the obvious question: has Zoë ever been like this before? It was like a slap - a moment of truth and remorse. Why had we shut our eyes to the obvious, letting Zoë suffer and degenerate on her own? For eight years we had let ourselves believe that Zoë's first episode had been her last. What was happening in Essaouira in March 2000 was a ghastly rerun of Bristol eight years earlier.

We left the psychiatrist talking to her in the corridor outside her room and went into ours. After twenty minutes he knocked to tell us that the encounter had gone badly. "Your daughter is super-intelligent and knew what I was."

However, he left a prescription, which we must try to persuade her to take. We scoured the Essaouira chemists in the late evening to assemble the four drugs he had prescribed and managed to get the last prescription at midnight from a late night pharmacy. We knocked at Zoë's door; she wouldn't let us in. "Go to bed," she said, "we are sorting some personal space." Her voice was dry; she wouldn't look at us. Wal gave Hicham 100 dirhams to buy her cigarettes. He said he'd persuade her to take the tranquillizers.

Next morning, Hicham said that she had taken one dose of tablets but refused the second. She opened the window that gave onto the corridor. "I hate you!" she spat at me. "Go on the bed and masturbate," she jeered at her father. She aimed a kick at his groin but he dodged; she knocked my glasses off my face again. I picked up the unbroken lens and Wal and I went for breakfast. On our return, the situation had escalated. The bedroom furniture

214

had been dragged into the corridor blocking the way. How could she have shifted the massive wooden double bed and enormous armchairs alone? Later, when I asked a doctor how she could have found such strength – the legendary strength of the insane – he shrugged – adrenaline. All her clothes were draped on the balcony rails. Apart from one orange sweater, they were dark-coloured and sombre. Leaning out of the window which overlooked the interior courtyard, she began haranguing the guests. From the floor above to the three floors below, everyone, guests and staff, could hear her proclaim, over and over, that her father had raped her sister for twenty years and she had herself suffered the same fate but only for four years. Her mother had connived in this. We tried to touch her but she attacked us so forcefully that she had to be dragged off by hotel staff. They urged us politely but firmly back into our room; we felt unsure and inadequate. The situation had spiralled out of our control.

The *sapeur pompiers* were summoned. By the time they arrived, Zoë had run out onto the beach. They caught up with her and carried her off to the hospital.

We went onto automatic pilot. Didn't think, just carried out the motions. For Zoë to be transferred to Marrakech, papers had to be signed by the prefect, who was out of town, so other officials had to be sought in their homes. This took most of the day as we traipsed from office to office. In the end, the papers were brought to the police chief for authorisation. Finally, our passports were necessary. Wal went back to fetch them, leaving me at the police station. Half an hour later, he came back, he was trembling, and "I'm hallucinating. I've just seen her. She walked straight past me!"

Could it be Zoë? It was. The hospital staff had left her and Hicham in an unlocked room and she had persuaded him to walk out with her.

Back at the hotel, Zoë was downstairs, standing in the centre of the courtyard well, chanting to various deities, including Allah. In spite of the humid warmth, she wore her grey woollen duffel coat. Her voice floated up to the top floor. Guests were hanging out of the windows, agog.

The hotel manager summoned the police and gave us an ultimatum, either let her be taken to the asylum in Marrakech or let the police take her to prison. Knowing how Zoë hated hospitals, I preferred prison but Wal argued that it would be easier to get her out of hospital than prison and we had already procured the necessary papers.

The Police chief arrived to find everyone unable or fearful of approaching her. He watched her chanting for a few minutes, lost his temper, seized her by the belt loops of her jeans and pulled her backwards down the alley into the square where the firemen's truck was parked. By now she was amenable, tired perhaps. The fire engine drove off. Then the hospital telephoned that they wouldn't drive a foreign national to Marrakech in the private ambulance unless one of us came too, for fear that she would sue them. Wal was exhausted, so I would have to go.

Before the ambulance set off, the psychiatrist sat in the back with Zoë and persuaded her to drink a little yoghurt. According to Hicham, she had hardly eaten or slept for seven days.

The ambulance arrived in Marrakech at midnight. The hospital director, a friend of the British consul was waiting on the steps. (Wal had phoned the British consul who had arranged for his friend to meet us.) The hospital looked clean. Zoë let me kiss her cheek but would not speak to me. When I asked to see where she was sleeping the psychiatrist refused; she'd been given an injection. Dr Ghazouan, a self-confident person with tiny hands, spoke perfect French.

I got back to Essaouira at three with tummy cramps (dysentery I reckon from tap water Zoë had poured into the whisky glasses on our first night). I had to crawl on all fours up the three flights to the bedroom in the dark.

The next morning, in the taxi to Marrakech, we discussed our responsibility towards our mad daughter; we were frightened and unsure what we should do. Marrakech was full with Easter tourists. We tried many hotels and landed up in something modern, inexpensive, not too far from the hospital.

That afternoon, we were let though locked glass ward doors into a dirty, paper-strewn patio garden. Round the walls were the barred windows of cells or patients' rooms. Zoë, calmer from the narcoleptic drugs, was still not speaking much sense. She hugged and kissed us both. She told me I was beautiful, made me take off my glasses and insisted that I sit upright and not move. When we told her she couldn't leave with us she became abusive. "If I have to stay here so do you. Why me and not you? If you locked me up, you can fuck off."

Wal said: "you'll have to stay at least a week." She burst into tears with what seemed to be the first realisation that her own breakdown had put her in hospital. We hugged. She said, "OK. I will stay." She massaged my hand; I massaged her foot. The horror lifted. She began to ask about other people, Hicham and her siblings. We had been told we could stay for ten minutes but we passed an hour and a half chatting until the nurse told us to leave.

Wal said, "You're the only one of my children I could imagine accepting to be here." He didn't add that she was the only one who would land herself there.

Zoë, during subsequent visits, harped on her obsession that Wal had sexually abused both her and Tanya. It upset him dreadfully. He couldn't understand my point that wouldn't I, as her Mum, be far guiltier than him as her Dad. We both knew that the origins of Zoë's accusation lay in the disturbed false memories of Margie but that didn't stop the pain for either of us.

During our visits, she insisted that we sit on either side of her. Physically she stayed close, lying in my lap or holding hands. The male nurse pocketed the cigarettes I had bought for her.

I wrote:

The chief psychiatrist whom we saw after the visit was courteous and friendly but vague. Zoë was speaking with her tongue behind her teeth, the words came out in a frothy lisp. "I'm sthpeaking like nana." She copied my mother's lisp.

The nightmare is maybe we could have avoided the hospitalisation if Zoë had taken the tranquillizers prescribed in Essaouira. Were the hotel staff right to prevent us seeing her after she had attacked us both on Saturday?

Poor little Zoë. Please come to your senses and let's leave this place.

Going through Zoë's papers. So sad. Cards from friends. Little Post It notes with babyish messages. Some one had given her a list of requirements for marriage in Morocco, a translation of the birth certificate and the father's permission were amongst them.

Will the hospital regime be too severe to allow her to recover her wits? I am in a panic that confinement will make her madder. Will she be able to stick it for seven days and not go crazier? Would we have coped better had we been stronger people?

My first angry reactions of hurt pride at our spoilt holiday were completely subsumed by pity for the state that she was in. She had tried to welcome us, ill as she was, and had been incensed by our frosty reaction. But her erratic behaviour confused and overwhelmed us.

218

Ben rang last night warm and sympathetic and eager to help. The support of the children is wonderful. We are still a family when a crisis happens.

We bought Zoë 3 dozen roses in a clay pot. We sat in the dirty little patio outside the locked ward. She acted crazy. We agreed to pray together our individual prayers. Zoë began to rant. She became angry but you could see the effect of the drugs. "You are not listening to me," she said and smashed the clay pot. She had given away the roses to the other patients.

Then she began clapping and improvising a rap. The song must have gone on for 30 or 40 minutes. I hated it. She brought in family members, "I've beena naughty girl," "mama Dorothee, and papa Walter Schwarz." Lots of new agery, "Bring on global peace." Wal was much better adjusted to the situation. He enjoyed the song for its own sake, admiring its skill and inventiveness but after nearly an hour, we sensed her anger growing. Wal went off to find the doctor. Zoë stopped the rap.

"Have you still got your sense of humour, Zoë?"

She laughed and said that a different part of her brain switched on. She was acting and talking normally. How can she reconstruct a version of the last eight or nine weeks that she can live with?

Wal and I are grating on one another. My fault? His fault? Neither probably. He fusses, is slow in his reactions. I am sharp and quick but spiky in mine. I hope that we will manage not to quarrel. The kids' support continues to be something wonderful.

Fredy, or a psychiatrist friend of hers, will call the hospital tomorrow. We want to get some sort of information on WHAT is wrong. I hope that Ghazouan won't think we are checking up on him. But we are - this IS the hidden agenda. What else can we do?

219

After she had spent a few days in the hospital, we regained some hope. The honorary consul, who in spite of Zoë telling him several times that, "my father abused my sister for twenty years," bowed to us and said "every family has its problems." He acted to help us in every way and sent us to a fellow business man, his friend, the manager of Air Maroc, who stroked his Hercules Poiret moustache, while examining Zoë's worthless expired ticket and our non-transferable economy flight tickets. We explained that our daughter had fallen in love with an unsuitable man. Whether it was a question of honour or not, he bypassed the rules and revalidated our three tickets for the following Thursday. Our task now was to persuade the hospital to release her in time for the flight.

On our visits, Zoë bragged about her exploits in Essaouira. She believed she was healing horses on the beach. She seemed reconciled to not seeing Hicham. At first she pushed aside the fruit and watch we had brought. "You are trying to ease your conscience." Later she accepted the watch but the nurses would not allow her to wear it, in case other patients became jealous. She had the humiliation of having it taken off from her wrist to be returned when she left. (She was wearing it when she jumped in front of the train at Marks Tey.)

Thursday. We have been here a week. Yesterday morning we managed to have sex (just). It does help. So now it is only a question of whether Zoë is SANE enough to remain quietly in that hospital for seven more days. Sometimes I think she is. Sometimes I think she won't. I am scared waiting to see her later today, If she makes the same progress today that she made earlier in the week, this panic will have been needless.

My stomach bug that gave me such cramps for four days has finally evacuated itself. May it rot!

We took Zoë yoghurt yesterday and asked nurse for a spoon. "We don't have spoons here." Oh the irrationality of institutions. Zoë ate half the yoghurt using a jagged shard of the rose pot that she'd smashed the previous day. Lost a lot of weight but in proportion. If her expression were less peculiar she'd look beautiful. She talked at length about Wal's 70th on the 20th May. Does this chitchat have a purpose? My primary emotion is pity spiked with daggers of rage. She is still so megalomaniac. Ugly sound bites. "My brain is like a vast computer." "I am super intelligent." "I understand everything that is going on in Morocco." "My writing will become famous."

Waiting.

The following day she seemed better still. She was in a curious state regarding Hussein, one of the male nurses, whom she accused of stealing her knickers. She began to walk down the corridor to the glass exit doors. Hussein called her back. She walked backwards towards him, facing the front. "See a robot."

The incident with Hussein, I couldn't know what the truth was. Maybe Hussein was a creep abusing his power. We'd seen him pocket the cigarettes we bought her.

She spoke of releasing a primal scream in Essaouira but never mentioned her physical attacks on the staff or us. She began to ask WHO had called the ambulance. I didn't know whether to tell her that it had been all of us. She had written a letter to Hicham. We decided that we would give it him but read it first. I had no qualms about reading their letters to one another in case either of them was planning anything wild. Both of them wrote babyish letters; Hicham's full of spelling errors, Zoë's full of childish drawings of heart and flowers, pathetic to read.

We advised Zoë to be strong and use her spirituality to keep calm. She seemed to agree. She sent me to the chemist to buy her sanitary towels. When I returned the nurses had sent her back to the locked ward. I had to hand the sanitary towels through the barred window. We could not kiss through the bars.

Friday 21st

Wal and I disagree on whether we should bring up her attacks on us. I want to keep it smoothed over; Wal wants her to admit them. After an hour of bitter wrangling, we agree to only mention them if she does. No one has told us what would be the best way to behave with her. We will try to keep her energy fixed on the future.

Fredy has phoned. Her colleague says the hospital is giving the standard drugs for a psychotic episode. So relieved.

In the rubbish-strewn garden, a lunatic in a locked barred room kept begging for cigarettes and coffee. We gave her one and she howled incessantly for more.

At 9 am Hicham, growing a wispy beard and wearing a floral shirt, arrives at our hotel. He denies taking Zoë out of the hospital in Essaouira. He says nothing of the future. Takes no apparent responsibility for anything that happened. He acts passively, first saying that he would go to the hospital and try and see her and then agrees he won't go, he'd write to her telling her she must go home. I have no idea whether or not to believe him.

We were unfair to Hicham. Nothing like this had ever happened to him before. He had fewer resources than we did to cope. He never asked for or took any money from Zoë or us. We emailed him, the day after her death and he replied, asking us to throw a rose in her grave. Would we please send him a photograph? We did but we've never heard from him since.

Some encouraging signs. Ghazouan says she will not need to be hospitalised on arrival in UK. Discouraging signs. He has not said whether he will release her in time for our flight on April 27th.

The 11 o'clock sun is hot without being unbearable. I sit in the ugly concrete enclosure of the pool and swim listlessly twenty lengths each morning. Neither of us have the heart to follow Zoë's instructions and visit the sites of Marrakech.

We are both reading a lot to fill in time between the daily visits.

Panic, fear lump in my chest. We both said independently that if Zoë refuses to board the plane we would fly off without her. Will we?

Friday evening

The best visit yet. Zoë looked frosty but spoke coherently. We were allowed to sit in the hospital grounds, orange trees and hibiscus at the front, a wilderness relieved with clumps of bamboo at the rear, hot sun in a furious blue sky. I rubbed an orange leaf between my palms and gave one to Zoë. She says that if she is in hospital then we should be too. My tactic was to try and bolster her up, which didn't work until the end when I hugged her and said her bravery was an example to us, which it is.

On our arrival we encountered petty spite from one of the female nurses, who would not let Zoë come through the locked glass door because it was five minutes to three. Zoë had the humiliation of staring at us through the locked door.

She rifled through the clothes, which we had brought her with great irritability. We were to read the journal she had been keeping in hospital. The handwriting was legible a great contrast from the big notebook of Essaouira. The contents were mixed, New Age physics, psychobabble and saccharine letters to her family. Not us. Weird statements, "If anyone harms Tanya I will kill them."

But oh, the relief to see her irritable, boring but almost normal.

Our daily chat with the psychiatrist went well. It seems that our bill will be minimal. Zoë won't like that. She is already fantasising "my important family" and "the rich people who are patients here." And so on.

I am so sorry for her threadbare dreams, her leaking illusions, and the lack of a future.

The young Schwarzes have sent us messages but they are all busy with their own lives and so many jobs. Both Tanya and Ben have offered to come to Morocco if necessary.

Oh, Zoë, Zoë, Zo. My final hug with her was partly sincere and partly manipulative. How brave you are, how we admire you. I will say or do anything to have you on next Thursday's flight. She complains that I act too worried.

As the narcoleptic drugs taking her down from the manic state took hold, Zoë's conversation became less disjointed. She insisted in trying to salvage some of the holiday plans she'd made for us; we must visit a magical spot where she and Hicham had plighted their troth.

We found the Mennora Gardens unmemorable, an olive grove with industrially planted rows of trees surrounding a large modern water tank bordered with cement walls. Busloads of tourists and carriages with ponies. A tame, unlovely spot. What pathos that Zo had found it a nirvana of beauty!

We walked into the Medina, passed booths selling oriental tat and Hong Kong plastics to find the hotel Amal where Zoë and Wal had stayed in October. Interior courtyard blue-tiled with rooms opening onto the courtyard. A 19th version of walled houses with no exterior windows. The two owners, Mustapha and Mohamed, like extras in a Kasbah film, smoothed their moustaches and brought us mint tea. They spoke well of Zoë; had seen no signs of illness, when she had stayed in February. That was her room, over there, bordering the courtyard.

Maybe if today she is still calm my uncertainties will vanish. How can you hold two opposing views at once? I am so angry that I want to hit her; I am so full of pity that I want to make sacrifices for her. She isn't nice though. Accusing Wal yesterday, "You are goggling at that girl" Wal had simply said, "Hello," pleasantly to a young female patient. Wal told her off sharply and she changed tack; her talk was full of dykes, wankers, motherfuckers, etc. He found it distasteful.

Pray for this afternoon. It must be all right. Zoë was much calmer on Sunday afternoon. But after one hour she picked a quarrel with me over her hair and said she was going back to the locked ward. Wal explained it by saying that Zoë could not bear the tension of all that has happened and semi-consciously brought the visit to a shorter end. She is exhausted.

We had a bitter discussion in our room. Wal thinks that if she wants to tear apart the family with her wild sexual accusations, then he wants to cancel his party. I am trying to tell him that Zoë is sick and so doesn't seem to be a very nice person but he can't stop thinking about himself.

By Monday Zoë had been in the hospital for eight days. Our flight home was Thursday. The director insisted that Zoë be driven straight from the hospital to the airport. He wasn't going to have her loose in Morocco for one second. He was watching his back.

Hicham turned up at the hotel. Hard to understand how Zoë could consider him as the love of her life, he looked so limp, so unappealing.

She gave us her hospital journal to read, a mixture of cloying sentimentality, New Age wobbly psychobabble and some strange angry messages.

I wrote in the diary that day: *a nasty experience to read what she wrote which did not match the verbose affectionate behaviour during most of our visits. The drugs semi-stun her.*

Wal and I back on course as a unit. The divisions of the last 24 hours have evaporated. Nice message from Hab and Tanya nothing from Ben, Zac or Fredy.

Zoë's cloying messages to Zac in her journal, where she calls him the most marvellous person she has ever met. As she is acting now I don't see how Wal and I can cope. She has this urge to control us. Wal is drained after each visit and can hardly bear to speak. Oh, why is she so ghastly? She makes me take off my glasses and sit bolt upright and not move. It is so creepy but I humour her. What's our responsibility in creating this raving egomaniac? But much of what she said was touching, poignant and sensible. She believes Buddhists have "no blame, no shame." But what is this mania for insisting that I am like a stuck record?

The ants: sitting with Zoë on the low wall outside the hospital, we watched a dozen ants carry a Pringles the whole length of the wall- 15 metres - to vanish with it down some nest. It seemed a symbol but of what?

<u>Zoë on Tuesday</u>

In 48 hours if nothing goes wrong we will be home. She was MUCH better today. Very slim, her hair in a French pleat. She was so calm and said, "Sorry I've been a bit short."

Wal and me have managed nine visits and not confronted her once. It is probably the hardest thing that we have ever done jointly. But each day she has been calmer. Today she seemed less doped up. The little doctor doesn't want closer contact with us. Refused our dinner invitation for Wednesday night

Wal isn't at his best. He is still stunned by Zoë's accusations.

226

I am full of fear. Wal is being very supportive. In the hospital garden the birds utter lovely songs. Zoë has been asking childish riddles. "What does the dog's bark say?" Her self-esteem must be in tatters.

A long email from Tanya describing in vivid prose the thrill of rock climbing. She is also in love. I pray that the sight of her in love won't exacerbate Zoë's pathological rage. [This was so unjust of me. When Zoë met Niall at Greenacres she was delighted for her sister. Envy was never a part of Zo's makeup.] *Rory sent a comforting message. Zoë's malady is more likely brain chemistry awry than psychological disturbance. She is probably the least neurotic of all your children. No, she isn't, Zac is.*

What have we done to deserve such a darling boy! He telephones to say that he hasn't done any studying and wants to go to London the next day after we're home. Arthur the parrot has turned out to be a hen. Both dogs and Merlin the cat follow him wherever he goes. He is probably nervous about meeting Zoë.

We never tried to influence Ghazouan, the psychiatrist's, refusal to let Hicham be admitted to see her. I regret that now. She had such a short time left to love him. Everyone in Morocco had treated us with courtesy and kindness. Only Hicham reacted with the same dreary, wet politeness he had shown from our first meeting.

What she wrote in the "mad" diary and in the hospital notebook, an exercise book that I had given her, shows her mind fighting against itself, trying with desperation to cling on; so many of her perceptions were acute, so many of her opinions wacky:

From an unsent email in the "mad" diary:

... small price to pay for the exploitation of Morocco by France and others. Like Dad says, a few extra dirhams are nothing to us but a lot to the locals. I think it can be vulgar for affluent tourists to over-barter or always insist on local prices. E.g.: if I buy yoghurt on my own, I'll pay 7 dirhams

227

for it. If H is with me, and he's paying, he'll get it for 2 dirhams.

...You can to a certain extent create your own existence in the midst of chaos. You can be surrounded by hysteria and fear but keep the oasis in your heart.

I have never seen my kids in a man's eyes. When Hicham's eyes twinkle with the sweetness of his soul I know that our kids would be blessed to have him as a father. I see children who are tough, free and very protected I hear them laughing and running about.

Some people might think that a woman with my load of a past would not go for someone like Hicham. But for me all the privileges of my life are - wonderful as they are - secondary to my need for personal peace (and GOD.)

I love Hicham because he is my piece of Goodness. He is graceful, creative and completely child-like. He also has the quietude of people who are very intelligent and not full of themselves. He is always joking and can talk about the most serious/powerful stuff without being serious or tedious.

The last time I felt this good with another living being is when Dad and I spent an evening listening to music shortly after Tigger's death.

Hicham sees me like Tigger did.

He adores me - he also thinks I'm a bit of a clot (my Western stress levels, my pomposity and babble) and I feel totally at ease and relaxed when he is around.

You are right, Mum, about God shining out of your lover's ass! But in Hicham's case God shines out of his eyes.

She wrote page after page in similar vein. To us, he seemed a gentle, shy boy with a nervous manner and a sweet smile. Maybe he was what she thought he was; we shall never know. She endowed him with marvellous qualities. But this wasn't a message she ever sent.

228

For Zoë and Hicham:

Hicham is nothing like my previous boy friends. He is perfect for me.

He is immaculate with my money. We live both of us cheaper than on my personal budget because he gets the prices and has got me off drugs. He has never taken a penny for himself.

But if I had to sum up why I love him it is because he is dripping with every pore of his body, mind and soul with what Mum calls divine fire.

.... I believe that he is strong enough to help me with my demons and not be like Grandpa with Nana. That he is as - if not more intelligent than me - which is fucking liberating I can tell you. He shares my faith/world view - loves God like I do. That he is a sweet genuine man and that he is trying his very best to understand this woman from another planet who's taken his heart.

Private for Zoë: the most extraordinary, creative and tender lover which was always my dream and I never had it even with Francis. On our first night in E he told me: "Tu es mon premier amour mais je n'ai pas beaucoup d'expérience." My heart melted and 24 hours later when I told him how happy I was he said, "Oui, je sais. Tu es mon professeur." Not like a disciple in front of his Goddess but with a wicked grin on his face.

Question is: can we unite the best of both our heritages and overcome the crap and all the technicalities. We believe so. But then of course we do because we are very, very deeply in love. Time will reveal if we can build a life and family together.

Tonight I smashed a couple of glasses in our hotel room and Hicham's response was to crack a marble slate. Empathy? Childishness?

229

There is nothing I find 'crazy' in the above, nor the passage following which was written in legible writing:

My biggest achievements have always been based on instinct. E.g. going back to uni not fully recovered from my breakdown which led to my getting a Distinction at LSE postgraduate school. Leaving a well-paid city job which led to my going to UR and being instructed in setting up and running a company... I am trusting my instinct again. It was the right time to leave UR and the UK. I am coming back at the right time...

But then her writing grows wilder and wilder and the sentiments angrier and angrier and she returns to this obsession of sexual abuse.

Keep quiet, eh? Little kids are little fucks, eh? Little kids can't speak for themselves often. Big ones can and I urge you to go fuck yourselves.

Go to hell.

And burn there until you are cleansed of your evil and deserve to be even considered for purgatory.

I feel guilty and responsible for the real pain willed into my foot for letting Zugi go. For torture of our minds... Cannot scream. Cannot cry. Can wallow in self-pity.

And then she wrote a short passage, centred in the middle of the page with its chilling foretaste of self-harm.

The hardest decision to commit to can give you real freedom.

I want to split.

I feel that I can do more good by not being. That in missing me and remembering me my inactive, chilled friends will be catalysed /galvanised into Positive Action...

I am hurting myself daily. Abusing my body with dope and cigarettes and peace *of mind is infected by paranoia, rage and neglect.*

Why?

I was raped.

How? By whom? When?

Why do the children cry?

Why when there are so many of us are there people still alone?

Our fear is that if we allow ourselves (myself) to be fulfilled we will be threatening. But on the contrary; if we are fulfilled and strong, we can discern and withstand bad from good.

I am afraid of being too attractive because being attractive attracts bad as well as good and I don't feel strong enough to withstand abuse.

I am abused and broke since a long time ago.

"I was abused and broke since a long time ago." My poor Zoë. By leaving us we have been stopped from asking you what you meant. And after writing such terror and horror, your mood lifts and you write a hymn of happiness about marrying Hicham. In French, too.

Jeudi 17 fevrier

Maman, papa et Mylène vont donner la bénédiction Hicham et Zoë arrange tout pendant le mois 2 et 3 comme il faut à sa place pour la security d'Hicham, Zouarah et leur enfants pour le mariage comme il faut, avec les 4 parents d'accord.

[Thursday 17 February. Mum, Dad and Mylène will give the blessing while Hicham and Zoë get everything ready as it should be for the marriage of Hicham and Zouarah and their children with the consent of the four parents.]

Poème de Zouarah pour Hicham

Probabilite renverse

1/billion devient 1/1

A Marrakech mon coeur est vrai/pure

Mon amour/amoureux est a Marrakech

Il est à Marrakech depuis longtemps

Dieu m'a mené à Marrakech pour m'emmener à lui et renversé la probabilté

Against all odds

One in a billion becomes one on one

In Marrakech my heart is true

My love is in Marrakech

He has been in Marrakech for a long time

God led me to Marrakech to bring me to him against all the odds

And on the middle pages of the "mad" diary, I read the following lines, circled ; the most heartbreaking of anything Zoë wrote in that book, as if she suddenly saw reality..

> *I want to go home.*

> *I don't know if I'm in a bed with my future husband, having a fabulous tender affair, or a rather sordid affair with this little seaside town sniggering because a local's having it off with a sexy tourist.*

> *We haven't had sex. I couldn't bring myself to do it.*

And then from another unsent email:

He is sleeping as I write. We wait for each other with patience and we share our tenderness and passion every moment.

I am so grateful to Florence for teaching me so much and I feel like the luckiest woman in the world to be the daughter of Walter and Dorothy and beloved of Hicham.

The next pages are full of disjointed notes and scribbling and suggest Zoë was stoned. But then the writing normalises and she writes:

.... I have explained to Hicham that my parents work hard and live well but relatively simply and that that is how I want to live. I want to make enough money to enable my parents to stop subsidising my glamorous "poverty" and have enough to secure my kids" future and share with my family, friends and deserving causes. Hicham thinks like this too.

In the notebook which we gave her in the hospital the handwriting varied, some childish, some neat, some wild. Much of what she wrote was gibberish. The narcoleptic drugs made her shaky, as her ideas and moods flowed and swung between perception and fantasy.

[Notes in very neat writing]

Where is our Spine?

Who loves this country?

Who makes "important" decisions?

Nobody starves; but approx 1/3 smothered/crushed

1/3 brave people who keep on trying

The land is generous and there is much beauty here; but corruption bribes and threats are common.

Leadership, such as it is not clearly visible.'

I love U

evolve-ing

evolution

How deep is Our Love?

Cannot define Love

Only spelt backwards it reveals the spirit of evolution

I love myself and the invisible. I know who my parents are:

Walter Schwarz - brilliant mind, His message is tolerance

Dorothy née Morgan (stein) - a great, fragile, weak and bewitching beauty

afraid of her own shadow - why?

Why do some starve while others metaphorically or literally wank over everything? Fear and sado-masochism are addictive. Freedom (after repentance and acceptance) is as simple as making a cup of tea:

With honesty and goodwill, tell yourself: I did: y, z, etc.

I am sorry. I understand how a bad action grows stronger: ripple effect. But if the originator evolves to better understanding, the sin is not only forgiven, it is also atoned for with patience:

God (or whatever you like to call it) grants a delay,

But never forgets.

All hail DOROTHY ..... I love she

Mum still whinges the same old stuck records, thinking superficially that she is being ever so clever. Remember, for fuck's sake the story of the horse with a pebble in its foot; and try even ONCE! Not to evade the issue by cowering behind a stream of words and alternating concepts.

234

Amongst all of this, Zoë wrote little memos to us and herself.

23/04/2000

The good doctor (Raswani) says: (I saw him this morning) straight from here (hospital) to airport. I will be ready; just right. We will have time to DISCREETLY thank hospital staff, and patients & bid farewell to all.

In England Dr Rasor* will follow my medical treatment till prescribed course finished. He is not in favour of psychotherapy during his prescribed medical treatment

* Raswani will write a report for Rasor using international medical coded language.

After comparatively sensible memos to us or herself, her words spiral again out of control and conventional meaning. Almost the last thing Zoë wrote in that exercise book was the following. Once back to UK she wrote almost nothing again.

My name is Zoë Sarojini Schwarz. I have been called all sorts of weird and wonderful names by those who know me well and those that don't ....

Whore/Tart/Saint/Beloved/ evil, etc.....

I wear them all with pride

I have a good feeling

Where I came from

Where I am going, etc.

I LOVE HICHAM

He is torn away from me

Have no fear, my love

We shall meet again

'cos THEY ha bloody ha..... cannot break the BONDS of LOVE

As Tom Grant put it: "Grand master(s) of instant bullshit"

The next generation (us too) cannot be BULLSHITTED around.

When the exercise book was full of writing on one side of the page, Zoë turned it over and wrote a series of messages for her family from the other end. They are full of hysterical affection.

She writes:

Zac = God has witnessed

All hail to the bestest, toughest, kindest and beautifullest human I ever had the privilege to know. Now, soon, we meet again and if manners allowed it, I would prostrate myself before Zac at the airport.

And what she wrote about Tanya was chilling. With part of her mind she believed Tanya had been raped or harmed, yet in other parts of her mind she knew this was not so.

Whosoever ever dares to hurt or even think of hurting Tanya will be accountable to I, and I may not be responsible for my actions. God will judge harshly <u>anyone</u> who hurts our Russian beauty because they don't make "em like Tanya anymore. Tall, perfect skin, her back symbolises victory and her beautiful long fingers and duck- like feet are perfect.

Tanya took 2 blows more. Now, NO blows for Tanya ever. Otherwise I will be like Phulan Devi, and I, Zoë, will kill in Tanya's name. No More blows for Tanya

You have all been warned!

And for Hicham she writes: *The tears of Allah. Hicham, my angel 'pon de earth. Walk tall. Walk how you will my love I cannot bear to look at the stars anymore because my star is ripped away from eye "n" I. Hi Cham : No-one has ever loved me like he did, and still does. When two people are already in love, the VILE OBSTACLES thrown in our path simply make our love stronger.*

During our visits to the hospital Zoë kept talking about Wal's 70th Birthday, handing me a list of thirty of her friends to be invited, seeming unable to understand that it was Wal and Tanya's joint party not hers.

I wrote the day before she was due to be released:

We intend to give the hospital a donation. The fees are £60 so £150. White magic thinking. If we are generous then Fate will be generous. I must remember that if I am gloomy now, wasn't I gloomy before Zoë went crazy? I must learn from this. Perhaps Wal and I can grow closer together. I hope so. I don't want to become some embittered old woman griping about past complaints and present woes.

On the penultimate visit to hospital on Wednesday, we found Zoë agitated. An old woman, a patient for twenty years, had hit her round the face. Zoë wanted to be let out to spend her last night in Morocco with us. The director wouldn't hear of it, He had arranged for the Honorary British consul to drive us to the airport at noon on Thursday. We worried that Zoë would not accept that final night in

237

hospital. She did after Ghazouan did his big chief act. We came back to the hotel convinced at last that the departure would take place tomorrow.

Thursday 27th April 2000

A new beginning. 11.15. By 12 noon the British consul is supposed to be at the hotel to drive us to the hospital fetch Zoë and drive to the airport. At 2pm we are supposed to fly to Stansted. Both of us fearful and nervous. Wal is tense and jumpy but he has done all the errands. The hotel bill 2300 dirhams only 800 for Zoë's stay in hospital and we have given them a gift of 3000. 2000d. for a present.

You feel your heart and your breath will stop with the tension of departure but it doesn't. My love for the sun is lessened but I still love it. The bringer of life and its destroyer. The endless need to make patterns and to mythologize. The details, which reveal what is happening and the details, that conceal it. What does it mean that he would rather spend his last moments reading the paper and drinking beer than with me?

Yes, the consul arrived promptly at 12. We found Hicham waiting outside the hospital gates: he'd shaved off the beard but wore the same shirt. Consul sent him away gently. He made a semicircle and returned. The consul spoke angrily to him in Arabic. He disappeared.

Zoë was tense, irritable, nervous and loving by turns. Consul whisked us through immigration and stayed an hour drinking beer with Wal. He must have been pleased we were going, although he never showed the least impatience. He said he'd visit on his next visit to UK but he never did.

In the departure lounge Zoë kept walking up and down, restlessly, telling me she loved me then saying "shut up". We dreaded she might make a scene and we would be taken off the plane before takeoff. But apart from her refusing to let us speak and going to the loo every few minutes, nothing untoward happened.

Zac had brought the car and was waiting at Stansted. We were home.

After Zoë's death, Louise, the Oxford undergraduate, who had tried to help us during our stay in Essaouira, wrote:

> she made me understand for the first time the power of charisma. Zoë seemed to emanate strength, glamour and excitement. When we met she introduced herself to me, saying "I have been watching you for days and I can see you are a genius and a poet". She was seductive, hypnotic, and all- consuming. For more than a week we were with her ... acting as willing participants in the dramas that were the actualisations of her instincts and imagination. Zoë saw a horse on the beach that she felt was in pain. She was convinced that [her friend] Mohammed was spiritual and religious enough to heal the horse. She made him believe he had the power to heal, and for several days he stood with the horse whilst a congregation of Essaouirian drummers and singers created spiritual songs to aid the healing process, again at Zoë's behest.... Zoë was the director or author of a world that was at once cultish and miraculous, but ultimately too fragile, too raw to survive... My abiding memory is of her dancing to a song by the "Mamas and Papas" which she had included on a compilation tape for her sister's birthday. She was dancing with her lover Isham in a way that I can only describe as ecstatic. She was performing, but she was so happy and in love that I know I was not the only person who had stopped dancing to watch her, and to think of my own comparatively realistic life as passionless and dry in the face of such intensity.

239

CHAPTER NINE

"... behind a glass wall."

Zoë, I've read books about the process of grief; they suggest that survivors talk to or write letters to the dead. How peculiar I used to think.

Your brothers and sisters don't often talk about you to me. Habie says they have not yet processed their grief. Tanya unlike me respects your decision. In the aftermath of your death, several people argued that someone making your choice is not using the sick part of their mind but is making a reasoned decision. You were ambitious and proud, they say and consequently couldn't accept a life which you knew would be haunted by recurrent episodes of mania and depression.

This view I've never accepted. During your last summer, no one managed to shatter the glass walls of your immolation, neither us nor your doctors, your friends, nor you yourself. If you were to return, I'd tell you how we misinterpreted what was happening during those last fourteen weeks of your life.

The last care review for your case was written after your regular Wednesday visits to the hospital. The young psychiatrist nurse noted in your weekly review:

Zoë continues to experience intrusive suicidal thoughts but says she would not act upon them. She is aware intellectually that she has a future but finds it difficult to feel this.

She wrote those words six days before you killed yourself. Do you blame her?

We arrived home from Morocco to find a clean house, a stocked fridge and the animals happy and well. Zac had looked after everything. Janet, the lodger, was her usual self, affectionate and awkward. Zac had changed the parrot's name from Arthur to Artha now that we knew she was female. Zoë seemed pleased to be home.

The next morning we had an appointment with our GP, Paul Rasor. We were kept waiting for thirty minutes. Zoë and I tense. She kept telling me to stop fiddling with my lip, Wal remained apparently calm. We translated for Dr Rasor the letter from Ghazrouan which listed the drugs he'd prescribed and his opinion that Zoë did not need immediate hospitalisation. Rasor agreed and reduced the dose of the anti-psychotic drugs. Overdose, unmentioned word. Zoë was adamant that she wanted to take charge of the drugs instead of me and the doctor agreed. He was to make an urgent appointment for a psychiatrist to see Zoë the following week. Ghazrouan had written the chilling phrase *traitable mais pas guérissable* [treatable but not curable]. I pushed this prognosis out of my mind. Of course she would be cured. Zoë must have overheard or read this life sentence.

The first complete day at home passed, surreal and uncomfortable. Zoë kept repeating that she was too old to be living with her parents and then say the opposite -she'd stay for the summer and bring Hicham over. She repeated grandiloquent ideas about them living in Brazil, without acknowledging that neither of them speaks Portuguese.

Her behaviour exasperated me. What money would she live on? She had £451 left over from the £2000 we'd given her for her piano. She wanted the whole sum at once. We said "No". After some discussion, we agreed on £60 cash and £100 a week. For years we'd complained about Zoë's irresponsibility with money. (One of the symptoms of bi-polar illness is during manic phases both reckless spending and a readiness to run up excessive debts.)

We asked the DHSS to give her a disability allowance. They granted £48 a week. I sensed that she resented our asking for the allowance, and disliked being qualified for it.

In her hospital notebook in Marrakech, Zoë had written eulogies to her little brother. She "adored" Zac. The only reason she was consenting to return to England was to see him. Once we were home, in spite of his love, Zac couldn't cope. The reality of a mentally sick sister overwhelmed him. He wouldn't stay at Greenacres and left for London on Friday evening. He masked his pain with brusque remarks. I felt bitter that Zoë's manic behaviour had effectively driven him away.

Just before she died, she took down the four photographs of him from her bedroom wall. We found them stacked against the wall. When had she done this? Was she disappointed at his cool reception or could she not bear to plan a suicide under his smiling gaze?

On her first weekend back from Morocco, Sarah and Kelly arrived as soon as they could. Mylène was abroad. Both girls' careers were going ahead: Sarah had accepted a teaching post in an American college; she and Kon were to marry in the autumn; Kelly was curator of the Stephen Lawrence art gallery in Woolwich. A humiliation for Zo to have nothing similar in prospect. Unlike the pages of her regular diaries, full of references to them, in the pages of what we called the 'mad" diary, Zoë rarely mentions Sarah and Kelly and has only a few references to Mylène, who'd had a vague plan to visit Morocco. Sarah and Kelly would have criticised her erratic behaviour in Essaouira so maybe she pushed them out of her conscious mind.

The three young women spent Friday evening closeted in Zoë's room. Next day, after they'd gone, Zoë said that they'd told her to behave with more equilibrium towards us. "If they say so they must be right." Zoë and I had an acrimonious discussion whether her pills moved her mood up or down. My obstinate denial of Zoë's condition operated strongly at that time: how can she be so ill, I reasoned, when she has such close, loving friends?

I wrote in my diary: *I think that we must move somewhere smaller and soon. Is Zoë chemically or psychologically mad? What does it all mean? Is she a calculating, lazy person or someone crying out for help? With such a lack of humility and gratitude how can we help her?*

An email arrived from Alexandra, the German girl, who was reportedly raped in Essaouira, the incident that is supposed to have sent Zoë over the edge. She grew excited and voluble and kept harping on the rape. Its details emerged: Alexandra had stopped penetration by jerking the guy off. Zoë and Hicham had taken photos of Alexandra's bruised neck. "They're secure. Locked up in a safe in Essaouira."

Wal said, "If penetration didn't happen, it isn't rape but attempted rape." Zoë shouted, "Are you calling me a liar?" And slammed out of the room. I told Wal, "Stop being so pedantic!" He and I quarrelled over whether an attempted rape was a true rape. A row with a hidden agenda; desperate for her to return to reality, he wouldn't connive with her fantasies; I was trying to avoid confrontation.

Next day, Zoë crayoned a babyish message decorated with hearts and flowers saying, "Sorry, Dad."

A few days later, we were sitting by the swimming pool and Zoë referred to one of the worst incidents in Essaouira. "I released a primal scream," she said, "and now it's over."

"That doesn't matter anymore," I said. We changed the subject (too painful to speak of) avoiding her accusations of rape and incest, her violence against us in the Hotel des Ramparts - as if we could poultice an abscess without draining the pus.

I wrote a week later: *none of her siblings have phoned her. She writes and rings Hicham. Her life is as empty as a muddy pond.*

The parrot goes from strength to strength.

But Zoë did make strenuous efforts to be her old self. My friends remarked how she would always ask after their kids and their concerns and show some of the empathy she'd been so admired for. A few days before she died she visited Janet in hospital for an operation. Janet later told me how Zoë had only asked questions and wouldn't speak about herself.

Towards me, after her initial bout of affection, she became more and more distant and irritable. I brought little presents back from the supermarket, mangoes, her favourite fruit, orange juice, her favourite drink, a beach towel. She'd accept them with a hostile "Thanks," and go back into her room.

What I didn't realise at the time was that my exaggerated care of Artha, the young parrot, was a substitute for the care I wanted, but could not, lavish on Zoë.

A week at home, Zoë still zonked with drugs, I deliberately told her Hicham was a fantasy. "At some point you've got to start living in the real world. He'd never fit in here." It was true but I shouldn't have said so. Hicham himself had told me in his pidgin French that he had no desire to live in UK; he'd wanted Zoë to stay in Morocco. I didn't tell her that. She slammed out of the room. A few minutes later she came back, "Let's not quarrel over men." With part of her mind she knew.

After Hicham had phoned her for the third time in two days, I told him. "Please stop phoning. Your calls upset her." My motives were mixed, not wanting Zoë upset but also, a mean-spirited reluctance to pay for her calls. Some years earlier, she had run up a £2000 bill phoning a boyfriend in the States.

Dr Rasor had arranged that the chief psychiatrist from the Lakes, Cahn Vasudevan would pay a home visit. I was away at the Swindon Literary Festival because I'd won a prize. Wal phoned with an account of the ninety-minute meeting. The consultant had sounded optimistic: sad episode in Morocco, possibly pot-induced; she is to be on reduced medicine for two weeks, then a gradual return to real life.

Prospects had brightened.

We didn't realise until after her death and read her hospital notes, that Vasudevan had seen her eight years earlier in her first episode of bi-polar.

At the School of Social Entrepreneurs, Zoë had made friends with a political refugee, a Rwandan lawyer called Fabien. We invited him, his wife Hyacinthe and his two sons and baby for Sunday lunch. The boys behaved like traditionally brought-up African kids, polite and reserved. The five-months-old baby never cried. Hyacinthe had arrived in England as a refugee, having lost mother, sister and most of her relatives, not knowing whether Fabian was alive or dead. He rejoined her after two years apart. A couple of times during the day she stopped reacting to everyone as if she were being sullen, only it wasn't sullenness. Fabien loved playing with the dogs and the parrot. He told us how he used to watch gorillas in Rwanda before the civil war. Zoë drove the two older boys to play tennis at a nearby park. Later that afternoon her friends, Michelle and Jide dropped in - tea on the lawn – children playing - everything almost normal. It was a happy afternoon.

Although the aggression that she'd shown in Morocco disappeared, I stayed wary. Her physical attacks in Morocco had frightened me. Zoë although not tall, was immensely strong. Her irritation melted into a babyish affection and obsessive behaviour. She wrote 'Dorothy, President of the World for Love' and pinned the paper up in my bedroom. When we went shopping together in

245

Colchester she insisted on shaking everyone's hand in the shops and startling customers with anecdotes about daily life in Morocco.

My diary entry read: *Zoë still full of I love you's but I doubt that we can ever trust her again.*

It does not look as hopeless for Zoë as it did in Morocco.

For those first couple of weeks, Zoë was able to join in our mundane daily activities: looking after pets, shopping, gardening, friends and local theatre visits; we felt optimistic, although Janet, upset by Zoë's brusque behaviour, would no longer eat her evening meal with us. Zac wouldn't come home regularly.

Tanya arrived from Jo'burg for a short break bringing her new man Niall - his first family visit. He was a big fellow in every sense of the word and clearly adored her. Zoë in spite of being on the threshold of depression was thrilled that her big sister had finally found the love of her life. She praised Niall so extravagantly that Tanya grew embarrassed.

We asked our family and friends for their memories after her death and Niall emailed: *we shared a sunset, sitting amongst the buttercups in the field at Greenacres in May - the weekend before Walter's 70th birthday party. The sun had been shining all day and we decided to watch it drift below the horizon. Initially just Tanya and I, and then Zoe joined us. The horses were wandering around the field minding their own business, as we sat quietly together. I remember Zoë's deep smile. She'd grin, and bubble with life for a brief moment when we hit on something funny. Her eyes were deep too, dark and mysterious. I sensed energy, and conflict, and fear, and power, and capability, and humanity. I can't remember what we discussed really. She spoke of the beach in Morocco. But she didn't have to speak much to say something.*

In those early weeks, she seemed a little better each day but still smarmy, repeating, "I love you, I love you," and then snappy. Her rapid mood swings made me edgy. She gave me amazing back massages. I'd been worried that once back home Zoë might attack Artha as she had done the receptionist in the hotel. But Zoë enjoyed playing with the young parrot before depression stifled her.

An ecology centre in Edinburgh advertised for an assistant and Zoë applied. Excited at this sign of progress, I barely acknowledged to myself and certainly not to her that her letter was exaggeratedly phrased and, as you might expect, no interview was offered. It doesn't matter, I said; just relax and wait to get fully better.

Walter's 70th Birthday party took place in May. Zoë had been home a little less than a month. Her depression had started on May 13th, ten days before the party. It was like a blind slowly rolling down. I wasn't worried. Hadn't we been told that depression follows a manic episode? It would only last a couple of weeks – four at the most.

Wal's party was a success, although Wal and I hade not fully recovered from the tense three weeks in Morocco. Zoë didn't help with preparations - just walked about the garden looking sad. Habie decorated the marquee. Diana and I cut bunches of fresh herbs for each table. Wal received an assortment of presents, trekking sticks, whisky, and books. Habie filmed the whole occasion - the last video in which Zoë would ever appear. In one sequence, she is explaining to Simon how to hold the parrot. Her voice is low and she's not smiling. In another, she is sitting close to me. Hab asked everyone present to write a comment in a Birthday Book. Zoë wrote, "Thank you, dad, for your unswerving love and support, Zoë."

The weather was cloudy with no rain. The young cook, Penny Campbell, arrived with plates of starters, melon balls and cheese, ham and figs. It was so stylish.

The whole family had arrived a few days earlier, Ben and Fredy with their three kids. Seventy people, champagne flutes in hand, were listening to Zac's short and funny speech. Wal's reply started OK then rambled; he'd drunk too much champagne. No one minded.

At one point, I asked Penny the cook, 'Notice anything odd about Zoë?

"No," said Penny, 'she's very quiet and beautiful."

But Penny didn't know the old Zoë, a focus of attention and a magnet for the kids. Today, wearing a black shift, she circled the party like an elegant somnambulist with Mylène and Sarah, staying close, unconsciously protecting her.

Peter Marshall, one of the guests, sent us a poem. His view of her death as her destiny was not one that I shared.

> *Zoë*
>
> *...At your father's 70th birthday*
>
> *You greeted me with warmth and care,*
>
> *Making sure that I had food and drink*
>
> *You introduced me to your friends*
>
> *As a friend from Wales*
>
> *But you were a little too polite*
>
> *Too good at playing the perfect hostess.*
>
> *Your beautiful dark eyes*
>
> *Did not engage*
>
> *You were already on your way*
>
> *Leaving us behind.*
>
> *Go well, Zoë, I will remember your grace,*

Your dance and your passion.

(Peter Marshall 16 December 2000, Birthday-
Guest)

A 70th Birthday party is packed with old friends and
relatives. Inda and I had been at school together in the
fifties. She had married John in 1955. Everyone enjoyed the
notion that OUR John Bunyan was a descendant of the
author of *Pilgrims' Progress.* We'd shared celebrations;
they'd been at our wedding in 1956, they'd come to our
Silver Wedding in France. John was looking seedy with a
yellow complexion but as charming as ever. He believed his
bad stomach was the result of giving up smoking. It would
be the last time we saw him. He died of pancreatic cancer
five weeks later.

Once the party was over, bad things started to happen.
We were trying to sell Amigo, the young horse. Zoë showed
no interest in him or where he was to be sold. We missed
these signs of incipient depression. On first returning to
Greenacres, she had shown an interest in the horses and
even gone riding with Penny Johnson who had bought
Wal's mare Kismet.

The day after the party Tanya drove Zoë to the Lakes to
ask for anti-depressants.

The next day I wrote: *Last night she went to bed
early as she always does. I asked Tanya the meaning of her
casual remark that all three girls had problems with men.
The two boys have picked stable seventeen- year olds as
soon as possible and appear to have stuck to them.*

Why, I asked?

You won't like the answer.

Tell me anyway.

Tanya gave a lucid presentation of her mental problems. Our upbringing had been too permissive. There was too much nudity and sexual freedom. It had made her too needy with men and lacking self-confidence.

What she complained off was lack of nurturing. "When I saw how Michael [her ex boyfriend] treated his kids I used to cry. I was never treated like that. Oh, yes, you loved us as infants but we were never allowed to be children. We were treated as adults. I have worked through this with therapists, one in London, one in Jo'burg."

And then she complained that I was not affectionate with my grandchildren.

"If you want intimacy with Ben you have to be more tender to his kids. When Max bounced a ball in the sitting room, you said - Stop that Max - with such ferocity in your voice. If that had been my child I wouldn't have accepted it."

It was true that I have never responded much to children's petty complaints and tears. If they cried I told them to shut up. I encouraged them NOT to cry. I'd always believed this was the result of what had happened to my first child Nicola in Great Ormond Street Children's Hospital. Nicola, placed in a side ward and suffering from meningitis, had screamed for so long without a pause that her vocal chords snapped and she screamed on, her mouth opening and shutting and no sound coming out. I could never stand the sound of children's crying after her death. In spite of that, I believed that our children had had in Winicott's phrase, "good enough mothering." Now that Zoë was so ill for the second time, our beliefs were being challenged.

Wal and I had compensated (some would say over-compensated) for the restricted attitudes of *our* parents by a liberalism that our kids now rejected. Our attitudes were shaped by the sixties, progress, freedom and all that jazz. A major part of our "freedom" being sexual freedom, without exactly having an open marriage, we both had affaires and thought ourselves dashing - extremely liberated. And felt rather smug that we *stayed* married to one another.

Fay Weldon put it well in her memoir, A*uto da Fay:*

If she [her Mum] *had contrived her life more differently wouldn't mine be more emotionally and practically comfortable? All children feel this about their mothers including my own about me. All mothers love their own children as best they can, according to their temperaments and circumstances, and all mothers should have done better, in their children's eyes, when the going gets tough for the children.*

I see now how our behaviour gave out mixed messages. My kids' attitudes were constrained by living in the AIDS generation and by the greater struggle to find and keep a job. Anyone from our generation (I always call us the last generation of women who were supposed to be virgins at marriage) who had been to university, had no difficulty in finding work. Not so for our kids. Zoë loathed the temping jobs she had to take and never seemed to quite know what her attitude to sex was. She could behave with brutal promiscuity in one phase and then advocate and practise celibacy before marriage in another.

After that talk, the first intimate one we'd had for years, Tanya behaved in her usual self-contained manner, busy with electronic messages. She and Niall contacted one another about twelve times a day. Tanya, like the rest of us, was optimistic that Zoë would soon snap out of depression. "Why did you take so much pot?" she asked her.

Zoë continued to be a humble, smarmy zombie. We had no idea whether it was the effect of the drugs or the depression. She changed her mind again and said she wanted to stay home for the summer. No more talk of trying to bring Hicham over. Wal was preparing for a working holiday, a four-week camping trip to France to write an

251

article about eco-villages. We discussed whether Zoë's illness meant he should cancel; we both agreed she would probably be better with just one parent. We were not getting on well anyway.

<u>*Sat May 27th*</u>

I am conscious of how disagreeable I am. He is not conscious of how disagreeable he is because he considers that passive silence has no repercussions.

Tanya left for Jo'burg with lots of luggage. Bridges have been built between us but I still irritate her. Artha continues to be adorable, biting the end of my pen as I write. She says Hi, Artha, and some gurgles. The weather seems to be clearing.

Zoë moping about, "Can I talk about my illness?" What a lack of sympathy I have. She feels "behind a glass wall." "Will I ever get better?"

I keep reassuring her - she doesn't listen.

Wal in France and the children have retreated to their various activities. Zoë keeps wearing the same outfit, torn jeans, a black tee shirt and a brown cashmere cardigan with a hole in the elbow. She complains that the drugs make her sweaty and constipated and manages to look pathetic, resentful, angry and unapproachable all at the same time.

The psychiatrist, Cahn Vasudevan, on weekly, then fortnightly visits, saw Zoë in private. When he left she would walk with him to his car, giving me little chance to speak to him alone. What advice he gave was simple; she can't do much; just ask for a few easy tasks each day; let her rest. He advised not to leave her alone for more than three hours - an unspoken hint that she might harm herself – the unspeakable, the unthinkable. He gave an impression of gentleness, calm and understanding; Zoë was in good hands, we thought.

I had two tickets for Rod Wooden's play in London; Zoë refused to come with me.

Rod Wooden wrote this a few days after her death.

FOR ZOË:

> *Lying awake*
> *I think of you:*
>
> *I am tired*
> *but I am here*
>
> *you are not here*
> *and you are not tired.*

The diary entry written on the train to London expresses my growing panic:

> *Wal rings every day. I'm not very friendly to him. ... Living with someone so depressed is depressing. I cannot imagine how she is feeling. How would other women react? Does Zoë feel the anger that surges up inside me? Sixty-three years old and not in control of my life. What WILL become of her? Are we doing all we can? Is Wal camping for four weeks being practical and spiritual or simply a selfish self-centred bastard?*
>
> *Zoë doesn't DO anything all day long. Just sits and stares with a slightly mad expression in her eyes. The mad look comes from certain rigidity in her stare. The only real smile she gave today was as I was leaving for Rod's play.*

Saturday 10th June.

The summer nights are long and I feel stiff and achey. A long call from Hab full of success for her Holocaust project. [She was doing the PR for a major exhibition] *...Why am I tied to this lump of misery sitting in the end room all day, grey-faced and morose? What efforts she makes or doesn't make, I have not the least idea.*

253

Zoë stopped making noticeable progress as the month wore on. Zac and his girl friend Maria came for the weekend. Maria offered Zoë practical help, offering to tidy up her bedroom. Zoë had a brief intermission. Her depression lifted for about twenty hours. She wrote Zac and Maria a fulsome letter thanking them, she felt better; they were "the world's most marvellous couple."

Janet sidled up to me, while Zac and Maria watched telly, "Can I have a word?"

Zoë had told Janet a few days earlier that she wanted to kill herself on June 29th, Zac's birthday. Janet had persuaded her not to be silly. I brushed Janet's revelation aside. If anything I felt irritated rather than anxious. Why was Zoë trying to worry and upset everyone? Zac, Maria and I had a two-hour talk, Maria implying tactfully that we ought to be more loving towards Zo.

The confusion which I felt over Zoë was shared by her own friends. Kelly, in the middle of a demanding job, came down by train twice for the evening to see Zoë, who didn't want to talk about herself. Kelly believed that since she'd survived her earlier depression eight years before, so she would this one. Mylène invited Zoë for a weekend to the West End flat. Mylène had taken over Zoë's old room. But the weekend wasn't a success. Zoë tried but couldn't communicate and Mylène and Zac were not sorry when she came home. Sarah was away in USA. A couple of other friends visited Greenacres but Zoë was unable to relate to them. Her outward behaviour was morose and unfriendly. She simply looked sulky and the friends went away. Her interior must have been bleeding but none of us could see her fear.

She developed a curious habit of staring. When I came back from shopping and brought her favourite fruit – mangoes, she would barely say thank you. Occasionally, she would ask, "will I get better?" Once she said, "why me?" The four anti-depressants she was taking were having no apparent effect. Her complexion was blotchy. She would sit for hour after hour turning the pages of a magazine but not reading the text. Watchijg her was creepy. But I never dared mention it.

That Thursday in June, I didn't go to the weekly playwrights' meeting at the Mercury Theatre, not wanting to leave Zoë alone for so long.

I wrote: *the longest summer night; the year is turning. I cannot say that Zoë is the root cause of my bitterness. Just so disappointed that the older children don't phone or answer emails. Wal phones every evening, breezy and enjoying his trip. Does he have the least idea what's happening?*

Zoë reiterated for 75 minutes how terrified she is. "I want to know what's going on in my brain?" But she didn't convince me that she can't help herself in any way. She went to bed disappointed. Am I lacking in empathy and compassion?

I felt happier - at least she'd shown some energy in door slamming when she went to bed. That evening, six weeks before her death, was the last time she and I had a real conversation. *I failed her.* She wanted to know *what's going on in my brain.* I was trapped in a rigid circular pattern of ideas that with the help of the medication, she had enough free will to overcome her low self esteem and feelings of worthlessness. Not only was I afraid that Zoë would pull me with her into her depression as she had done years earlier but also, I couldn't see that this brilliant woman was unable to help herself. I couldn't see that at this stage, she *had* no free will.

"Depression is flat, hollow and unendurable. It is also tiresome. People cannot abide being around you when you are depressed. They might think they ought to, and they might even try, but you know and they know that you are tedious beyond belief; you're irritable, paranoid and humourless and critical and demanding and no reassurance is ever enough. You're frightened, and you're frightening,

and 'you're not at all like yourself but will be soon,' but you know you won't."

That was how Kay Redfield Jamison in *The Unquiet Mind* described what Zoë was going through. But I didn't read those words while Zoë was alive.

On his following visit, Vasudevan changed the pills to another "newer drug", the initial effect of which exhausted her. She lay facedown on the grass, hardly eating, not smoking and not speaking.

Between us lay no communication, no warmth.

"Am I mad?" she asked.

"Of course you're not. Mad people never ask that." I look back and shudder at my self-delusion, at my deliberate blindness; I couldn't accept that her behaviour was due to illness; it wasn't simply her refusal to accept reality.

I wrote: *the Zoë scene is deadening. All she wants to do is a sort of Ancient Mariner. Seize someone and talk about her depression. She told the shrink, "My mother is angry she thinks that I am lazy. She just wants me to be better so I can help her do housework."*

This attack delivered in a monotone appalled me. Perhaps some truth in it because you can't get angry at something that is truly preposterous. But I cannot rid my mind of the idea that Zac shares to some extent – that she likes to sit on the bottom of her depression. It is too painful to start to claw her way up. Oh the weight of this woman lying down all day. Tanya [Zoë's aunt, Tanya Morgan]) tells me that a paralysis of the will is sure sign of depression. I must try to be more sympathetic. I am so weary ...

Zac made her weed some paving stones two days ago but since then she has done nothing. Just sits. She watches Neighbours at one o'clock. Is this her depression

256

or a subtle attack on us? I don't know. She keeps flicking over the same pages of Red magazine. It's driving me nuts.

For the first time tonight I miss Wal. Would he be of any comfort? We die alone.

The sun smell of Zoë's room and person. Her wild dark eyes lacking in expression and the way her mouth turns down at the corners when she smiles.

I couldn't understand what was happening. Why I couldn't touch her, when we had been so close. Tanya Morgan never said outright but implied that I was lacking in sympathy. She invited Zoe to London. After a couple of days, Zoë drove herself home and Tanya telephoned me, "I see what you mean. She's impossible to reach."

Wal returned from France and drove Zoë and me to London to see Nana. When she was first put in the old peoples' home by Mickey she had complained bitterly about the demented people sitting in the lounge. Now, two years later, she had become one herself. Zoë sat on a footstool, sweaty and silent, holding her grandmother's hand. Nana noticed nothing wrong. Around them various old women and a few old men gibbered and moaned, one old lady nursing a baby doll. Almost every member of the caring staff was a foreign worker - affectionate and showing patience with their fretful patients. The smell of disinfectant barely masked the smells of urine and old age. The old Zoë would have radiated good heartedness and made everyone smile. This one appeared oblivious to the surroundings. It was the clearest signal since Morocco how ill she was. *We did not register it!*

We tried to continue normal lives, although with hindsight that was a mistake. Wal and I were both incapable of appreciating that Zoë simply could *not* alter her morose behaviour. It seemed against every urge of common sense that this beautiful young woman could *allow* herself to do nothing all day long. I made attempts to cheer her up. "Try and laugh, Zo." She couldn't. "Take the dogs for a walk." She returned within ten minutes. This might be the most telling incident of all. I gave her *The Unquiet Mind* to read, the book that tells how Kaye Redfield Jamison came to terms with bi-polar and continued with her life. A book considered inspiring. Zoë gave it back to me the next day and said coldly, "There you are you see. You never get over it."

A couple of odd and ominous incidents happened around this time. Our family has always loved swimming and sunbathing naked. But we would always be dressed around the house. One morning, Zoë, stark naked, started sweeping the sitting room floor. I said nothing. After half an hour or so she went back into her room and re-emerged dressed in the torn sweater and jeans she had been wearing for days. And she did something similar a few days later, when Wal came back from France. She emptied her wastepaper basket into the dustbins. In the nude. Whatever signal those brief flashes of nakedness were meant to convey we missed them. A brief thought flashed into my mind, "she's gone bonkers." Then I wiped these thoughts from my conscious mind and never told Vasudevan while she was alive. Was she making a plea for help that we couldn't understand, that didn't reach us?

One of my friends, Pauline, who herself had suffered from severe depression after a messy divorce, came to lunch. Her attitude – that Zoë would pull herself out of depression by will power when she was ready - corroborated mine and Florence's, who'd said "Zoë is cunning. She'll get better when she wants to." That was the line most of us took and one that gives us so much regret.

July 5th Wednesday

Pauline brought her parrot to lunch. Artha adored this other African grey. Pauline and Zoë talked for one hour. Pauline insisted to Zoë that, "You must pull yourself off your own lap." I really like that phrase.

My mother's had a heart attack. They moved her to hospital for three days. She's back in the Lady Sarah Cohen home, in her room where she seems much happier.

Wal said: I've got some bad news. I thought that my Mum had died. John Bunyan has pancreatic cancer that has spread to his liver. Then we watched a sexy Ally MacBeal. That's life. In the middle of imminent death you are in the middle of a witty USA sitcom. Zoë stays much the same - a taciturn, closed face. It's so hard to love her. She showed no reaction to the news of John's cancer.

One reason why we did not see the depth of Zoë's growing desperation was that during that period, she made strenuous efforts to sort herself out. Michael Young, the founder of The School of Social Entrepreneurs, was one of Zoë's many admirers. She displayed towards him the ambivalence she often showed towards men. At times she called him "a dirty old man," (he was 84) mostly she admired his work and character. During her illness that summer, Michael Young telephoned and wrote several times. He made various suggestions to help; he offered his own doctor. He lent her £1000, "to establish yourself in London." He invited her to a meeting at the House of Commons. She refused but accepted the money. After her death, we found she had kept his letters in her bedside drawer alongside Hicham's love letters and the Get Well cards from her siblings and cousins.

In July, Lord Young fixed Zoë up with a six-week research job. It failed; she only managed to get herself to Bethnal Green for three mornings, complained of migraines, said the job was Noddy and busy-busy work. "I wouldn't do a silly project like this if I was well so why should I now." By the Thursday she had phoned and resigned. At the time we thought she was being pettish and ungrateful. In reality, her depression was too severe to allow her to communicate or work. As she, herself, wrote in her suicide note.

"I used to work and see friends, now I can do neither."

After the fiasco with Michael Young's job, Zoë decided she'd go to Glastonbury and stay with a friend of her cousin, Daisy, herself a diagnosed bi-polar.

Zoë said: "she only needs money for food. I can stay on longer if I like."

Wal and I were dismayed. Suppose she went to Glastonbury and ended up with an unsuitable bloke or on drugs or pregnant or all of these. We persuaded her that she must inform the hospital before she travelled. She agreed to see the young psychiatrist Sally Mathieson.

July 22

Zoë saw Sally yesterday, who persuaded her to come into The Lakes as a voluntary patient. Zoë sick and shaking. Angry with me. "You think that I am just lazy."

"I don't. But I think you must give the hospital a try."

She doesn't want to. Terrible to leave her there. She seemed absolutely hopeless. Sally was upbeat and cheerful.

Zoë said bitterly, "you've blocked off my last chance of escape." I felt so bad when she said that. But we can't let her go running all over the country in the state she's in.

Zoë hasn't rung me from the ward. Florence is elected carer-in-chief. I feel resentful. It's nicer at Greenacres without her.

Rows with Wal. We slept outside last night.

Wal and I often sleep in the garden in the summer nights. The kids used to sleep alongside us on mattresses but they stopped years ago.

Artha stood on the edge of a Kilner jar and tried to get biscuits out of bottom. Got stuck in as far as her wings.

Once she realised that she couldn't she didn't try again. I reckon that is a sign of intelligence.

No emails from our kids. Tanya must have got ours 'cos she sent one of her multi-recipient messages with her new address. I wish they didn't leave us alone like this. All my efforts with Zoë end up with shouting and unpleasantness. Why doesn't she seem to care that John is dying?

The weekend in the hospital was a disaster. Zoë had been admitted on the Friday evening and there were reduced staff on weekend duty and no activities scheduled. She stayed in her room and would not talk with staff or patients Wal and I visited separately each day; our conversations filled with more spaces than words.

Monday, July 24ᵗʰ 2000

A quiet, dead, airless atmosphere in The Lakes. A male nurse in civvies fetched Zoë who looks pale, thin, pasty-faced and unhappy.

"Am I doing the right thing to stay here?"

I keep repeating that she doesn't get any better at home and she should give the hospital a chance. If she agreed to go as a voluntary patient she must have some strong unconscious reason.

A sort of flat despair. What can we do for Zoë? The long summer continues grey and cold. Won't be very nice having a poetry workshop in the garden next Saturday.

Zoë had been in hospital for five days. The staff nurse suggested I took her into town for the afternoon; she needed new trainers. Zoë drove. We walked through the shopping precinct. We bought the trainers; we had tea in a café. Zoë remained silent throughout. I'd taken Artha on her harness and having a parrot on your shoulder provokes friendly comments and smiles. Zoë's mobile features never moved. It was like walking with a zombie.

261

Her week at The Lakes had made her no better - if anything a bit worse. Sally Mathieson, the young psychiatrist, who was in charge of her while Vasudevan was on a three-week leave. Sally was the same age as Zoë. Zoë didn't register any emotion, when Sally told her that she would not be seeing Vasudevan until Wednesday, August 23rd. But she knew that he was considering a more drastic drug treatment which would entail being in hospital so that her blood could be regularly monitored. Zoë feared hospital.

Sally, Zoë and I had a long chat in Zoë's room at the Lakes. The grapes and chocolates were untouched; the books and magazines in the same piles I had left them. Zoë asked to be given ECT [Electro Shock Therapy]. I was horrified, remembering the result on Jack Nicholson in *One Flew over the Cuckoo's Nest*. Sally said cheerily, "Oh, no, we're a long way up the road from that." I was relieved and Zoë didn't persist. After her death, I kept wondering whether Zoë *knew* what would help her and we had bypassed her request. I learnt of several bi-polars whom ECT enabled to come through depressions, including Daisy, the woman Zoë had wanted to stay with in Glastonbury.

Each time I visited her at The Lakes, Zoë pleaded to be taken home. "I feel safe there," she said. I refused, stuck with the memory that during her last stay in hospital eight years before, she had snapped out of depression as if by magic. In the garden at The Lakes, an elderly man, presumably on a heavy dose of tranquillizers, shuffled past us, head bent. "Don't let me get like that," said Zoë. "Oh, don't be so silly," I replied. I didn't realize that Zoë was terrified.

When Florence visited her next day, Zoë begged to be taken away. Since she was a voluntary patient and not sectioned, no one could stop her going. She had stayed in hospital less than a week. The next day Wal phoned the Leaders. They appeared relieved that he would come to fetch her home immediately.

On the first evening at the Leaders, Zoë had been relatively well and communicative but the next day became withdrawn again. The Leaders didn't want to keep her anymore than Tanya Morgan had. The glass wall surrounding her was at sub zero temperature, chilling anyone who came near. Habie, away in Scotland, sent long distance advice. "Zoë wants unconditional love," she said. We tried, unable to show our tenderness, baffled by her behaviour.

Wal was becoming desperate, too, as the weeks went by and Zoë's depression never lifted. He phoned a psychiatrist friend who suggested Zoë could live in a London hostel. She rejected the idea outright; she refused to show any interest in self-help groups or the Manic Depression Fellowship. That remains one of our most haunting regrets, had we insisted - would it have done any good?

The same weekend that Zoë left the Lakes, the Essex Girls, a local poetry society, held a Saturday workshop in our garden - fifteen lady poets and a picnic lunch under the trees. Zoë, back from the Leader's house, went to bed early. Sheena, a family friend who often had done exercises with Zoë and me, tried to give her their usual hug; Zoë was rigid in her arms. She had loved Zoë dearly and wrote after her death:

It's her voice I keep remembering,

throaty and conspiratorial,

whispering shocking secrets in my ear.

Zoë aged 25

About 6 pm a friend rang that John Bunyan had died. Later Inda rang – her voice calm, matter of fact. We went through the tail end of the workshop knowing that one of our oldest and dearest friends had died. Zoë just stayed in her room. I felt disappointed with hr lack of emotion. Hadn't she always been as fond of and admiring of John as us?

I missed signs that Zoë's condition was worsening not improving.

My diary entries read: *the medication appears to be finally reacting on Zoë. She is still withdrawn but I don't imagine that she will stay slim. She eats sweet things without stopping.*

I am happy and unhappy at the same time. We have made Greenacres amazingly beautiful with the roses and the potager which is lousy for edibles but full of shapes and colours. 63 already. John had just 2 more years. We must be happy otherwise what is the point of living?

Although she remained so morose, speaking to us less and less, Zoë applied for another job as a recruitment manager. A job she'd done briefly but with success a few years before. She got through the first two of three interviews and failed the final one. She said something about role-playing. "I wasn't in the right mood." She had bought herself a too-tight lavender suit for the interview. We thought the fact of applying, even if unsuccessful, indicated improvement. We clung to tiny signs, enabling us to continue our blinkered optimism: until the final week of her depression, she bought weekly lottery tickets. I reasoned that she must be thinking of her future. She epilated her legs and plucked her eyebrows. I reasoned she must be thinking of her appearance. We watched a programme about dinosaurs and she joined us. I offered her a foot massage and she accepted. Because of the riding accident she had had with Zugi, she often had pain in her foot. Vasudevan had told us he was arranging cognitive therapy sessions– "just as soon as she is less depressed." We pinned our hopes on that.

Had a stranger met Zoë for the first time that summer, they might not have seen her as ill, simply a mute, mournful, beautiful woman. She wouldn't come to Thakeham the following week for John's funeral service. Nor give any explanation.

In August I wrote almost nothing in my diary; I had become depressed myself.

Every summer, Ben and his family spend a week at Greenacres - so the other kids try to come and we have a family reunion with plenty of psycho-drama, quarrels, kisses, fun and food. Most Schwarzes and their partners are good cooks. Fredy makes the world's best brownies; Zoë can cook Nigerian pepper stew. We take turns. This year Zoë didn't but she was no trouble to anyone - simply absent. She hardly played with Chloe and Max, or Noe the new baby of whom she took little notice. I overheard her reading Chloe and Max a story, her voice hollow with no inflections. The children were puzzled by her changed behaviour but accepted in the way kids do. At the funeral Fredy said, "If she'd been a patient I would have seen how ill she was but as one of the family, I didn't." And she said that when she asked Zoë to hold baby Noe, Zoë had said, "Are you sure? I've been so ill."

The last weekend of Zoë's life had typical English summer weather, dull, cloudy with outbreaks of sunshine. On Friday night the siblings decided on a pub dinner together - the five of them. Zoë wasn't her lively self but then she hadn't been for weeks. They even said she'd told a couple of jokes.

My friend Diana, a Samaritan of many years standing, had mentioned casually, that when a deeply depressed person appears a little better - watch them carefully. She meant that in a deep depression you haven't enough energy to kill yourself. You must recover sufficiently to have enough energy to organise your death and choose the method.

About ten days before she died, Zoë told me she was going to drive to Florence's. She came back sweating and nervous. Florence had not been at home. I didn't ask her why she was gone several hours when driving to Florence and back would only take thirty minutes. Now I believe she had gone to Marks Tey Station and found out what time the London express hurtles through.

Saturday night was the last meal for the ten of us to be together. A few incidents stick in my memory. Habie was sitting in Zoë's usual seat. When Zoë came to the table, she leaned over, kissed Habie's cheek and took another chair. For pudding, we had fruit and ice cream. Zoë cut an apple into three sections and gave one third to me and one third to Wal. It was the first friendly action she'd made all summer. She gave me a proper smile. For the rest of my life, it will haunt me that I did not smile back. She took no further part in the family evening and went to bed early. That last weekend, I believe that Zoë's apparent calm came as a result of her final decision.

By Sunday lunch time, the visitors gone, the house in turmoil, beds unmade, floors dirty, Wal said after all the hurly-burly, he needed a siesta. I started the massive clean up. Zoë, unasked, began to help. By four o'clock the floors were washed or hovered and most of the sheets in the washing machine. I was so pleased that she'd helped even though in an unfriendly silence that I sent emails to the kids that night - Zoë seems *much* better.

Although we never acknowledged it aloud, Wal and I were aware of the risk of suicide. In case she had taken pills, Wal asked her every morning - how do you feel? She replied each time with the blank stare that had become habitual, "the same." He was sure that she knew why he did it.

On Monday, she spent the day reading a Myra Syal novel. I thought that a good sign but when I asked her about the plot she snapped, "I don't know. I haven't finished it."

Walter had a medical test in London the next morning. He rang up at lunch time to say he would be late. Trains were delayed because of "a fatality on the line". He came home at tea time and Zoë still wasn't home. We were more puzzled than anxious. In her bedroom she had pinned over the bed a handwritten list of people. "That's sad," said Wal, "why hasn't she got an address book?"

Our defences against the unthinkable are impregnable. Wal had already told me on the phone that someone had thrown themselves on the railway line. Neither of us imagined that it might have been her. During our long conversation of June 29th, she'd said categorically, "Suicide isn't an option. I can't do it. I'm not brave enough to jump in front of a train. If I took pills someone would find me." She must have remembered her first attempt.

Wednesday August 23rd 2000

Zoë died yesterday. She threw herself in front of an express train at Marks Tey at 12.40pm. I was in Colchester putting the money from Amigo's sale in the bank. The funeral will be on Friday if the coroner releases the body. They wouldn't let us see it. It was identified by fingerprints from her handbag mirror. They won't let me see the photos. Maybe I will some day. My last conversation with Zoë was.

"What are you doing today?" She was sitting in the sitting room wearing the same clothes she had worn for three days - blue jeans and shirt and trainers.

"I'm going to see my friend Tammy."

"Ring up if you're late."

"Yes."

"You could visit the Colchester labour exchange and find a waitress job now you're so much better."

The last words she spoke to me were:

"I'll give it some thought."

CHAPTER TEN

"She took a considered rational decision ..."

Three weeks after Zoë's death, at my mother's meagre funeral in Bushey Heath just outside London, her brothers found Nicola's headstone covered in lichen in the children's section, where the mounds are the size of pet graves. Nicola was thirteen months old when she died forty years earlier. Ben in his thirties, a young dad with three kids, and Zachary at twenty, sobbed in one another's arms. Zoë would have given a wry grin, knowing that they were really crying for her.

On Tuesday, August 22nd, Wal came home around 6 pm. I'd expected Zo home at lunch time and was fretting about her lateness. Around tea time I'd driven round to Tammy's street but her car wasn't there; no answer at the door. Maybe they had gone out together? By 7 pm we were anxious and searched her bedroom. Zoë's wallet lay in her bedside table drawer. No passport. Had she gone to Morocco? We still made no connection between her disappearance and the 'fatality on the line'.

At 7.30 pm. we were eating sweet corn and bacon. I meant to watch *Big Brother*. We had decided to wait until 8 pm to inform the Police that she was missing. At 7.50 pm. a police car drew up and parked outside the gate. The officer said something about a car number. It was her car number. Where is she? Has she had an accident? Has she crashed? Is she in hospital? One of the policemen said - not exactly, the car is parked at Marks Tey and we both knew. Total unreality: to the Police - can I see her? No, there is no body to identify. We have to use fingerprints. They took away Zoë's handbag mirror. Asked what clothes she was wearing. "Blue jeans and shirt and fawn trainers." They nodded. No hope after that. But the mind won't accept. I kept interrupting the police, "Stop talking. I know what you're

269

doing. You're only on a training exercise about how to break bad news with compassion. You've done it very well but please leave now. My daughter will be home soon." As they were speaking, a car drove down the lane and Wal rushed outside, crying, "She's back!" I remember screaming at one point, "What about her children?" The police were gentle, polite; they arranged for a female officer to visit Zac in his London flat and tell him.

I made some phone calls.

Zac arrived weeping uncontrollably about 11pm. Ben was there next morning. Tanya flew back from Jo'burg on Thursday. Habie and Simon drove from Glasgow. Less than a week after they had gone away, the children were reunited again minus one.

On Wednesday morning, Cahn Vasudevan arrived with Sally Mathieson. The young Oz doctor thrust a bunch of flowers at me. She was crying hard. I held her in my arms; it felt bizarre, me comforting her. She had believed that Zoë was not considering suicide; it wasn't an option. They had discussed it together. They were about the same age. Bi-polar affective disorder. A name. A diagnosis. So why no fucking cure! Zac was angry with the shrinks. It's their fault, he kept saying, so we kept him away from them.

Just after the doctors left, a secretary from United Response telephoned asking for Zoë. Ten days earlier, she'd asked (typical Zoë, not telling anyone at home) whether there were any job vacancies. They apologised for not getting back sooner. There were two vacancies; she'd be high on the list of candidates. What if they had called on Monday? The call joined the list of 'if-onlys' and 'what-ifs' that accumulate around a sudden death.

Flowers began to arrive. In her room, the highly-scented lilies mingled with Zoë's own smell; she didn't seem gone, her clothes draped on a chair back, her bed unmade, an opened packet of ten bikini briefs from British Home Stores on the floor. Three had been taken out. So she hadn't meant to die? Surely you wouldn't buy ten pairs of pants the last week of your life!

Under the bed, I found a *Boots* till receipt. Quinine - the same pill she had taken in 1992. So she did mean to die. The receipt was dated August 15th. The same day that Sally Mathieson at the Lakes had noted, 'a slight improvement.'

The funeral was to be Friday, if the Police could identify and release the body by then. Wanting to celebrate her life as well as mourn, we held a wake on Thursday evening. I don't know who arranged the food; I don't know who contacted friends. I expected only a few extra people - about fifty turned up. Some had to stay overnight. There was a typical Schwarz cock-up. With our house full with our children, Kelly, Sarah and Mylène and other people in tents, two student friends of Zo were sent to sleep in Rachel's caravan. About one in the morning, one of these girls arrived crying into my room that she couldn't stop in the caravan - there was a rat in a cage.

We lit a bonfire on the lawn - a late summer evening. Zoë would have adored hearing her family and friends telling stories about how much she related to everyone; how much she helped them with her time. Penny a riding friend said, "Zoë could always make you feel you were capable of anything."

After one hour or so, the stream of eulogies irritated Wal. "Hang on a minute, Zoë was no saint; she had a terrible temper. She could rage enough to smash windows and doors." I knew what he was thinking of - the glass panel in the kitchen door, still cracked across the middle from where Zo slammed it in 1997. Had her friends seen her in a rage? None had - or wouldn't say so on this occasion.

Kelly remembered when Zoë first arrived at school, how exotic she was because she came from France. "She used to run around the netball court at great speed, very frustrated when the rules of the game meant you had to stop."

Zoë used to tell me a Buddhist teaching when I was moaning about my life. "Buddha sat on a hill. The village was half-burnt down and half the inhabitants burned to death. But Buddha was smiling. Someone asked, 'How can you smile when half the village are dead?' Buddha replied, 'I am smiling because half the village are saved.'" That was Zoë's philosophy, her tragedy that she could not live up to it. But however much we tried to celebrate Zoë's life, the ending of it kept intruding. Several people spoke out about the survivors' guilt.

Jane Grant, Tom's mother, an old family friend has suffered from depressive illness and made two attempts at suicide. She almost succeeded on both occasions.

She said being in that sort of depression was like living behind a glass wall, as Zoë herself had said. "It feels like you will never be able to get out. No one can reach you and you can reach no one."

Tom, who had been Tanya's first proper boyfriend added. "Zoë was a bright, bright star, too bright maybe to go on burning as she did."

Several people said several times that Zoë was too incandescent to burn for long. I've never agreed, neither then or later.

Zac recalled Zoë's passion for Tigger. "He was quite a haughty cat who only came to you if he was in an especially good mood. They adored each other. They had a real bond, like a respectful love affair." Zac said, "If there's some place where you go after death, Zo has to be there with Tigger and Daisy." He thought of his sister like a rock & roll star without the music; she had all a star's passion and unpredictability.

Inda, John's widow, had driven three hours from Sussex. John had died only three weeks earlier. Zoë hadn't reacted to his death with any show of feeling. I didn't realise that at the time what an indication of how she must have been feeling. She had cared a lot for John. Of all the people in our lives, John and Zoë had the most charisma. And John, too, had a fiery temper that his family knew but outsiders never saw. Someone imagined them charming each other, wherever they are.

Not everyone spoke. There were some silent presences around the flames. Fabien, the Rwandan lawyer and refugee, travelled up from outer London. He, who had known so many losses, came to mourn a friend and colleague.

The stories circulated until well after midnight. There were an immense number of shooting stars. The bonfire was still smouldering next morning. The circle of charred grass left on the lawn grew out a year later.

Such kindness from family and friends, food appeared, meals cooked, a funeral arranged. My brother Mickey, our son Benjamin, Habie and Simon arranged the service. Wal and I could not have coped alone. In those first days, we were both more dazed than anything else. Jan, Mickey's wife, just out of hospital, prepared most of the meals. Every room in the house was filled with flowers and Habie pinned photographs of a smiling Zoë up on the walls.

The physical paraphernalia of death is further complicated when a person dies of murder, accident or suicide. You have to deal with the Police, the coroner, the press. The bald announcement in the Essex evening paper that a thirty-year old woman had died on the Marks Tey railway line had upset Zac. We wanted to redress the balance and contacted *The Essex County Standard*. Wal and I told a sympathetic young reporter about Zoë's illness. At this stage we wanted to talk about her all the time; we almost babbled I think. We didn't blame the health service; we said how beloved and brilliant she was. The young reporter wrote an accurate piece.

I kept counting hours: now Zoë has been dead for twelve, twenty, forty-eight, seventy-two hours. Her funeral took place less than one hundred hours after her death. Our family huddled on the gravel and watched a little woman, high-heeled, dressed in black with a hat and veil walking in front of the Rolls Royce hearse (Zoë would have loved the Rolls) down the drive. *Zoë is stuck inside that box under those beautiful lilies and she is not coming out.* The hearse reversed and started back down the drive, the veiled woman walking in front. The drive is two hundred and fifty metres long and uneven. It couldn't have been easy for her. At the road, she nipped back inside next to the driver. This pale imitation of old-fashioned funeral rituals was strangely comforting. Where did the swathe of white roses and lilies decorating the coffin come from? Habie said cousins Julia and Andy had ordered them.

I found an outfit of Zoë's, a black skirt, a black tee shirt and her high wedge mules that fitted me because I hadn't been eating much. I still do not recognize what the action symbolized. The chapel at the crematorium was full. I don't know for how long the grounds have served as a burial ground; its trees are fully mature, copper beeches and oaks and yews. Habie and Simon handed each mourner a photocopy of Zoë smiling on the telephone and printed below was the suicide note left in her car. Three sentences printed in bold type were those that she overwrote for emphasis. The letters are small; the lines clear and straight. A terrible proof to me that she was calm when she wrote:

No one is to blame for my death.

I love you all; but I can't live like this.

I'm sorry. Please forgive me.

At the funeral service, I read the dirge from *Cymbeline,* a Shakespeare poem that Zoë and I had loved.

Fear no more the heat o' the sun

Nor the furious winter's rages;

Thou thy worldly task hast done

Home art gone, and ta'en thy wages.

Golden lads and girls all must,

As chimney sweeps, come to dust.

The last verse didn't apply because Zoë has no grave.

No excorciser harm thee!

Nor no witchcraft charm thee!

Ghost unlaid forbear thee!

Nothing ill come near thee!

Quiet consummation have,

And renownèd be thy grave!

Zac spoke first out of the siblings - brave of him because he is shy. He read from a Native American book that he and Zoë had both enjoyed.

"I think what Eagle Chief of the Pawnee says sums up my sister.

'All things in the world are two

In our minds we are two – good and evil

With our eyes we see two things – things that are fair and things that are ugly

We have the right hand that strikes and makes for evil, and the left hand full of kindness, near the heart.

One foot may lead us to an evil way; the other foot may lead us to a good.

So are all things two, all two.'

"I also want to say that I love her, and I miss her so much…"

Tanya wore a blue dress, one bright note amongst all the sombre clothing. She concentrated on Zoë's achievements at school and at work but she concluded: "What I will remember Zoë for, over and above all these

275

worldly achievements, is her ability to touch all those around her. She treated us all as equals, and helped us to see what was special in ourselves."

Ben turned his back to the mourners and spoke directly to the coffin. *"Excuse me turning away from you, but I want to talk to Zoë:*

"Zoë, last night at the wake I learned more about you in an evening than I had in a whole life time. However I look at it, little sister, I did fail you as a big brother. Maybe we just had too much in common emotionally to not drive each other up the wall. Although I was always here for you, we only made intimate contact on rare occasions, Zoë. You remembered that the old snooker cue at Nana's was mine, so you obviously remembered my joy at the game. I will now carry on playing pool for you too, to carry on our all too rare precious moments of bonding.

"I thank you for your wonderful friendship with my wife Fredy, a real sisterly relationship. Through Fredy, I stayed intimate with you in your last days.

"For my children, you were the most fun aunt ever! Noé will be very envious when Chloe and Max tell him about you, and sing your special song, on lawn romps without you.

"My darling sister, the five members of my new family will treasure your memory forever. We'll miss you, Baby-Ji. We trust you are now at peace."

Habie's voice is light and musical. Zoë's was husky. They both often spoke with passion in their voices.

"I always talked too much, and lately you hardly talked at all."

And then Habie did something that cost her pain and effort. In the two days since she had flown back from Glasgow,

276

she had sorted through the piles of papers in the cardboard boxes and extracted excerpts from Zoë's writing. Many of them I've quoted already and Habie finished off by saying:

"Zoë, I want to believe in God and Heaven, but whatever is true, wherever you are. My baby, you will be alive as long as we are, here with us, with your lovely thick hair, laughing your head off, or maybe silent and sad.

"Please, please, please, don't ever be ashamed again. We are proud to love you…"

My brother Mickey wrote a poem. He was one of those who believed that a person who commits suicide has made a choice that we must respect.

It ended with the lines:

And we who loved her need but close our eyes

To see her as she was.

Our lovely, shining Zoë, finally at peace.

Walter read parts of a Buddhist prayer, which contained many of Zoë's highest aspirations:

'Let your love flow outward through the universe,

To its height, its depth, its broad extent,

A limitless love, without hatred or enmity. …

Our friend Heather, who's known me and Wal before any of our children (twelve between us) were born, wrote a prayer with her husband Bernard. They are both devout Roman Catholics.

"We pray to God, our loving Father….

"Only you really knew and understood the agony of mind she suffered before her tragic death. … May she, who

277

believed in you deeply, now find with you the peace and happiness that she could not find in her last months on earth.

"And may she now rest in peace.

Amen."

Although, we had stopped attending services at the small Jewish community in Colchester some years earlier because no one in the family was practising any form of Judaism, several of the congregation came to the funeral. Maurice Sunkhin, one of the community members read the following prayer, which Zoë would have appreciated:

"As for man, his days are like grass, he flourisheth like a flower of the field; and the dust returns to the earth as it was, and the spirit returns to God who gave it. Whom have I in heaven but you? And loving you I desire nothing else on earth."

Sarah, who looked like a ghost after a transatlantic flight and little sleep, said: "Zoë, last weekend I wrote to you from the States. I told you about my summer, I told you that I loved you, and that if simply the love and will of your friends would make you better, you would be well instantly.

"That's not possible, and you did not receive this letter. But I know you already knew all about my love for you, and yours for me. Perhaps that's the most extraordinary thing about you: there were no *'non-dits'*. You created love and loyalty all about you. You taught me about the possibilities of friendship. When we were 15 or 16 you said we would always be friends, I believed you – you made that possible. You touched every part of my life, and you were the brightest thread of continuity. Whenever one of us had been away, we would come back together and tease and tell each other new stories, and retell the old ones. Your stories were always about the people around you – your family, or Kelly or Mylène or a new friend – you would bind us to other people as well as to you.

"I will miss coming back to you, Zoë. But I – we – will keep telling the stories and re-telling the stories, and re-telling them again."

Sarah looked over to the family, made a loving gesture and gave a sad smile, "Thank you for Zoë."

Florence and Sheldon both spoke. I envied Flo's belief that she and Zo would meet again. "I wait for the day when I see you again to run and jump with you in the joy that is yours today; love you with no shadows and receive yours with the purity you were always looking for."

And Sheldon who felt, like so many of us, that we failed her, said:

"Zoë was not a saintly person. She was more like us than that. But she was also not like us. For there was an extraordinary range of life that coursed through her veins. It did so sometimes involuntarily and sometimes as she willingly embraced all that existence had to offer. She was a crossroads of experience of extremes that most of us will never know. …

"Hers was an intelligence of the eye. It saw things.

"I had an experience of that. Several years ago I had the privilege of helping her in a difficult situation. As we sat and talked, I was groping for a way through – trying this and that idea and approach. She came back with her own. The conversation carried on, and then there was an instant where her gaze caught mine and held it steadily. It was no more than a split second, but it was enough; she had found a way through. She didn't need to say more, nor did I."

Sheldon had referred delicately to the dreadful time during her first illness when Zoë had said she was returning

279

to Bristol to work in a brothel and the Leader family, principally Sheldon, had dissuaded her.

I can't recall the moment that the coffin slid behind the green velvet curtains. Most of us were crying. After a minute's silence, one of her favourite songs was played *Nothing Compares to You,* by Sinead O'Connor. The congregation filed out and looked at the flowers laid out on the paving stones. Everyone said what a beautiful funeral. Meanwhile, the mourners for the next one were arriving.

The sun shone with a late August brassiness. Jan and Mickey had arranged a picnic lunch on the lawn at Greenacres. Zoë was more *there* than she had been during her last weeks alive.

The following day, Sarojini arrived, having rerouted her journey back home from USA to Bangalore. She stayed a week.

Zoë's first surviving diary, written when she was nine during a trip to Sri Lanka visiting her godmother, contains the first of her many lists that have survived. She listed every tree, every animal and bird she saw. She wrote: *Sarojini lives in meetings now. Sarojini is new Buddha solving everyone's problems.*

Sarojini, who has indeed spent her life solving problems (on the macro scale for the world's children and on the micro for all her friends and family) wrote a tribute to her goddaughter: *Zoë was perhaps too good for this world, wanting perfection, demanding much of herself. Yet those she loved, she saw as bigger than life. Life itself was seen through a magnifying glass. Like Alice, she, too, wanted to live in her own Wonderland. The world could never measure up, and she couldn't wait.*

It seems so symbolic that she chose a train to rid herself of her frail body. Her spirit wanted to fly, be liberated, and be elsewhere.

We want to believe that her spirit is happy, that she is elsewhere. For us, it is a comfort.

A few days later I wrote in my diary: *Lots and lots of flowers gradually wilting in Zoë's room. She said she had "no clothes". She'd bought several outfits for job interviews. She was not selected. It must have been a desperate effort on her part. How could she have convinced the selectors in the role-play? She was too depressed.*

What mother lets a child commit suicide? This mother.

The family went in separate groups to Marks Tey platform. Rod, Tanya, Niall and I went on Saturday. As the express train thundered through, we instinctively jumped backwards. Experiencing that thunderous onslaught, you realise how brave or how desperate someone must be to countermand every instinct for self-preservation and JUMP. I screamed and we all hugged. Zac had left a note and some flowers stuck into the railings for 'my little sister'.

Bi- polar affective disorder. Does anyone have two *dead daughters? Zoë's enthusiasms. Her 18 month-long Cordelia behaviour. No more Zoë. No more Zoë. More Zoë. Zoë forever. Her name means life but it didn't help her live a normal lifespan. Wednesday's visitors: Florence. Sheena, Cora and Shamir, all shaken. Dot the earth mother consigning her daughter to the flames. I can't forgive myself.*

Zoë's papers show a happy busy schoolgirl. Zoë's mad diary doesn't.

Who can I blame? I can't find anyone.

Clutter and chaos. The summer is coming to a close. Throwing away things from Zoë's room. Not letters just pieces of paper. Her Walkman. I can't bear the sight of these objects. She's kept all the notes Zac wrote to her. Oh Zoë, why did you leave?

<u>*Sunday September 30*[th]</u>

281

Those who will never grow old. My baby daughter and my grown up daughter. Food tastes like sawdust. Wal and I went for a walk round the field and wondered whether our other children will eventually blame us. Our daughter has thrown herself in front of a train - no body to identify.

In one of Zoë's diaries written at the age of sixteen, she has sellotaped a lock of everyone's hair. She went to church with Florence and wrote that one day she'd be an old lady like all the other old ladies in the church praying.

Wal and I reply to the warm messages. I put them in a shoe box; there are hundreds. A message from all the cleaners at one of the football clubs – big wavy handwriting. The fine weather continues. So ironical. Mylène said sweetly before she left to return to work that Zoë was looking after us and sending warm weather. At noon today Zoë has been dead for 14 days. I don't know how to assimilate this. I don't know how to behave. Clichés are true. Mad with grief. Numb with despair. Drowning in sorrow. How wonderful to be religious. Oh, you little liar, Zoë. I couldn't enter your mind set; it seemed implacable. So stupid your reiterations of "why won't the pills work?" My inadequate answer. "Just wait. It takes time."

Zoë's room starts to look stripped, clothes in bags, papers in boxes. So little left. Debts at the bank. Barclays paid her cremation bill from one of her accounts that had £800 odd left in it. We planted 125 trees in Caledonian forest. And planted a rose at Bushey Jewish cemetery where her grandparents, sister and uncles and aunts are buried.

Fredy wrote to Tanya a few days later: ... *Zoë's death has made us more fragile. You know when you hear somebody had something terrible; something in you thinks it always happens to other people. This time it happened to Zoë and to us. We don't feel protected anymore.*

<u>Sunday</u> *The effect of tragedy is that it concentrates and narrows the mind. What is happening in the news, the weather, and the telly become trivial. I would rather watch tragedy than live it. The central mystery of Zoë's decision.*

282

Artha continues a comfort. The bird's reaction is extraordinary. Every morning I open her cage door at 10 am and she flies around the sitting room. The morning after Zoë's death, I opened the cage door and the parrot remained on her perch. She kept her head tucked under her wing until the afternoon when she began to eat and drink as usual.

Leah is also acting odd. When I say the name Zoë, she starts to whimper. Why the hell didn't I know that I was living with someone in a suicidal frame of mind? Think of Virginia Woolf. Think of Sylvia Plath. Cousin Heimer rang up. Apparently Zoë is the fourth Schwarz suicide within the wider Schwarz family in 40 or 50 years.

Thinking of Zoë - her 30s her 40s her 50s her 60s her 70s. Imagine the children she might have had. The jobs, the illnesses, the madnesses. Was she an ordinary woman, or a 'sensation; as Sydney Bayley [her counsellor] wrote? Never to be a bride. Never to be a mother. Never to know the death of a loved one. When I am not sad, anger is what I feel. How could she have done such a thing to herself!

This pain is unbearable. If her pain was worse than this – no wonder she killed herself. How brave to have lasted 14 weeks. Why did no one help her?

Within the week the house emptied of kids and guests and Wal and I began the active business of grief. The kids, living their separate lives, sent lots of emails to us and each other.

A couple of days after she flew back to South Africa, Tanya sent memories of her sister:

I remember my first conversation with her on the phone in April after she returned from Morocco. I was driving back from the Northern Cape and she spoke about her hysteria in Morocco - it was no big deal she assured me. It started she said when she read my email about rock-climbing and my new-found happiness. She thought, "If

Tanya, who has suffered so much, can find happiness, so can I." My "suffering" was of course part of her manic fantasy. She went on to quote Mandela - something like "if you are happy and radiant, you give others the right to be so." She said that my happiness had been a big inspiration ....

We lived together a while in Golders Green. ... She was seeing a number of men at that time, and I disapproved. She was usually out in the evening and back after my bed-time.

I remember her and Zac coming for dinner at my home in Holland Park, late '98. We got very stoned with Josh and the three of us siblings laughed in the way we do when we are stoned and Josh felt excluded. Zoë and Zac were making fun of him, in a way which he could not understand). He admired the closeness the three of us shared.

My best memory of Zoë is getting stoned with Zac at family reunions - at night either with the rest of the family, or after the others had gone to bed. We would laugh in a way that I have never laughed with anyone so much, about absolutely nothing.

I remember admiring her ability to engage with all and everybody, and treat them as equals. I was always amazed at the variety of friends she had, while remaining close to her three best friends, Sarah, Kelly and Mylène.

Above all, I remember certain gentleness, a caring about those around her. The expression on her face when I told her something was not quite right in my life. There is a gap, a void, in the world that Zoë has left. I feel her absence most minutes of the day. I feel confident that she is in peace wherever she is - if "she" still is. I believe that she took a considered rational decision to end her life, and I respect her for it. My regret is that she did not discuss her reasoning with her loved ones first - so that we could have had a chance to make her change her mind and urge her to try to survive a little longer. If she had then killed herself, *after we had all done our best, I would feel more at peace with her decision. As it is, she - who asked for advice about everything always, from cooking to careers, took the ultimate decision completely alone. That saddens me greatly - that the rift she felt with the world was so great that she could not let anyone in.*

A friend had warned me at the funeral lunch to be wary; that suicide could break up a family. We were fortunate. It didn't happen to us.

Tanya concluded her memories: *Thank you all for being such a lovely family and so close over the last ten days. Zoë would have been so proud of us all! I have never known the Schwarz's and their partners to be so united.*

Zac the youngest and the closest to Zoë found grief almost impossible to share but he emailed the family just before Zoë's 28th birthday-

Just writing to say that I'll be thinking of you all tomorrow. I don't know how I'm going to feel, but I am seeing Gabrielle [a therapist] *and that should help. I'm going through a very weird phase of grief: half bewildered by it, half not believing/thinking about it. I don't feel guilty about not crying about her death or carrying on, because she is never far from my mind. I don't really believe in heaven or alike, but find myself imagining she is in another better place.*

People still tell me how amazing she was and it makes me feel so proud of her life and no longer ashamed of her madness or her death. A couple of days ago I rang our insurers John Kilcare, and he asked about us and told me he thought Zoë was amazing from what he knew - he had only ever talked to her on the phone!

And his older brother emailed that he was thinking of him: ... *I don't even know if it's a day to mourn or celebrate Zoë, both I suppose....*

Love, Ben

And I wrote to the kids the following day:

December 7, 2000 **Subject:** *Birthday*

It all went much better than I could have expected. Good chats with Kelly and Sarah and Mylène. It helped that we as a family don't make much of birthdays.

The future Zoë-less seems more of a possibility and less of a nightmare. I keep thinking that if she had lived and suffered more attacks she is better off without them but on the other hand ...

Christmas will be fine with the kids and all our blessings before us.

Habie replied: *As I see it, our future won't ever be Zoë-less, it's Zoë who is futureless. We have Zoë with us – yesterday I felt her presence so clearly I swear I could smell her. Along with Henry James and Francois Truffaut, and apparently the whole population of Mexico, I do believe our dead live alongside us.*

Zac continued with his college and finished his degree. He emailed: *I often allow myself to see her and chat to her as such. I remembered taking the tube with her and chatting. I remember that Xmas when we got stoned with Tanya and even Ben had a little bit. We were all sitting in corners. Tanya was laughing so much she was crying! Habie was telling us about her "bestest" something or other. It was probably one of the funniest moments of my life. Later Fredy pulled me out of the fridge, twice!*

Love, Zac

And Hab wrote about this time - still frantic with grief.

Was there one big secret, sister, or just lots of little ones, trivial, dreadful but manageable in sister imagination? ... How can you be dead from a jump, little one? Why did you stop riding horses and jumping over wooden logs? Why have you broken off a part of us? At your funeral, your gazelle best friend called you

*'l'indomptable' and said 'au revoir, princesse Zoë…' Your
big brother apologised for not getting to know you better,
your mentor's husband admitted how much he had learned
from you. Your mother read Shakespeare's most beautiful
poem. Couldn't you have stuck around for that? To see that
we* finally *satisfied your craving, admired you and loved
you as we should have and became worthy of your ideal of a
family? You finally brought out the best in us, when there
was nothing left but a coffin and flowers.*

A few weeks later she could be more reflective.

*Zo knew how much I loved her, as the storms in our
volcanic relationship were never about love, only
intellectual or emotional compatibility. The problems in the
last few years were, interspersed with moments of closeness
and friendship. I feel bad about times of neglect, only
consoling myself with thought that they didn't affect her too
much, as we always ended up having it out and making up.*

Wal and I continued to grieve in our separate ways;
he stiff upper-lipped, me weepy and ill-tempered. He
needed to keep busy. He drove to Wales and wrote an
article about the Centre for Alternative Technology. He
visited Tanya and Niall for ten days in South Africa.

Hab wrote to Sarojini's daughter that her father:
*keeps his emotions where they have always been, deep
inside. But he is spiritual and profound in many ways, and I
think he has the tools to cope. He came with me to put
flowers on the railway track where Zoë died, and to pay
respects to her last journey. He also cried several times (for
the first time in his life), once with your ma in the car. So I
believe he will let himself feel what is to be felt, and not
bottle it up.*

Did Zoë have to die? The question without an
answer. Wal wanted some reaction from the Health Service.
He wrote to Vasudevan after we had decided not to make
any formal complaint. What had gone wrong during Zoë's
treatment, we believed was due as much to ill luck as poor

care, although we didn't think that during that brief stay in the Lakes in July she had been particularly well-cared for.

Cahn Vasudevan, after his initial condolence visit, came several times and tried to answer these criticisms. I quote his response almost in full because it sums up both the strengths and the inadequacies of the system of health care.

Wal emailed the kids: *There is still no escape from the feeling that her death might have been prevented ...*

Vasudevan stayed for two hours and appeared prepared to stay longer if we had wanted him to. He was clearly still very involved in Zoë's life and death and both he and Sally Mathieson were still extremely upset. He took a detailed interest in every aspect of her story, her character and her relationships.

Later this week there is to be a review of the way Zoë was handled by his service, involving a senior psychiatrist from outside the service. This is usual practice after a suicide. He asked permission for our submissions - in our letter to him and the material from the funeral and the wake - to be used in this review. We readily agreed.

He dealt with the points in the letter he received from us.

1. Lack of effective continuity in Zoë's treatment after he went away (nearly four weeks before her death). He admitted this had not been satisfactory. He had worried about Zoë before leaving and continued to worry during his absence. He seemed to admit he could have set in motion more effective handling of Zoë during his absence. He implied that the senior man left in charge, Dr X, had not performed well. "He's a bit ... " he was saying, agreeing with Zoë's negative impressions, but did not finish the sentence. Significantly he spoke all the time of his own involvement in Zoë's treatment and the relationship he had developed with her - thereby tacitly admitting that tragically this relationship stopped because of his absence and was in abeyance in the last three-and-a-half weeks of Zoë's life.

The clear implication was that if he had been present Zoë might have been saved.

2. The contact with Zoë's carers (i.e. her parents) had not been adequate.

He agreed there should have been more intense and effective discussion on the risks of suicide and how to counteract them, and on the way depressed patients feel they are behind a glass wall and cannot communicate, cannot react to parental care and affection in a recognisable way. However, he did not suggest there were reasons to think there would have been a different outcome if we had acted differently with Zoë.

3. He acknowledged that the regime at The Lakes needed improvement. He agreed with us that there was far too much empty time there, when nothing happened to distract depressed patients from their lonely despair. He said he would now recommend changes and would seek the resources for a more active, hands-on regime at The Lakes.

On whether Zoë's suicide could have been foreseen and prevented, he said Zoë had said to him, as she said to us, that suicide was "not an option". However, she had half jokingly asked him if her drugs could have been taken in overdose to commit suicide, and when he had said - no, she complained he wasn't being very generous. At the time he thought he had successfully "negotiated" with Zoë not to commit suicide. He had been aware before his absence that Zoë was not responding to the chemical treatment and needed more intensive use of drugs, with a number of drugs used in combination and in heavier doses. The problem was that such intensive medical treatment required close supervision, blood tests, etc. which could only be done in hospital and Zoë had convinced him that hospital was not the right place for her: she had told him she felt safer and better at home. She appreciated her parents, care and concern and felt sorry and ashamed of the things she had said and done in Morocco. That shame was part of a more generalised feeling of stigma which was at the heart of her distress and despair, as expressed in her suicide note. The stigma attached to hospitals was a factor in her preference for being at home. The stigma of depression isolated her from her family and friends, which exacerbated her despair. She was also painfully aware that she was an affliction and a hindrance in her parents' lives.

Throughout, he had "negotiated" with Zoë - about her being at home instead of hospital, etc. He had tried to convince her that she would surely emerge from her depression. But in the end she appeared to have come rationally to the conclusion that the odds were stacked against her: even if and when she came out of the depression, she was aware that she could never be quite free from this torment. It was significant that Zoë had clearly suffered from manic problems months before she went to Morocco last December. Indeed her success at proselytising in her job could be seen as a common trait in manic conditions - as could her violent quarrels with some of her siblings and her refusal to take a normal job. Her resort to excessive pot smoking at this period was a characteristic reaction to the onset of mania: another way of seeking solace from agony in self-medication. Even before 1999, in the years between her first episode and her second, he felt sure Zoë had from time to time showed symptoms of mania.

He thought it significant that four suicides had occurred within two generations of Wal's family: a recessive gene could cause a predisposition.

The three episodes of Zoë's uncharacteristic nakedness around the house during her last weeks were probably "regression" into childhood. It was safe to be naked with Mummy. He noted that clinical depression after a shameful bout of manic behaviour was itself a form of childish regression, a return to the secure simplicity of childhood which was free from blame and responsibility.

He showed much compassion and sympathy and offered to visit again whenever we asked him to.

Love to you all, Dad

Vasudevan has now left the Health Service and returned to India. His last words to us were in a report he prepared about Zoë at our request.

He concluded: *Psychiatry does help a lot of people. However it remains terribly imprecise and inadequate, particularly when it comes to helping people with personal pain, anguish, despair and fear. I believe that we did all that could have been expected of a professional team in such very difficult circumstances, and yet we failed to deliver – for Zoë Schwarz.*

He had tried his best.

For me, as for other mourners, the worst time comes in the dark as you turn out the light. During the day you've kept busy answering letters, doing stuff; at night there's only thought and memory. For those who don't fall asleep easily, the horrors begin. Mine was one specific image - Zoë driving to Marks Tey *alone*. What had she felt? Anger, loss, abandonment, grief? The torment of that image was alleviated when Maev Kennedy, a *Guardian* colleague of Wal's, told me the story of her father Maurice's suicide. It had *never* occurred to me that there might have been a strong sense of relief. He had suffered throughout his life with episodes of recurrent depression. He tried to kill himself by letting carbon monoxide into his garage as he sat in his car. As he lost consciousness, his foot hit the accelerator and the car shot through the garage doors. He recovered consciousness in hospital but died a week later from his injuries. Maev was able to ask him what he had felt while he was executing his plan. "Ever the man," she said, "to choose his words with care," he thought long before saying, 'comfortable'."

*

Zoë's bedroom has become my study; a new blue vinyl floor covering replaced the old green carpet. As the sharp edge of grief grows smoother over time, the pain stemming

291

from her permanent absence remains, the sadness of never being able to tell her about the family or the animals.

<u>*December 7th 2000*</u>

The day after Zoë's 28th birthday. Friends and family remembered and sent messages..... My eyes are permanently red and sore.

Helping the bereaved is a delicate art, which I've never been good at myself. Rory, far off in Adelaide, sent advice one month later:

.... However deeply we love someone, I don't think we have the right to use that love as a form of blackmail to keep the other person alive if they do not wish to live. And even we did regard ourselves as having this 'right', it would be pretty futile. If the urge to kill yourself is really strong, you are not going to go on living, day after day, just to be accommodating to other people who want you to live.

If bi-polars were given to killing themselves while temporally spectacularly manic (as Zoë was in Morocco) there would be a much greater argument in favour of forceful intervention with a view to returning them to their primary personality structure - what I suppose you could call their 'real' selves. But they don't - they kill themselves while rational and depressed.

I can understand Rory's argument but never agree with it.

Just before Christmas I wrote: *Zoë has been gone four months. How feeble our hearts are or mine is. Why did she HATE me in some of her diaries? Do we all hate one another? Gone through lots of old stuff in boxes, letters from friends and Wal and my first love letters.*

2 am. Christmas passed well. Fifteen at table. Our four kids with Simon, Niall, Fredy, Maria and the grandchildren. Fredy weighs 43 kilos and is thin as a rake. Ben must weigh double; I am almost stout myself. People must have missed Zoë in their own way. No one has

292

mentioned her much. I have gone off to the caravan to
weep. 15 people - there must have been more than 100
presents. ...

The candles at dinner - a pretty healthy glow. Zoë is
28 but only in my head.

Thursday January 3rd. 2001

A year that Zoë will never know. Zoë wasn't spoken of at
Christmas but everyone was thinking of her. Her presence is
still in the house. Everyone behaved more kindly and gently
towards one another.

Zoë has stayed with the family as a gentle presence
although she is little spoken of. When Tanya married Niall
in 2002 in the garden at Greenacres, Sarojini conducted the
marriage service devised by the young couple, based on
Hindu and Buddhist religious vows. As Tanya and Niall
came hand-in-hand to meet the guests waiting on the grass,
two nieces scattering rose petals and Ben playing a recorder
with Max his nine year-old playing the clarinet preceding
them. Tanya and Niall exchanged vows under a garland of
flowers hung between two poplar trees. Their son Aaron
aged five months went from one person's arms to another's
with his habitual sunny nature. It was so easy to imagine
Zoë at that celebration. Not the morose Zoë of her last
months but the younger Zoë who enlivened any social
occasion, got the children playing, bringing out shy guests
and always flirting with at least one male guest. The
wedding was the sort of family occasion she excelled at.

Three years after Zoë's death, Habie wrote:

.... Zoë in life was a seeker of truth and would have wanted
as many of us as possible to try and express how we feel
now that she has gone. Zoë's death undid years of therapy-
generated confidence and fulfilment, took away the
possibility of pure joy, and left sheen of sadness and fear

over everything. I can't bear the phone to ring at night, I panic if anyone I love is on a motorway, I don't trust contentment to last more than a second at a time, and cannot remember what 'carefree' could have felt like. Since Zoë died others have died too, including my two unborn children. Each time I wonder if it will be possible to sit up straight again. I no longer know what is a Zoë moment, or a consequence of Zoë, and what is just the rest of life, the parts of life that were never Zoë in the first place.

... I've stopped expecting her to come back. The extreme pain has become muted, more a continuous effect with occasional moments of either disbelief – or overwhelming sadness and missing her until my skin crawls from the longing. But mostly it's just there, in the background, something that has changed me as a person in so many ways and all of them are bad.

'I don't know for sure 'why' she did it, but I have some instinctive idea. She didn't want to face a lifetime of emotional trauma that was beyond her control. I think she believed in an afterlife and assumed the illness would not follow her there. She definitely did want to die; she knew that if you jump under a train at full speed you die for sure. No chance of waking up in hospital with a sore tummy, to anxious faces full of love. She wanted oblivion, and didn't want to tell us why, other than an anonymous kind of note covering all the expected suicide bases and revealing nothing.

I had always felt so close to Zoë, emotionally. We were both hyperbolic, unlike our other siblings. Everything for us was the absolute best or the absolute worst at all times. But she had an extra dimension of intensity. She didn't flick her hand to express irritation; she slammed a door until it broke. She didn't glare at you; she punched you in the stomach. She didn't say, "You annoy me." She said, "You have ruined my life" (and two days later, "you're the most amazing person I know, you're the bees' knees and the dog's bollocks - bugger me!" with a burst of sexy manic laughter). So when she actually jumped under that train it

294

seemed as if, destroyed by the life sentence of a manic depression diagnosis, she just waited until she was 'better' enough to function and called on those reserves of extreme Zoë-ness to do physically what others only ponder, in moments of stress or sorrow, but never really consider. She was so extreme that her sorrow was extreme (was that her nature or the effect of the illness, or both? Will there ever be answers to such questions?) Her anger was extreme too. Suicide must be in some part an angry gesture towards those left behind, an acknowledgment that they were not good enough. But at the same time, I don't believe Zoë actively thought through the pain she would cause everyone she loved (and the distress she would cause the train driver who would kill her). She was far too loving herself for that; she will have blocked it out, all but perhaps the most vague half-notions of "so there!" and "I 'm sorry..." – if we her family couldn't make her better then we would be better off without her. She often asked in those final weeks, "Will I get better?" None of us could convince her she would. I could tangibly feel that glass wall of hers, could feel us all operating behind it as she watched us, dead-eyed, from the other side.

My saddest memory is of a moment a few days before she died. The family were by the swimming pool on a hot day, chatting and jumping in the water and playing with the kids. Zoë was standing some distance from us at the other end. I was watching her, though she couldn't see me. She started to slowly unbutton her top to get ready to swim and then after one button, she just folded under the effort of the gesture and there was a kind of visible hopelessness about her as she seemed to remember there was no point in anything; she stopped what she was doing and listlessly sat down again. No one noticed. I don't remember if she did the button up again or not. We all left the family home to go back to our own homes, and there was just Zoë and Mum and Dad and she had two more days to live.

EPILOGUE

"Goodbye Zoë."

This was the note the Police found pinned to your dashboard at the railway station where you killed yourself; the handwriting was neat.

To my family and friends and Hicham (their addresses are on a list pinned up over my bed.

No one is to blame for my death.

I am killing myself because the circumstances of my life are unbearable.

I love you all; but I can't live like this.

I am in too much pain and I am just deteriorating.

I'm sorry. Please forgive me.

I used to work and see friends a lot; but now I can do neither because I can't function nor communicate.

I've been in hell for 4 months and I can't bear the pain any more.

Zoë

When I had finished reading your diaries, my diaries, your notebooks and hundreds of emails from friends and all the medical reports, I found no answer. Weren't you yourself swinging between *yes* or *no*? You wrote that last summer in the brown notebook I'd given you:

Reality: Morocco/Hicham - can't go back. So you knew, as I guessed you had, that Hicham was a fantasy.

> *Most probably have to accept a more humble job and more humble living arrangements than I would like - if*

I don't get better, but make the most of things - I can work my way up.

Have to accept that at 27 I am not 'set up' job/house/relationship-wise. My friends will not reject me if I don't reject me. The challenge is to be happy and true to my nature, through deep self-esteem because I don't have any strength at the moment and may not have for a long time if ever - bad luck.

I feel myself trembling on the brink of understanding your leaving like that - the essential mystery of suicide. You killed yourself – doesn't make sense. Killing is someone does to something else – an enemy, an animal, an accident. Not to yourself!

There is no pain to compare with the one suicide inflicts. Nobody who is healthy wants to die and nobody who is healthy wants to burden his or her loved ones with this kind of pain. And what was going through your mind during the confusion of your last weeks and what was going through our minds - not seeing that you were growing worse not better?

"No one is to blame for my death," writing in your suicide note those eight words in biro then tracing over the letters so that some letters are thickened and others have two parallel lines from top to bottom. They are like railway tracks foreshadowing your implacable act.

Your friend Lizzie sent an email a year later saying that she'd dreamed about you. She couldn't remember details but you were giving her useful advice. When people dream of you sometimes you frighten them, sometimes not. Julia dreamed that you held a menacing rifle but Tanya dreamed that in our sitting room, a wind blew through your hair and you turned into a butterfly in a cloud of other blue butterflies that all flew outside.

Your father went to Scotland the spring after you died and saw the trees that we had paid for. Six hundred of them. No plaque or anything. In the forest book, there's a grid reference for the actual spot. He took photos. They are just young native trees, a good memorial for you.

Most of your ashes (you'd be as surprised as I was, the volume of ashes one body makes) are under a mossy stone where Tigger is buried in the front garden. I sometimes fight an urge to raise that stone and see what's happened to them. Are they mixed with earth? When Tigger died you were pleased that I wrapped the cat in white muslin instead of burying him in a dustbin liner.

When the vet opened his bag, I ran out of your room, too squeamish to watch the final injection. You held Tigger your arms. When I came back a few minutes later, he looked asleep and peaceful.

No one held *you*. The police sergeant insisted that you could have felt nothing. That can't be true! You must have felt something as your body smashed against the window of the driver's cab. The train driver said at the inquest that you jumped high. He was sent to hospital with shock. Remained there for several days, I believe. A friend of a friend of yours said: "what an egotistical way to die. Didn't she think of the train driver?"

"At that moment she wasn't thinking of drivers." I said, "Fuck off!" I've never seen him again, nor want to.

"I can't bear the pain any longer," you wrote in that note. I've laminated it, a souvenir together with a lock of your hair.

Why couldn't you wait? Fourteen weeks of pain should not have been unendurable. You slept a lot.

But there are other ways of looking at your tempestuous life – your friends, your lovers, your writing, your enthusiasm, your joy.

Perhaps you were too fine for us? The music of the drum you danced to didn't suit our drab, calculating world where what someone *has* counts more than what someone *is*. Or was it simply random chemicals misfiring, turning your reactions from vivid to florid and shocking the sensibilities of everyone around you? I had never seen a mad person until I saw you when we came to fetch you home.

Sensitivity – we lacked it. Honesty – we bamboozled ourselves. And you – the silent, sullen one behind the glass wall retreating; we thought you were improving but you had already decided to go.

I don't know what doppelganger took you.

I hate her.

You accepted her; the two of you must have worked out careful plans to arrive just as the London express hurtles down the tracks; hid behind a concrete pillar, dash down the platform and leap at the precise moment.

To be loving is not enough when we are also ignorant. Your father phoned from Liverpool Street to say that his train was delayed." Apparently there's been a fatality on the line."

Neither of us guessed that it was you.

Zo, my beloved daughter, stay in our memories as long as we're alive and the others who remember you - even if it's not for so long. Sometimes, Zo, I go places and I don't tell them about you. Every parent who loses a child to suicide has to accept that the dead fade from active daily consciousness; they have to or none of us could carry on. There comes a stage when grief must subside or life becomes subordinate to pain.

"Please forgive me," you wrote. When I forgive you, will you forgive me? You left an unexpected legacy. You used to complain in letters and conversations and emails, that I moaned too much about my life. Now that the next to worse thing has happened, I moan less.

So is there an answer?

299

You killed yourself because your brain grew too disordered to give you enough time to wait for the anti-depressants to take effect.

You killed yourself because you couldn't face returning to hospital. Or as your elder sister says: you just wanted to stop the pain and thought that you could come back later.

Life itself is a mystery – why should death be clearer?

APPENDIX ONE:

Other People

Immediate grief prevented us from looking much deeper into manic depression. In those first two years we transcribed onto a computer the diaries Zoë had written for most of her life and many of the papers she had kept. I found myself affected by her diaries: usually just the day to day comments of what she was doing and with whom and then in later years those black and mad entries of someone fighting literally for their life. Sometimes I would be laughing, on other times, it was like entering a pit of darkness. How could she have maintained that smiling exterior and written those agonizing words?

Wal and I wanted to do something to mark her passage, to commemorate Zoë and help other families by exploring our mistakes and omissions and those of the mental health services who, in spite of all their care and concern, had allowed Zoë to die. We sent a jointly written article to *The Guardian* telling Zoë's story in 2,500 words. Not all the family was in agreement. Zachary didn't want our private grief expressed in public.

Losing Zoë appeared as the cover story of the G2 supplement with a picture of Zoë radiantly happy, and another of her depressed. At the end of four days we had received more than 350 replies; a year later as I write this, they are still trickling in. It would take another book to describe fully the many replies we had to our article but in this chapter I have tried to extract the main themes.

We discovered: young people struggling alone, unable to convince their GPs that anything was wrong beyond the usual teenage upheavals; families dogged by multiple cases of mental illness, multiple suicides; parents whose son or daughter was locked up ("sectioned") for months, so full of drugs that they had been reduced to a shadow of themselves.

Some people barely able to cope with manic depression and not knowing to whom they could turn appealed to us for advice. So we began surfing the web, discovering a network of research and hands-on agencies - the Manic Depression Fellowship, Mind, the Institute of Psychiatry, the Mental After-Care Associations and some others.

I had thought that writing such an article would bring much criticism. It was the contrary. Only one correspondent, I'll call her Elizabeth, herself a sufferer, complained that we had no right to violate Zoë's privacy by exposing her in public. I replied that Zoë had not burned her papers so I guessed wanted them read. Inevitably, neither of us convinced the other and I went ahead with this book.

Many readers wrote to thank us for giving them the courage to fight on. Others said they were managing to live with the illness with the aid of medication and psychotherapy, and that made us wonder, if Zoë, too, had found the strength to persevere, how she might have coped? Yet others suggested, a view which we've heard from different sources, that in ending her suffering and escaping from a future with an illness that was treatable but not curable, Zoë probably made a "rational choice".

Many people wrote and emailed us that our article helped counteract the stigma of mental illness by our efforts to understand Zoë, and by linking manic depression to someone who was beautiful and talented.

The responses to the article showed sympathy with the guilt we felt over the sterile and scratchy relationship we had with our daughter in her last weeks. These readers pointed out that people who are clinically depressed cannot respond to family and friends. Such people live, as Zoë herself put it, "behind a glass wall."

We replied to every email, received supplementary answers from many and became friends with some of them.

Parents "left out of the equation"

Nearest to our own experience was that of Jean Fellows who wrote to say her daughter Melanie's manic depression had remained undiagnosed until far too late. Melanie took a fatal overdose at the age of 27.

Jean, who is a city councillor, spoke for many frustrated parents who were not listened to by the doctors because their manic-depressive offspring were adults. Melanie, after an outpatient appointment at which she denied being ill, fled from her home town to avoid scrutiny and criticism. After that, her mother's efforts to get help were consistently rebuffed because Melanie was an adult and did not always show obvious psychotic symptoms.

Like Zoë, Melanie was "intelligent, great fun, much loved, creative and idealistic. The only thing that might have helped is if she had been given hope that treatment could work."

Jean Fellows found the doctors unwilling to listen to her concerns. They said Melanie must first realise that she is ill and needs help.

But it looked to us as if the illness made her unable to realise anything of the sort - until the moment when she was "coming back to herself", and then she felt alone and unable to cope with how she had behaved (appallingly to friends who still were ready to help if only given the chance) and unable to accept that a "normal" life might be possible even with manic depression.

Jean could have been writing about Zoë in her last months. She thinks GPs need to be better trained in recognising the signs of mental illness, more ready to listen to family and friends and more willing to intervene when treatment is evidently necessary. 'Public awareness too is vital: this is still a taboo subject, people are frightened by mental illness and there is considerable stigma attached.'

Jenny Day is another agonised and ignored parent we could identify with. Her 26 year- old son had been diagnosed as a manic depressive four months before she wrote us.

Since then I have lived every day on a knife edge. Have I got enough information? Am I doing all I can? Will I recognise signs of distress? So many questions and I feel that the mental health services are only scratching the surface of treating my son. He is just one of many they see every day, such a familiar sight to them, such a devastating experience for me and him.

Jenny wanted to know if there was a support network for families. "I know there isn't one locally and I have thought of setting one up. What would have helped you?' We passed on what we had learned and wrote to her three months later for news.

So lovely to hear from you both. Jim is OK at the moment.

He tried twice to go back to his job and after the second attempt rang me from his bed in the middle of the night in tears saying he couldn't cope. This was the first real admission that he had to make a serious attempt to get back his life. Since then he has finished renovating his fishing boat and I have bought him a new engine. He is waiting for the better weather to launch it.

Jim was now seeing a counsellor whom he liked. "He plays around with his medication but seems to be quite stable nonetheless". Jean had got no further in setting up a support group.

Richard Bates is another parent who felt "left out of the equation" by the mental health authorities, resulting in severe and needless suffering for the patient and the parents. His twenty-year old daughter Maria shared the article with him when he visited her in the hospitals' Psychiatric Unit.

As you can guess, Maria is a manic depressive and has just survived a second major breakdown whilst studying. Like Zoë, Maria is vibrant, charismatic and highly intelligent. Her breakdown, which happened when she was editing the college magazine, was no doubt made worse by stress, alcohol, cocaine and not taking her medication. Whilst in the unit, she has also attempted suicide and self-harmed in various ways. Thankfully she is now home with us and we are gradually trying to pick up the pieces.

Maria's parents felt needlessly excluded from her care. After her first breakdown it was three days before they were informed. Maria had tried to take her life twice in a two-week period and the second time she was transferred automatically to a psychiatric unit where she was held without a section but against her will.

The conditions were awful and she was almost blind without contact lenses and had no access to a phone. She finally persuaded a nurse to ring us so we could get her out. Her flatmates had covered for her and the university authorities didn't feel it appropriate to inform us.... Carers (in our cases the parents) need to be much more involved in the process. It is crazy to let someone who is mentally ill determine their destiny and deliberately not include those who care for them the most. I also wish Maria's friends had been better informed about her needs and tried to help her control her lifestyle.

Three months later, Richard Bates reported a breakthrough. He had found the course called STEADY run by the Manic Depression Fellowship, available free to the under 25s. Maria had done only one session but it had made a radical difference.

It is all about self-management and even the facilitators tend to be sufferers rather than healthcare professionals. The chance to meet a group of fellow sufferers of about the same age has been tremendously encouraging. So many things she feels guilty about are things all the others have done too. She is already much

*more confident about the future and really looking forward
to the other sessions. Thanks to the course, she now has a
peer group she can phone, email or visit.*

Zoë, too, might have had that opportunity. Had she emerged
from her final depression, she might have overcome her
antipathy for the company of other mentally ill people and
joined a support group. But then, she would have had to
acknowledge and decide to cope with permanent disability,
involving a character change – a Zoë we have never known.

How can parents help a manic patient who, like
Zoë, is an adult? Vera Doughty' daughter Gail is 21, with
an English degree and a diagnosis of bi-polar. She is also a
bulimic, self-injures and sometimes has hallucinatory
episodes.

*There must be more of us, shut out from so much of what is
happening to them and being on the 'edge' of the services
given to them. It's such a hard role to play – the parent. I
was told that she is an 'adult now', when she reached 18
but who the hell cared for her and listened in the middle of
the night and in between juggling work and other family
responsibilities? On the scale of time, how much more we
spend with them and have so much to offer those who sit in
judgment of them and us.*

Like Zoë, Gail's problems seemed to start with
glandular fever. She described her daughter as "incredibly
creative…. musical, plays piano and sings. Is an ardent
defender of the less able and has spent time over the years
with children who have learning disabilities. She has a
wicked sense of humour and shows great kindness to
others"

Liz Miller wrote that reading our article had
encouraged her and her husband in their determination to
show their son, Samuel, who is bi-polar, "just how much we

love him, and not, as one of Zoë's psychiatrists advised, to leave (him) alone."

Samuel is 21. Like Zoë, he is a wonderful person to be with - most of the time. He too is very intelligent, lights up a room with his wit and charisma, and is so loving and giving. We can never know as parents whether we are doing the right thing. All we can do is follow our instincts (and perhaps some advice) and hope for the best.

Liz, who is a health care professional, agreed with us on the issue of confidentiality, and said she would be using Zoë's story "to underline a message that I, colleagues and carers have been trying to get across to medical, nursing and social services staff for many moons. Carers need the right kind of support and more information, to help them to help the person they care for and hopefully, to prevent further tragedies."

'Thank you for sharing your story. I, for one, will be taking your advice and never be complacent about Samuel's depressions, and indeed, will kiss him more often.'

Unaided and alone

We heard also from bi-polars themselves. Some, like Cliff Harris, felt unaided and alone.

I am 30 years old, have not really spoken to anyone for close on two years, have burned bright, fast, hard and with much acknowledgement from my peers...but it's been gone for some time now and my pride is the cornerstone of my problem - to return to that which I know I can be... 'I know that I don't have the courage to commit suicide, so I rather keep away from society, not having to engage in the terrible truth of my life...I see little prospect of recapturing the intensity of my life.

Cliff Harris had tried meditation as a means of quietening his mind's delirium and keeping at bay his urge for suicide. Meditation has permitted this quietening, but at the expense, he felt, of his spark and his spirit.

I too have read about manic depression and how it creeps and devours the afflicted and it is the inevitability of this that really makes any effort seems futile and the prospect of deferment through drugs simply a state of delusion. Should you know of any permanent manner of dealing with the condition I would really appreciate your help...

John Wallace could not manage a bipolar life either, and was encouraged by our article to return to treatment.

As I read about Zoë, I saw a lot of parallels between her and me - it didn't make for easy reading. Two years ago I made a conscious decision to stop my course of medication and counselling. I wanted very much to be able to lead my life as myself and I believed that I should be able to deal with any problems by myself.
Recently I've been relapsing and I've been told by friends and family that I need help. After having read the article and having thought about this for a long time I've been back to see my doctor (for the first time in 18 months) and I will be trying to draw up a new plan with her to help me deal with my illness.

Three months later we asked him for news. John replied that he was now working with a psychiatrist to develop a long term strategy to deal with his illness.....

I'm finding this challenging, monitoring my moods, sleep and diet, not drinking, no drugs, regular intensive exercise and severely reducing my caffeine intake (probably the hardest thing to give up). I am however starting to feel a lot more positive and in control of my life (apologies if this last line reads like something from a self help book...)

Julia Melford had developed bipolar disorder after contracting meningo-encephalitis while backpacking in China. She feels lonely and misunderstood and wishes there was a campaign to get rid of the stigma of this and other mental maladies. .

My parents found it very difficult to deal with and the whole family remained in denial... I battled on with it for years without telling anyone at work: I just took tranquillisers and anti-depressants. At times the anti-depressants made me go high. Sometimes I would get into a rage at work and nobody could understand why. I include myself in this as I didn't believe in the diagnosis and didn't realise temper was part of it. I wasted thousands of pounds on therapy which did little good. What I really needed was the right medication.

Julia had her worst episode after her father died: she made abusive phone calls to her elder brother and sister who concluded that she was vicious and evil.

I made the decision to try and 'come out' to friends and the fact that it is no longer called 'manic depression' has made a great difference as it means people do not have such erroneous ideas about it. I think we really need a campaign to try to get rid of the stigma. People should be encouraged to let their friends and workplace know. I was just too frightened I would lose my job. I found the website for bipolar condition very helpful and the diagnostic criteria they put on the web made me feel sure that I did have the illness and stopped me being in denial. Fortunately I was quite honest to the doctors about smoking pot at times. The psychiatrist warned me never to touch it again. It is a shame your daughter never got this advice. We need to campaign for this too.

Hetty Manfred identified closely with Zoë and offered acute insight into the heaven of mania and the hell of depression.

I would like to have met her. I think we would have been friends. You see, you were also describing me. I am manic depressive and two years ago, aged 27, I was admitted into hospital for the third time after a suicide attempt. After being manic I had hit a long and severe depression. I, too, have two brothers and two sisters; I have a first class degree and have had my (intermittent!) share of varied and odd success! However, to be blunt, I am still alive. And I know that I am fortunate.

Hetty was "dragged to a doctor" by a friend and promptly sectioned, but she feels this would not have happened if her mother had not been away on holiday. When her mother returned she tried to get Hetty released from "the filthy, Victorian psychiatric hospital" but failed.

Though Zoë is not with us here anymore, I am sure she is definitely around somewhere, spiritually, in some form. And I bet my bottom dollar she is having a ball! The thing is, when the depression hits that bad and you believe in an after life, you feel as though you have just naturally come to the end.

We do not know whether Zoë still kept her religious belief at the end of her life. There is little evidence one way or the other. In any case, her deep depression probably allowed no space for faith, as Hetty herself suggests.

The pain is unbearable; you cannot talk, concentrate, think, bear to be touched or even to be seen. Your whole existence becomes one of non-existence. You want out and even though you would never verbally admit it, all you think about is death. All you see is blankness and all you want to do is die. As you mentally fight (and it is a hardcore, fuckoff fight) day in, day out, you realize that you exist purely for the reason of not existing.'

Hetty's message was precious to us because it helped us to understand why Zoë in her last weeks had been able to show so little affection for us, the rest of the family and her friends. That in turn assuaged our own feelings of guilt that we had not been able to show her more affection.

You stay non-existing for those you love - but you know that you are hurting them.... You wish that they would leave you alone, act normally, ignore you, be happy, and get on with their lives. You are a burden. A burden unto yourself, your family, your friends, your pets, your family's friends, your friend's friends, the nurses, doctors, consultants. A universal burden...

At those times Hetty felt that the possibility of her depression lifting was one that only existed in other people's minds, for this was not just her illness; this was what she had become. She felt her life was over.

I am sure Zoë, after much intense, constant deliberation and grief came to the conclusion that whether she left, or stayed, her family would be sad. But she had the option and release of death and the enticement of freedom and happiness. Hugs and kisses are beautiful, but they would not have held Zoë here. Unfortunately, I believe the only thing that would have possibly made her stay is medication and, as you know, that's a whole long saga of its own.

Hetty got little help or understanding in her family, but eventually, during her last "hospihell," she put her trust in a consultant who prescribed a "medley of medicational concoctions" which eventually stabilised her moods. Hetty now accepts her illness and even talks of it with affection. She is on a level of understanding and acceptance that poor Zoë never reached.

Manic depression is, like some other illnesses, a kind of gift. It swans eccentrically down generations, torturously teasing, chronically belittling, egotistically inflating, and pompously pampering our little minds. It is scathing, brutal and unforgiving. It is awesome, orgasmic and thrilling. It is what it is and holds no reason, barriers or justification 'I am so very sorry it took away your Zoë. But I like to think it might just have taken her someplace fantastic. Compassion and empathy are so important in this world and without illness how would they begin to be instigated?

311

Zoë felt frustrated and shamed at being "left behind" while her friends and siblings seemed to go from strength to strength. So did Linda Hale, who wrote to us about her eight-year struggle with cyclomythia, a milder form of manic depression. She is twenty-five.

I too had seen graduate friends off to high paid jobs in the City, while I struggled to find something I could actually cope with, despite being a straight A / First Class graduate. Being told I'd never be able to cope with a full-time job (proved them wrong on that one!). And feeling guilty for hating the lows but loving the highs, experiencing emotions of an intensity you knew other people couldn't. Longing for some stability, but despising it when it came, never knowing which feelings were real and which were lies - my body's cruel conspiracy against my mind. ....

Linda seemed able to identify with us, the parents, as easily as with Zoë.

You can give all the love and support in the world and say all the right words, but you can't change what's in someone's head. I remember my own parents making gestures similar to yours - fixing up Zoë's car (that's such a sweet thought!) - but in my ingratitude all I could see was them try to fix the wrong problem, kind of wondering why they were wasting their time. I didn't need a new car, I needed a new head! I felt sorry for them. Some things you just can't help with. BUT, those kind words and gestures are probably what sustained her as far as they got.

Linda's message showed us better than anyone else why Zoë could not communicate the anguish which drove her to suicide.

The best way I can describe it is like really fuzzy, faint filters of light a very long way off in a thick, penetrating darkness. Even if you can't banish the darkness, it's better than no light at all.

312

We asked Linda how she had learned to live with her illness: she said recovery could only be defined as self-management –

...: learning what your triggers are, putting coping mechanisms and support networks in place for future episodes, learning to recognise the warning signs, learning certain avoidance techniques (for me that might be not drinking too much /not going to crowded places like nightclubs - in other words, know your limitations), and fully utilising the support networks available to you THAT WORK FOR YOU (be that medication, psychotherapy, friends, religion, art, exercise etc)

For Linda, self-management could only come through self-acceptance – "accepting that you are ill, that ignoring it won't make it go away, that you aren't a freak - you are simply unwell, and that illness is more often than not chronic or recurrent."

There ARE ways of reducing the effects of mental ill health on your life. What is needed is mass re-education of society as a whole, from school curriculums to medical training. MIND, in my opinion, do a fantastic job of normalising' (by which I mean not dramatising) mental health. The media on the other hand, by and large paint a painfully inaccurate picture of mental health.

Rob Dibben wrote consolingly that we could not have helped Zoë more than we did. "She simply would not have reacted to your displays of affection, to your hugs, to your caresses, to your obvious love and concern."

I have suffered from manic depression for many years. During the depressive phase one cannot react, one feels dead inside emotionally which leads to great feelings of guilt when emerging from the depression. You both and your other children could have been killed in a tragic accident and Zoë would have been able to feel NOTHING. She did not want to be in that state. In the blackest of moods one has to focus on the fact that a manic phase will

313

eventually return. Unfortunately at 27, Zoë had not experienced sufficient cycles of the condition to appreciate this. Because she had come out of two depressive phases perhaps she thought that she would never be able to function as a 'normal' adult with a family of her own.

Rob understood that Zoë could not bear the prospect of a life with lithium because it would diminish her.

It is true that most manic depressives would try to avoid treatment with lithium - because during the manic phase they experience such periods of creativity, of sensitivity, of inspiration, of love for others that to be 'normal' is less preferable than enduring the periods of depression. It is as if the mind burns itself out during the manic phase and then shuts down in the depressive phase so that the body can recuperate... I hope that there is something in what I have written that will at least allow you to eventually forgive yourselves. Even in her depressive phase she loved you dearly but was totally incapable of expressing it and perhaps in her manic phase she was so busy helping others that she neglected to tell you just how much you meant to her.

Catastrophes even worse

And then we had those really heart-rending messages telling of catastrophes worse than our own.

Hello, there. My name is James Beaufort and I read your article in the Guardian yesterday with great interest and obvious sadness at the same time. I can really empathise with you as I also have a daughter, Sarah, who is now just 27 and suffering from bi-polar disorder. Currently she is in a secure ward and sectioned under two counts, one for her illness, and secondly she is still serving a 4.5 year prison sentence for misdemeanours in 2000.

Sarah had been ill for 13 years. She was due out on parole in a month but had no idea what she wanted to do.

The total lack of any sort of help for me or her mother - we are divorced - is very plain to see, probably

314

because in the eyes of the law she is an adult! I know that is not the case as she has missed a great chunk of her teenage and "20's" years being in and out of homes, psychiatric institutions, prison, etc. Her mentality is that of a 14-year-old which is when all the alcohol and drug induced psychosis started. The point I am making is who to turn to for positive feedback on Sarah?

Two months later we wrote to James for news. Sarah was back in prison and about to be moved to another psychiatric hospital.

Leila King wrote to say she identified with us as 'a middle-class professional family.' We identified with her too, although her daughter Penny suffers a worse fate than Zoë did.

Like us Leila had grown up in the tradition that equated psychological problems with neurosis which, in turn, we linked to early environment – and the mistakes of our parenting. Hence, wrote Leila. "We are almost considered the guilty party as the causative factors of this terminal and cruel brain disease. That hurts, when what you have tried to do is to give all your children the same springboard to leap from."

Leila's 20-year-old middle daughter, Penny, had a rapid-cycling schizo-affective mood disorder – similar in essential ways to manic depression, but worse: at 21 Penny was sectioned and detained in hospital. Like us, Lucy and her husband asked themselves: how could this happen in our happy family? Did we miss anything?

Now we realise that unbeknown to any of us, the very first warning signs - the amber alert - must have appeared from the early age of 12 onwards, but they were sporadic and, as you put it, we must not become too hysterical and overprotective as middle-class parents! The summer she sat her 11 GCSEs (and got 8 A* and 3 A grades), I as her mother saw that something was not right. She became very withdrawn, depressed, lost her initiative, became afraid of people. From then on, in her sixth form

315

year, the depression and suicidal plans became a permanent state of mind. I spent nights with her trying to console the inconsolable. There was something so immeasurable in her fragility and so terminal in her existential despair. This was clearly different from run-of-the-mill teenage angst.

Penny went through A Levels but that was as far as she could go: she started hallucinating and hearing voices. She confided only in her mother.

I tried to persuade her to see a doctor but she convinced me that it was nothing to do with doctors and they would not be able to help. She then withdrew from the outside world completely, seldom left the house or her room, became pathologically interested in death, and murder investigations on television.

Penny was seen by a psychiatrist and prescribed antidepressants and mood stabilisers but there was no improvement.

By April she was so psychotic, believing she had supernatural powers, could fly like birds, stop aeroplanes and cars by her glance and receive commands via television and newspapers. At times she believed that I, her mother, was passing on information about her in a coded language over the phone to the police and the Government.

And then the worst happened for Penny and her mother – the nightmare Zoë had always feared most.

Six days after her 21st birthday they came and amidst screams of protestation from our poor child she was sectioned into a mixed age, mixed sex acute psychiatric unit, where she has been languishing for nine months to date. She has been drugged out of all human emotion, almost all cognitive function, and her slim body has layers of acne, her long blonde hair falling out, her mouth drooling, hands and feet trembling, periods missing for seven months.

Penny was detained under Section 3 of the Mental Health Act, which she and her mother experienced as "the most archaic bits of English legislation."

To end up on her Majesty's Pleasure for 9, 12, 18 months when you are so young and all your friends are getting on. And you remain without any control in any decision, encouraged to attend workshops of omnipresent pottery or creative writing week in week out. You become just a number to be 'observed' through the glass in the door (if you are lucky enough to have a single room - it may be only a flimsy pair of bedside curtains round your bed in a dormitory!), a receptacle for pouring potfuls of pills into three times a day.

Leila found her daughter lacking in any empathetic psychological support while agency nurses came and went.

Her psychiatrist is from Sri Lanka and has the typical attitude of the males from his culture to all females. He seems to be able to ban the family from all communication and information - against the requests of our daughter.

Perhaps without meaning to, Lucy Lane seemed to suggest at one point that her daughter, who was obsessed with death, might indeed be better off dead.

What I am trying to convey to you is my feeble offer of comfort to you - you did everything possible for your Zoë. She herself tasted the life under lithium and weighed the benefits of being 'controlled' by drugs, which then deprived her of the compensatory highs of her manic spells. Like your Zoë, like our Penny, the victims of this illness have to work out the balance sheet whether they wish to continue with their 'risky' swings, with the helter-skelter, facing the inevitability of the final 'accident', or whether they accept the career of being a drugged mental health 'service user' (what an awful term, reminding me of a car park or launderette user or the services offered by a prostitute to her users!). If I had known what I committed our daughter into by agreeing her to be sectioned in April, I would not do

317

it again. I would or should allow her the basic human right of choosing the place of her death - unfortunately, the time should not be of our own choosing but in terminal illness compassion sometimes forces even the professionals to shorten the agony and hasten the end. And I speak as a nurse with a long experience.

Later, Leila wrote with better news. Penny's section 3 had been rescinded and after a year in hospital she was discharged into community care.

We were celebrating liberation - like the Iraqis - but it seems so hollow when the poor girl's mental condition is not that different from what it was a year ago. Her depression, withdrawal into her bed, isolation, lack of any interest in appearance or activities continue without relief; the manic spells are removed, so it is even bleaker this way.

And Leila sent us a poem written for us by Penny, called A Cancer of the Mind.

I could not see the sun,

It had gone out.

I could not feel what love was,

It had left me.

My heart became a tomb,

My hands were clay.

And people came to visit

but they could not reach me.

I, a trapped nerve,

A gut spasm,

I who read seaside as suicide,

I who wished

to raze me from life,

cried with the hole of my heart.

and Jesus heard me

and reached down

for He poured out his blood

to raise me to Life.

My Lord, my Love, I cried

and I flew to the moon and the stars.

Under the Stigma

For Hetty Parsons, the stigma attached to mental illness was hard to bear.

> *My brother died 10 years ago from an accidental heroin overdose. He was 28. He was manic depressive. He was a musician and because of the circles he moved in he found it easy to get hold of anything he wanted. He wasn't a heroin addict but used it when the depression became too much. Of course, we too discovered this after his death.*

Hetty's brother was diagnosed with the illness when he was 18. By this time he was already in a rock band, touring far from home and very independent. He did not talk of his illness to his family until he was 26 when he could no longer avoid it.

> *Dealing with the loss of someone who is manic depressive, especially if you have only known about their illness for a relatively short time, is devastating. All the people I know who suffer from it are very special. They do and say the things you wouldn't dare to, they achieve incredible feats. They are such a bright light in a grey world that when their light goes out all your world seems pitched into darken. Manic depression needs to have the stigma stripped away from it and care of people with mental illnesses needs to be exposed for the outdated sham that it is.*

The Carers' burden

Partners, or just friends who find themselves unofficial, de-facto carers, also wrote to us of the heavy burden they carry. **David Gates** wrote of his bipolar partner Maria who, just like Zoë, had had her first manic episode when she was 18. Mike's misfortune was living through the second one, which caught them unawares.

Although I would say she is quite stable, after reading your article I know that I have been ignoring some signs. Maria is Spanish and one of the kindest "full of life" people you could ever meet. She has many friends, and finds it easy to make friends. Completely opposite to me! For a long time she had problems with her medication. No combination of antidepressant and mood stabiliser was ever quite right.

After the suicide of a bi-polar friend, Maria deteriorated.

She had been slowly trying to come off lithium; she was being supervised by her doctor, who I personally think was wrong to think that Maria could leave lithium. She could not sleep at night and had panic attacks. Then everything blew up, she bought plane tickets for total strangers and told everyone – except me - that she was going to Spain. The next thing I knew I was told that she had been found on the roof of Liverpool airport, and had been taken to hospital. I went straight there to find a very different Maria to the one that I had known for five years, I knew that she was bi-polar, but I was totally unprepared for this. She refused to see me, and was adamant that she didn't ever want to see me again.

Reading David's account we remembered how Zoë, too, had turned against us in her final mania. We assume the reason was that a manic state is fun to be in and a familiar figure from normal life may not be welcome.

I was devastated, kept asking myself what I had done wrong. Then to add pain to injury the hospital managed to let her run away in the middle of the night.

Precisely what Zoë did, twice, in Essaouira!

Luckily she was found OK back at Liverpool airport trying to buy another flight to Spain. She was arrested and taken back to the hospital, where she was sectioned. Her mother came over to help me look after her. After a week Maria was allowed to come home. I was glad to have her back, but it was hell, she slept two hours a night and kept talking all the hours she was awake. I knew I could not cope so she went back to Spain with her mother.

Now she was due back and David Gates is apprehensive.

I dread the coming months because I don't know what lies ahead. Will she cope with going back to work? And how can I help? I think of things like 'is it OK to leave her in the flat by herself while I go to work?' And suicide, well she has always said that she would never do that and has never tried (as far as I know), but it will now always be in the back of my mind. What really worries me is that there seems to be very little aftercare, except for a visit to the doctor once every few weeks there is nothing. Did you have the same experience?

Yes, David, we did. After Zoë's first manic and depressive episode, she had no medical or psychiatric follow-up or supervision.

Comfort from an "expert"

We heard from several people who had become experts on their own mental illness or that of their loved ones and offered us their comfort. Oggie Freeman had some original insights, yet his conclusion is uncomfortable: if those last muddled months had turned out differently, if Zoë had been better served by her professional minders, she might have made it to the other side.

321

Your story will surely help a lot of people facing crises to be aware that they are not alone as they face the shortcomings of the mental health system, the powerlessness against the rollercoaster moods of their loved ones with manic depression, the limitations of medication, and the gulf that can grow between the person who is ill and family/friends. As a 'survivor' of manic depression (I had two severe psychotic episodes and many years of mood swings) I would like to challenge some issues you deal with.

Oggie, a bi-polar survivor, told us that we should not blame ourselves for refusing to see Zoë's eccentric behaviour as a bi-polar relapse.

Manic depression is like a drug on its own...pot and cocaine would certainly not help...but just like anyone with a drug habit or alcoholism, it is that individual who needs to gain insight. All the love and desire that you had for her to be well could not reach her directly but I am sure that your love would have been a constant fixed beacon, a lighthouse on the stormy sea of manic depression.

In our article we had written of Zoë's final, dismal weeks: "we cannot now forgive ourselves for reacting, during some of that time, like normal parents when their unsmiling child is surly and irritable." Oggie replied that if we had reacted like "abnormal" parents that would surely have been unreal for Zoë.

Manic depression can have the characteristics of a religious cult in taking an ill person away from their family through weird ideas, feelings of being a messianic figure, the drug of mania. Family are an annoying reminder that there is an unchanged stable life that the ill person was a part of before they became super-human. To react 'like normal parents' was probably the best thing to do.

Oggie reported that to a bi-polar, other peoples' worry could add additional strain.

I used to feel the concern of those close to me. If I felt elated one day I knew they would be thinking, 'Uh oh,

*he's going a bit high' or if I was depressed I knew a little
network of concern would be whirring away in the
background. This could feel claustrophobic, this constant
concern and observation.*

Oggie, with help from the Manic Depression
Fellowship (MDF), was now stable, as Zoë, perhaps might
have become if she had had more patience and humility.

*Why have I survived when your daughter has not? I
have been 'well' now for over 10 years. I stopped taking
medication – lithium - in co-operation with a cautious
psychiatrist, many years ago. I am very happily married
with a two year-old daughter (I reject the notion that I
should be afraid to have children because of passing on
manic depression genes) and I am able to work. Like your
daughter I accepted that I could not have a high-flying
graduate career because the illness had scuppered that start
in life and stigma, sadly, would be another obstacle.*

For Oggie, the MDF had not contradicted Zoë's
notion that "you never get over it", but had taught him that
you can live with it.

*The overriding message I got from MDF was that
this is a life-long condition – but a disability that people
were living with. The trouble is that, because of stigma,
those who are back living full lives usually do not come out
and say: yes I had manic depression in the past but I am
better now. I believe that there are prominent politicians
and others in the media glare who would give great
encouragement to people in the worst stages of manic
depression and their families if they could only speak about
their experiences and how they recovered.*

Suicide is not an option

Beware of depressed people telling their carers that suicide
is not an option, wrote Susan Beeching

*I always tell my mother the same thing: it is not an
option. I'm far too strong and far too much of a survivor to
even think about something like that! Although even while I*

reassure her, there's a dark side of my brain wondering if I
really am so sure.

Like Zoë, Susan fell into a depression while at
university – "so bad, I didn't even want to brush my teeth or
wash my hair, and my family doctor wanted to hospitalise
me." The doctor sent her to a psychiatrist, who put her on
Stellazine.

*It didn't make me happy, and it didn't make me want
to get up in the morning. I refused to be put in hospital,
figuring, well, how is having electric shocks and endless
drugs and hanging around other unhappy people going to
make me better able to deal with day-to-day living? That
said, I didn't want to live my life in a half-dead state, not
wanting to get up in the mornings - not even really wanting
to wake up in the mornings. Even now, quite often when I
am falling asleep, I sometimes think how peaceful it would
be just not to wake up the next day, and leave the whole,
messy frustrating business of life for other people who like it
just to get on with without me.*

Could anyone have reached Zoë? Our
correspondents sent us a mixed message. I have reached a
conclusion that hurts to accept; that she *could* have been
reached by people who had more compassion and insight
than ourselves.

'You weren't Mother Theresa,' friends said. 'You
did the best you could,' remarked others.

Just weeks before her death, she herself wrote what
her illness felt like:

*The most frightening thing is not knowing when the
depression will lift. There is a type of depression which is, I
believe, organic. It is when the biochemistry is so
unbalanced that it cannot rectify itself and hence the need
for medication. Like a broken leg in plaster, an unbalanced
biochemistry requires medication. It is a terrifying place to
be in - it's very difficult to describe which makes it harder
for others to understand.*

The stigma is hard too, when you're in a depression, it's hard to imagine being out of it. State of mind is so altered; you feel you've gone mad even when you're lucid.

Don't know what to do with myself. What to think. Where to start. Cannot envisage improvement in the future. Everything is quite frightening.

Zoë showed us both this passage. I remember how fast I read it, wanting the reading of it over as soon as possible. But denial was operating at full strength. I caught no sinister hint in the phrase 'cannot envisage improvement.'

That a bi-polar disorder is *not* a terminal illness needs to be stated and restated. And it does not have to carry the stigma and shame that so many feel. This final testimony comes from someone who gave us permission to use his real name.

Robert Westhead has suffered since his late teens until his early thirties and has finally reached an equilibrium. After finding our article in *The Guardian* archives, more than a year after it was written, he commented:

…. The echoes with my struggle with illness and the suffering of my parents are painful. I was diagnosed with bipolar at the aged of 19. I too managed to struggle through Bristol University despite being in the grip of illness, qualify and work as a journalist. Now, aged 31, I've struggled for many years to get the right treatment - baffled and deceived by this terrible condition - and have put my parents through a similar ordeal to the one you've endured.

The day after Boxing Day, I took an overdose of Lithium and crawled into some undergrowth in woodland near my parents' home in [a rural area] to die like an animal. Fortunately, something made me change my mind before it was too late - and somehow I'm still here. My family and fiancée have narrowly escaped the tragic loss

325

that you have suffered. New medication, I think, seems to have restored my mood to normal, as if by miracle. Please don't blame yourselves. No-one is to blame for bipolar – it's just a curse.

On May 15th 2004 Robert married Suzanne his fiancée.

[Some names have been changed.]

APPENDIX TWO:

This Illness

When you're high it's tremendous. The ideas and feelings are fast and furious like shooting stars, and you follow them until you find better and brighter ones. Shyness goes, the right words and gestures are suddenly there, the power to captivate others a felt certainty. There are interests found in uninteresting people. Sensuality is pervasive and the desire to seduce and be seduced irresistible. Feelings of ease, intensity, power, well-being, financial omnipotence and euphoria pervade one's marrow (Kay Redfield Jamison: The Unquiet Mind).

Kay Redfield Jamison might have been writing about Zoë. This is the stuff of manic depression, or bipolar affective disorder as professionals now call it because patients swing between two poles. The disorder affects as many as one adult in a hundred at some time in their life. *(1)* One in five bi-polars eventually commits suicide. *(2)*

On a "high" you have tremendous energy, racing thoughts, euphoric feelings and unusual insights. You talk too fast, spend too recklessly. You may be sexually promiscuous or extremely irritable, or both. You may, as Zoë claimed to have done in Morocco in her last, disastrous episode, let out a primal scream.

But, somewhere, this changes. The fast ideas are too fast, and there are far too many; overwhelming confusion replaces clarity. Memory goes. Humour and absorption on friends' faces are replaced by fear and concern. Everything previously moving with the grain is now against ...

Down in a "low" you are deeply depressed, unable to communicate and terribly anxious. You feel worthless and empty. You feel, as Zoë said, "behind a glass wall."

327

Jamison gives an inspiring account of her struggle with the illness which did not prevent her becoming and remaining professor of psychiatry at John Hopkins University.

This, I decided in the midst of my indescribably awful, eighteen-month bout of it, is God's way of keeping manics in their place. It works. Profound melancholia is a day-in, day out, night-in, night out almost arterial level of agony. It is a pitiless, unrelenting pain that affords no window of hope.

Bi-polar episodes most commonly start during or after the teenage years. The illness can be precipitated, but probably not caused, by viral infection, as it apparently was in Zoë's case, or by early trauma or stress. The first onset may be followed by long periods – typically eight to ten years - of being 'well'. Only a fifth of people who experience a manic episode do not get another.

Manic depression often runs in families, hence most professionals now think it has more to do with genes than with upbringing. Researchers in the USA have found that the prefrontal cortex area of the brain is smaller and less active in people who have hereditary depression, but no bi-polar gene has been isolated. Virginia Woolf's grandfather, mother, sister, brother and niece had all suffered from recurrent depression when her own famous manic depression ended in her suicide; her father and mother were cyclothymiacs (a milder form of recurring mania), and her cousin James also died in an acute manic episode. In our own family histories we know of four suicides in three generations.

Touched with fire

Manic depression is an ancient and well-documented illness. Excitement and depression were associated with a single disorder in the second century AD. The term *manico-melancolicus* appears in the 17th Century and in the 19th Century two French doctors described "circular insanity."

328

The illness has long been associated with charisma and exorbitant energy, often with genius. Famous bi-polars of our own times include Winston Churchill, Graham Greene, Virginia Woolf, Auguste Strindberg, Spike Milligan, Otto Klemperer, Stephen Fry, Vivien Leigh, Kurt Cobain and Francis Ford Coppola. Leaders and innovators of every age have had a disproportionately high incidence of mental disturbance which bears the hallmarks of manic depression: Martin Luther, Oliver Cromwell, Horatio Nelson, Napoleon Bonaparte, Abraham Lincoln...

Poets and novelists have been especially prone to "that fine madness.... which rightly should possess a poet's brain," as Michael Drayton called it. Byron, whose life was vitiated by manic depression, wrote of his "savage moods" and claimed: "We of the craft are all crazy. Some are affected by gaiety, others by melancholy, but all are more or less touched".

He might have cited Rabelais, Coleridge, Goethe, Blake, Burns, Melville, Poe, Kipling, Gorky, Tennyson, Lear, Elizabeth Browning, Swift, Samuel Johnson, George Eliot, Wordsworth, Thackeray, Dickens, Charlotte Bronte, Tolstoy, Shelley, Keats, Balzac, Victor Hugo....

Byron's violent mood swings, profligate spending, sexual promiscuity and terrible rages were classic bi-polar behaviour. Edgar Allen Poe, one of many bi-polars who sought refuge in recreational drugs (like Zoë) or alcohol, wrote: "As a matter of course, my enemies referred the insanity to the drink rather than the drink to the insanity."

Coleridge felt his manic depression as a stigma as well as a curse:

Instead of manfully disclosing the disease, I concealed it with a shameful Cowardice of sensibility, till it cankered my very Heart. How many hours have I stolen from the bitterness of truth in these soul-enervating Reveries – in building magnificent Edifices of Happiness on some fleeting Shadow of Reality! My Affairs became more and more involved – I fled to Debauchery – fled from silent and solitary Anguish to all the uproar of senseless Mirth!

Coleridge's anguished words are quoted by Kay Redfield Jamison in another distinguished book, *Touched with Fire*, where she argues for "a compelling association, not to say actual overlap, between two temperaments – the artistic and the manic-depressive." Jamison asks: "is there something about the experience of prolonged periods of melancholia – broken at times by episodes of manic intensity and expansiveness – that leads to a different kind of insight, compassion and expression of the human condition?"

Zoë, even when she was not manic, had charisma - a rare capacity for exuberance combined with compassionate insight, and she left behind some good poems and essays.

Jamison recommends the positive aspects of the illness she herself would rather have than not, despite its terrible downside:

Who would not want an illness that has among its symptoms elevated and expansive mood, inflated self-esteem, abundance of energy, less need for sleep, intensified sexuality and – most germane to out argument here – sharpened and unusually creative thinking and increased productivity?

We would guess that only minority of bi-polars manage their illness well enough to agree with Jamison's judgment. Yet the astonishing prevalence of manic depressive symptoms among artists is undeniable - Michelangelo, Rubens, Van Gogh, Ruskin – and among composers - Bach, Handel, Berlioz, Liszt, Wagner, Tchaikovsky, Elgar, Mozart, Beethoven, Rachmaninoff, Chopin and Schumann- and among great scientists and philosophers - Newton, Leibniz. Schumann, who died in an asylum, wrote of his amazing energy in his manic episodes: "But if you only knew how my mind is always working and

330

how my symphonies would have reached opus 100, if I had but written them down."

We are trying not to romanticise this agonising and tragic condition. For every bi-polar admired for charisma and competently treated, many more are undiagnosed and unaided for long periods, or, even if treated, see their lives disintegrate in ruin and deep despair.

Is there a remedy?

There is no cure for manic depression but treatment by medication, therapy and long-term self-management can all help. Cognitive behaviour therapy helps patients to identify connections between thoughts, feelings and behaviour and encourages problem-solving techniques and coping mechanisms. The more controversial ECT (electro convulsive therapy) is used with some success against the most intractable mania or depression; Zoë in her despair seemed to favour it but we discouraged the idea because of its negative associations.

Professionals do not always agree on the relative importance of physical and psychological causes, so naturally there are differences about the roles of medication and therapy in treatment. Ideally, treatment follows early diagnosis and consists of a judicious, constantly reviewed mixture of therapy and medication – the latter also kept as flexible as possible.

The first problem for the therapist is to get the patient to admit there is a serious, long-term illness and that treatment has to go on, even after the end of an episode. Prof Graham Thornicroft, who runs mental health research at the Institute of Psychiatry in London, might have been talking about Zoë between her two episodes, when he told us*: "When they're very unwell they seek treatment but as soon as they feel they're coming out of it they don't want to dwell in the past, don't want to be seen as having a disability, persuade themselves they've recovered and convince others. They pretend to be better than they are because they need to re-establish self-respect and the respect of others. Also they're fighting to preserve their sense of self. They get suspicious or even paranoid. They won't show any weakness or doubt."

Before therapy can start, the urgent priority is medication to control inordinate mood swings. Larry Rifkin, a psychiatrist who treats bi-polars at the Maudsley Hospital in London, told us that high and low mood extremities have to be controlled differently for each individual and for the same individual at different times.

Antidepressants correct the chemical imbalance which accompanies depressed mood. Unlike tranquillisers, they are not addictive but some have side effects like dry mouth, drowsiness and blurred vision. Anticonvulsant drugs are also used because they do not appear to have the same side-effects. Anti-psychotic drugs are used to control manic moods. While older drugs can cause stiffness, shakiness, dizziness and dry mouth, newer ones often avoid such side effects.

Lithium, the most commonly used long-term mood stabiliser, is a naturally occurring substance which takes three months or longer to work and often has intermittent side effects including staggering, blurred speech or vision, unusual thirst, muscle weakness, trembling of the hands and weight gain. These effects can often be controlled by changing the dose or supplementing lithium with other drugs.

The underlying problem with lithium and other long-term mood stabilisers is that patients can feel they are "not themselves" and many bi-polars at some stage come to hate the drugs more than the illness. Larry Rifkin said medication needs to be the subject of a constant dialogue between the patient and the therapist. "The therapist has to be able to say: if you stop taking the drug I'll still see you." Using antidepressants without adequate balance from mood stabilisers can actually be may be dangerous because a bi-polar patient may pass rapidly from depression to mania.

Jamison, after many experimental changes in the doses she took, found that lithium worked for her - and for many others. But Larry Rifkin, more cautious, said lithium, although is usually worked, could not be seen as a fundamental solution. "One should not generalise from the experience of Jamison; her experience is not that of many others. A problem is that proper research involving long-term studies on volunteers are almost impossible to organise."

Therapy cannot be used during a deep depression, as we found with Zoë. Had she emerged from her depression she would have been put on cognitive behaviour therapy, a new technique which is designed to identify connections between thoughts, feelings and behaviour. It aims to enable patients to develop skills which will act as coping mechanisms.

Electro-convulsive therapy (ECT) is usually a last resort against intractable depression or mania. It involves placing electrodes on the temples and delivering an electric current through the head to produce a seizure or fit, under general anaesthetic. Its advocates defend it as an effective life-saving treatment; critics describe it as a crude and barbaric procedure and complain that it is often administered without adequate understanding and consent by the patient.

A patient who is very intent on suicide and who would not wait 3 weeks for an antidepressant to work would be a good candidate for ECT because it works more rapidly. In fact, suicide attempts are relatively rare after ECT. – Joy Inkleman's website.

However, in a campaign to restrict ECT to patients who are fully informed and have access to a mental health advocate, the health charity Mind points out that even people who have experienced it disagree on how helpful it is.

Some have said that it helped them beat depression where nothing else worked, while others say that it created

333

real and lasting problems. The immediate effects of ECT can include headache, confusion, disorientation, nausea, muscle ache and physical weakness. Far more worrying, however, are the possible long-term effects: memory loss, apathy, learning difficulties, loss of creativity, drive and energy. These serious side effects can last for weeks, months, or even be permanent.

Recent surveys carried out by MIND discovered only 14% of people who had ECT had been given information about it beforehand. Almost half the patients who had ECT thought they could not refuse it. Anyone detained under the Mental Health Act can legally be given ECT entirely against their will. – The Shocking Truth about ECT, Mind pamphlet.

But Mind's pamphlet leaves unanswered the problem of severely disturbed patients who may not be in a position to weigh the pros and cons of ECT.

In the long run the best hope for bi-polars is self-management, a technique which may take years to master. Self-help groups, notably those run by the Manic Depression Fellowship, and a wide variety of dedicated websites, like Joy Inkleman's, advise bi-polars to be their own health care advocates, to be forceful with doctors and psychiatrists and in effect to take charge of their own treatment.

Research shows that if we are able to recognise the early triggers and early warning signs of an impending episode, and implement appropriate coping strategies, then we can gain greater control over our mood swings. Examples of coping strategies would be: reducing stressful activities, relaxation exercises, maintaining a regular sleeping pattern (for mania) or exercise and cognitive therapy techniques (for depression). We know that circadian rhythm, especially the sleep/wake cycle, are very important in manic depression... Another useful tool is keeping a mood diary which can provide an early warning of a mood swing and can also help to identify any patterns to the episodes. People who self-manage often provide an action plan which lists coping strategies to be put into effect if the triggers and warning signs should appear. - MDF pamphlet:

The MDF runs a network of 140 self-help groups, meeting monthly, employs 24 legal advisors and publishes a monthly magazine called Pendulum. It provides its bi-polar members with help getting and keeping jobs, travel insurance, car insurance and life assurance in which they claim a 30 per cent success rate for people who can't get it elsewhere.

A network of regional groups for young people, called Steady, offers support and training in the handling of elation and depression. Steady groups discuss what matters to bi-polars: the warning signs and triggers for mood swings, action for coping, self medication, negotiating with doctors, problems with parents and other family carers. Later the groups go on to plan long-term changes to life patterns, complementary therapies including yoga and massage and the role of sport and diet.

Long term self management would have been Zoë's only option for survival. It would not have been easy, as Larry Rifkin pointed out. "The problem always is the hurt pride, the stigma and the loss of autonomy. This is hard. Proud and successful people are not used to seeking advice and help from professionals, or parents. Long-term arrangements for manic depressive patients will have to include changing aspects of their lifestyle, such as working less, drinking less, and learning a new humility. Management of the condition very often requires a new approach to relationships with parents, family, partner etc. In all this there is probably a significant loss of autonomy.

Family and friends as carers

Because bi-polars behave so wildly when manic and sink into such deep and dangerous depressions, they pose a huge problem to their families, friends and other carers.

It is not always easy to offer sympathetic support to someone who may have been behaving erratically, angrily, recklessly or thoughtlessly. It is difficult not to take such behaviour personally and to react to it ..... Family and friends often feel they have been rejected by the individual concerned, and are unsure how to respond.....Manic Depression Fellowship pamphlet.

Similar advice is offered on the Royal Society of Psychiatry website.

It is often difficult to know what to say to someone who is very depressed - it may seem that you can't say anything right because they interpret everything in a very pessimistic way. It can be very difficult to know what they want - this is hardly surprising because often the depressed person does not know themselves what they want. They may be very withdrawn and irritable but at the same time unable to do without your help and support. They may be very worried but unwilling or unable to accept advice. So try to be as patient and understanding as possible.

At the start of a manic mood swing, the person will appear to be happy, energetic and outward-going, the 'life and soul of the party'. They will relish being the centre of attention and will enjoy social occasions such as parties or heated discussions. However, these will tend to increase the sufferer's level of excitement and will tend to make their mood even higher. So, it is a good idea to keep them away from such situations if possible while you try to persuade them to seek help. They will benefit from information about the illness, advice about how to help, and practical support.

If a manic swing has become severe, the person may become hostile, suspicious and verbally or physically explosive. Don't get into arguments but get professional help immediately. You should keep a contact telephone number and the name of a trusted professional handy for any such emergency. There may be times when it is necessary for the manic person to have a short admission to hospital to protect them from getting into trouble.

336

Trying to be carers for Zoë, we experienced much of the agony and perplexity of trying to look after our child who in one state was violent and abusive and in the other state morose, irritable, uncommunicative and resentful. To make matters worse, the consultant treating her did not feel at liberty, because of patient confidentiality, to tell us what she was telling him. When she began talking to her professional carers about suicide while telling us that suicide was "not an option," this became a life-threatening problem.

Suki Khaira, the manager of The Lakes acute psychiatric admission unit at the time, told us after her death that the confidentiality issue was "tricky because some patients have difficult family carers and we could be sued if we override confidentiality." But Larrry Rifkin agreed with us that carers of bi-polars must be told what they need to know despite the requirements of confidentiality. To guard against suicide, carers need to know the signs, the risks and the right preventive action to take. But he warned that family carers such as we were could also complicate the situation because their worry is itself a pressure on the patient. "Preaching a gospel of hope to a clinically depressed person is not going to have much impact. The amount of love bestowed on a person in this state does not radically alter the situation. Their moods are independent of that. Love disappears from their experience – they are incapable of experiencing it.

Larry Rifkin was able to offer us some consolation for the frustrations of our sterile communication with Zoë in her last weeks, when she seemed to want to be somewhere else. He told us some of his bi-polar patients feel "the worst thing is for the family to be there because the family adds to the anguish. It's so very difficult when you were beautiful and brilliant and people invested all sorts of hopes in you. Also, the family can seem to restrict or even remove the individual's autonomy."

The carers' greatest responsibility is keeping their patient alive. We heard from several relatives and friends who had tortured themselves for their lack of foresight, for allowing themselves to be deceived by bi-polars who declared, like Zoë, that suicide was not an option.

In Zoë's last weeks a friend who works with The Samaritans told us somewhat casually that when a depressed person begins to feel a bit better suicide risks are higher. "You should watch a deeply depressed person when they appear a little brighter," she said. It makes sense because when they are down in the depths people lack all drive and initiative. Zoë did indeed come out of the depths before she killed herself. That we did not heed this warning is our most agonising regret.

Counter intuitively, those who killed themselves had been assessed by their doctors as "calmer" and "in better spirits" than those who did not. In fact, nearly one third of hospitalised psychiatric patients "look normal" to their doctors, family members or friends in the minutes or hours before suicide ... They may be calmer because, having decided to kill themselves, they are relieved of the anxiety and pain entailed in having to continue to live. They may also be deliberately deceiving their doctors and families in order to secure the circumstances that will allow them to commit suicide. - Patty Duke & Gloria Hochman: A Brilliant Madness – Living with Manic Depression

The state of the mental health system

Zoë had been relatively privileged but not lucky enough. She had a high level of support from family, friends and, in her final illness, a sympathetic consultant provided by the Health Service, whom she liked, visited her once a week. Except of course during the three last weeks of her life when he was away on holiday and not adequately replaced. In spite of her relatively privileged experience, Zoë suffered from the defects of the mental services. These are many, despite a long history of reform and improvement in recent decades.

The huge Victorian asylums have been emptied and mental patients are now dealt with as far as possible in the

338

community. Mental health has been taken into the mainstream with psychiatric units like The Lakes, community mental health teams in every population centre, day care centres and crisis houses operating with full time staff in a homely setting. Home treatment teams may visit patients two or three times a day...

A new category of staff includes primary care psychotherapists to whom GPs can refer patients for assessments. Link workers – between GPs and specialist services – have begun to operate nationwide. Some 50 "early intervention teams" aim to treat people in the first three years of psychotic episodes. A national suicide strategy aims to bring down suicides from their current rate of 5,000 a year.

That is the theory and the slowly emerging structure. But the demand for services is bottomless and resources and staff are short. In everyday practice, the mental health services can still be shockingly inadequate.

On a typical day 100 people in the UK experience severe mental illness for the first time. A year later over half have still had no specialist help at all. Many will have tried to get help and been turned away. Others will have been so frightened by the stigma and by misreporting in the media that they will not even have tried.

The average delay in getting help with a psychosis in the UK is 12-18 months. Half of people affected become so ill before help is offered that a compulsory section is their first experience of mental health care. – 2001/2 annual review of the mental health pressure group Rethink.

In theory every GP knows about manic depression as well as schizophrenia and must refer patients to the mental health services. In practice, as we have seen from many of our e-mail correspondents, many bi-polars slip through the net and diagnosis, if it happens at all, can take years. One study shows many bi-polars wait six months or more from initial presentation to a GP surgery and referral to a psychiatrist, there is then a further potential delay of

339

welve months for a correct diagnosis. It could be eighteen months before treatment starts. Six years ago the average age of manic depression diagnosis was 32. Now it's 19 – which suggests there was a lot of misdiagnosis. According to Zoë's health service notes she was not diagnosed manic depressive until December 22, 1992 – six months after her first suicide attempt, nineteen months after she first reported feeling depressed.

Bi-polars will often fight hard against being labelled as mad. Zoë's kind and friendly GP, Paul Rasor, admitted to us after her death: "It's difficult for us doctors when patients are more intelligent than ourselves." Another difficulty is that most young people presenting mental problems are victims of recreational drugs. Staff at The Lakes told us that it is often hard to distinguish between a drugs problem and schizophrenia or manic depression.

Dr Rasor said GPs generally have some working knowledge of at least one branch of what he called "psychological medicine (it depends which college you go to)" and the team in his surgery had good access to psychiatric help.

All of which worked well in Zoë's case. But then there were problems. Considering what happened in the end, Dr Rasor said gravely that the loss of support when her consultant went on holiday "could have been quite overwhelming."

And yet, Zoë was far better treated than most young bi-polars in Britain.

Most psychiatric wards are frightening places. They are noisy, people out of control, young and old, abusers beside the abused, not enough staff to cope. I would feel safer in a high security ward in Broadmoor than on most inner city wards. If your first experience of the mental system is of compulsion and being over-medicated – drugged up to the eyeballs – you are never going to use the services again – senior mental health official, quoted in

Pure Madness – How Fear drives the mental health system, by Jeremy Laurence.

Every year 26,000 people are being "sectioned" (detained in secure wards) – twice the figure of ten years ago. An underlying complaint against the current mental health system is that it is increasingly driven by fear of violent maniacs, especially schizophrenics but bi-polars can also be violent. In recent years many people have been taken into wards as voluntary patients and are then told that if they leave they will be sectioned. The result is that many now resist hospital treatment.

The current emphasis on coercive treatment was accelerated in 1992 after a man was murdered by a complete stranger on a railway station. Jeremy Laurence, a journalist on The Independent who was moved to undertake a national inquiry, concluded: "From that point the focus shifted from the care of patients to the protection of the public. The psychopathic murderer- the mad axeman of popular myth – became the new monster in our midst."

What I found was a service driven by fear in which the priority is risk reduction through containment – by physical or chemical means. ..... As the numbers detained in hospital have soared by 50 percent in a decade, the protests have grown louder.

Although services have improved, standards remain lamentably low, especially when compared to the quality we have come to expect in physical care. Psychiatric wards are often unpleasant, dirty and overcrowded and there is violence. Community care is geared to dealing with crisis and support services are patchy at best and non-existent at worst. London's psychiatric service was said to be a powder-keg waiting to explode (Jeremy Laurence; Pure Madness – How Fear drives the Mental Health System).

The shortcomings of the system were tragically obvious in our own town. Zoë's consultant at The Lakes, our acute psychiatric admissions unit, went on leave at the worst possible time for her – and her case was not taken

341

over by another consultant. After her suicide there was an internal inquiry. Suki Khaira, the manager at The Lakes, told us the inquiry resulted in a better anti-suicide strategy and a better system for handing over the care of patients when a consultant is away. Another consultant must now take proper responsibility in a more assertive way.

Zoë did not like her experience of The Lakes. Its bright rooms and pleasant garden are a vast improvement on our huge Victorian mental hospital which is being closed down. But its atmosphere of lethargic hopelessness only increased her depression. Heather Castillo, who works there as a mental health advocate, admitted that coming into The Lakes can be a shock. "The company of the obviously mentally ill and then the anticlimax when for long periods nothing happens to you. We are working to provide more activities." But The Lakes is still grossly overcrowded – people going on short leaves come back and find their space has been occupied by someone else. "Good reforms are in place but lack of funding often makes things move backwards: our local crisis centre has been suspended for lack of funds."

No doubt lack of funds in the health service contributed to Zoë's death, because there was no effective replacement during those three crucial weeks when her consultant went on holiday leaving her desperate and alone. But blame and regret cannot stop here. The deficiencies of the health service do not absolve her parents and most of her family and friends when we stuck firm in our denial, when we refused to admit that our beautiful and brilliant Zoë was going mad again and, in the end when she was in despair, we might at least have hugged her more often.

The Manic Depression Fellowship: Castle Works, St. George's Road, London SE1 6ES. Tel: 020 7793 2600 Fax: 020 7793 2639 Email: mdf@mdf.org.uk
Scottish office: 87 Holborn Street, Aberdeen, AB 10 6B

Tel: 01224 590435 Fax: 01224 211721

Fellowship of Depressives Anonymous: 36 Chestnut Avenue, Beverley, Humberside, East Yorkshire HU17 9QA. Tel: 01482 860 619

Depression Alliance: 35 Westminster Bridge Road, London SE1 7JB. Tel: 020 7633 0557 Fax: 020 7633 0559

AWARE - Helping to Defeat Depression: 147 Phibsboro Road, Dublin 7, Ireland. Tel: (01) 830 8449 Fax: (01) 830 6840

The Samaritans: 10 The Grove, Slough SL1 1QP Tel: 08457 909090 in the UK or 1850 609090 in Eire (local branch telephone numbers in the telephone directory) Confidential emotional support to any person who is suicidal or despairing.

RETHINK severe mental illness: 30 Tabernacle Street, London EC2A 4DD

Tel: 020 7330 9110

Saneline: 1st Floor Cityside House, 40 Adler Street, London E1 1EE
Tel: 0845 767; 020 7247 6647 Mobile: 07718 735 121

National out-of-hours telephone helpline for anyone affected by mental illness. 12 noon to 2am every day of the year.

Mind: Granta House, 15-19 Broadway, London E15 4BQ Tel: 020 8519 2122 Fax: 020 8522 1725 Email: contact@mind.org.uk
Mindinfoline: 020 8522 1728 (London) 08457 660163 (outside London)

PAPYRUS (Prevention of Suicide)

Rossendale GH, Union Road, Rawtenstall, Lancashire BB4 6NE

TeL &Fax 01706 214449

Web: www.papyrus-uk.org

The Internet can provide some helpful sites and forums. We found the POS (Parents of Suicide) network a great help in some of the bad months just after Zoë's suicide.

Parents of Suicides - www.parentsofsuicide.com

Friends & Families of Suicides - www.friendsandfamiliesofsuicide.com

Suicide Memorial Wall - www.suicidememorialwall.com

Suicide Reference Library - www.suicidereferencelibrary.com

Suicide Discussion Board - www.suicidediscussionboard.com

Notes

1. Royal College of Psychiatry 1997 report

2. Goodwin and Jamison: *Manic Depressive Illness*

Printed in the United Kingdom
by Lightning Source UK Ltd.
135242UK00001B/20/A

9 781904 697206